Decentralization in Mexico

Decentralization in Mexico

From Reforma Municipal to Solidaridad to Nuevo Federalismo

Victoria E. Rodríguez

University of Texas at Austin

Westview Press

A Member of the Perseus Books Group

Copyright © 1997 by Westview Press, A Member of the Perseus Books Group

Published in 1997 in the United States of America by Westview Press, 5500 Central Avenue, Boulder, Colorado 80301-2877, and in the United Kingdom by Westview Press, 12 Hid's Copse Road, Cumnor Hill, Oxford OX2 9JJ

Library of Congress Cataloging-in-Publication Data
Rodríguez, Victoria Elizabeth, 1954–
    Decentralization in Mexico : from Reforma Municipal to Solidaridad
to Nuevo Federalismo / Victoria E. Rodríguez.
        p.   cm.
    Includes bibliographical references and index.
    ISBN 0-8133-2778-4 (hardcover).—ISBN 0-8133-2779-2 (pbk.)
    1. Decentralization in government—Mexico.   2. Mexico—Politics
and government—1970–1988.   3. Mexico—Politics and
government—1988–   I. Title.
JL1229.D42R63   1997
320.8′0972′09048—dc21   97-20387
                                                                        CIP

The paper used in this publication meets the requirements of the American National Standard for Permanence of Paper for Printed Library Materials Z39.48-1984.

10   9   8   7   6   5   4   3   2

To Peter,
for all the things you are

Contents

Tables and Figures

Figures

Acronyms

ANMEB	Acuerdo Nacional para la Modernización de la Educación Básica (National Agreement for the Modernization of Basic Education)
BANOBRAS	Banco Nacional de Obras y Servicios Públicos (National Bank for Utilities and Public Works)
CANACINTRA	Cámara Nacional de la Industria de Transformación (National Chamber of Manufacturing Industry)
CDS	Convenio de Desarrollo Social (Social Development Agreement)
CIDE	Centro de Investigación y Docencia Económica (Center for Economic Teaching and Research)
CM	Concejo Municipal (Municipal Council)
CNC	Confederación Nacional Campesina (National Peasant Confederation)
CNEM	Centro Nacional de Estudios Municipales (National Center for Municipal Studies)
CNOP	Confederación Nacional de Organizaciones Populares (National Confederation of Popular Organizations)
COFIPE	Código Federal de Instituciones y Procedimientos Electorales (Federal Code for Electoral Produres and Institutions)
CONAPO	Consejo Nacional de Población (National Population Council)
COPLADE	Comité de Planeación para el Desarrollo Estatal (State Development Planning Committee)
COPLADEMUN	Comité de Planeación para el Desarrollo Municipal (Municipal Development Planning Committee)
COPLAMAR	Coordinación General del Plan Nacional de Zonas Deprimidas y Grupos Marginados (National Plan for Depressed Areas and Marginalized Groups)
CUC	Convenio Unico de Coordinación (Coordination Agreement)
CUD	Convenio Unico de Desarrollo (Development Agreement)
DIF	Desarrollo Integral de la Familia (Integrated Family Development)
FDN	Frente Democrático Nacional (National Democratic Front)
FFC	Fondo Financiero Complementario (Complementary Fund)

FFM	Fondo de Fomento Municipal (Municipal Development Fund)
FGP	Fondo General de Participaciones (General Revenue-Sharing Fund)
IFE	Instituto Federal Electoral (Federal Electoral Institute)
IMPLADE	Instituto Municipal de Planeación Urbana (Municipal Urban Planning Institute)
IMSS	Instituto Mexicano del Seguro Social (Mexican Social Security Institute)
INDETEC	Instituto para el Desarrollo Técnico de las Haciendas Públicas (Institute for Technical Development of Public Treasuries)
INEGI	Instituto Nacional de Estadística, Geografía e Informática (National Institute for Statistics, Geography, and Information)
ISSSTE	Instituto de Seguridad y Servicios Sociales para los Trabajadores del Estado (Institute of Security and Social Services for State Workers)
IVA	Impuesto al Valor Agregado (Value-Added Tax)
LCF	Ley de Coordinación Fiscal (Fiscal Coordination Law)
LGAH	Ley General de Asentamientos Humanos (General Law on Human Settlements)
LOPPE	Ley de Organizaciones Políticas y Procesos Electorales (Law on Political Organizations and Electoral Processes)
MT	Movimiento Territorial (Territorial Movement)
PAN	Partido Acción Nacional (National Action Party)
PARM	Partido Auténtico de la Revolución Mexicana (Authentic Party of the Mexican Revolution)
PAZM	Programa de Atención a Zonas Marginadas (Marginalized Areas Program)
PDM	Partido Demócrata Mexicano (Mexican Democratic Party)
PDR	Programa de Desarrollo Regional (Regional Development Program)
PFCRN	Partido Frente Cardenista de Reconstrucción Nacional (Party of the Cardenista Front for National Reconstruction)
PIDER	Programa de Inversiones para el Desarrollo Rural (Program of Public Investments for Rural Development)
PND	Plan Nacional de Desarrollo (National Development Plan)
PNDU	Plan Nacional de Desarrollo Urbano (National Urban Development Plan)
PNR	Partido Nacional Revolucionario (National Revolutionary Party)
PPS	Partido Popular Socialista (Socialist Party)
PRD	Partido de la Revolución Democrática (Party of the Democratic Revolution)

PRI	Partido Revolucionario Institucional (Institutional Revolutionary Party)
PROCAMPO	Programa de Apoyos Directos al Campo (Program in Support of the Countryside)
PRODES	Programas de Desarrollo Estatal (State Development Programs)
PRONASOL	Programa Nacional de Solidaridad (National Solidarity Program)
PST	Partido Socialista de los Trabajadores (Workers' Socialist Party)
PT	Partido del Trabajo (Workers' Party)
SAHOP	Secretaría de Asentamientos Humanos y Obras Públicas (Ministry of Human Settlements and Public Works)
SEDESOL	Secretaría de Desarrollo Social (Ministry of Social Development)
SEDUE	Secretaría de Desarrollo Urbano y Ecología (Ministry of Urban Development and Ecology)
SHCP	Secretaría de Hacienda y Crédito Público (Ministry of Finance)
SNCF	Sistema Nacional de Coordinación Fiscal (National System of Fiscal Coordination)
SNPD	Sistema Nacional de Planeación Democrática (National System for Democratic Planning)
SNTE	Sindicato Nacional de Trabajadores de la Educación (National Union of Education Workers)
SPP	Secretaría de Programación y Presupuesto (Ministry of Programming and Budget)
SSA	Secretaría de Salubridad y Asistencia (Ministry of Health)
UNAM	Universidad Nacional Autónoma de México (National Autonomous University of Mexico)

Preface

This book uses a specific area of public policy, decentralization (*descentralización*), to analyze the distribution of governmental power in contemporary Mexico. Although Mexico was once recognized for the stability of its strongly centralist one-party political system, events since the mid-1980s have raised expectations that it will successfully decentralize in response to the demands of its ever-changing political environment. Increasingly, these demands have clustered around issues of political empowerment and democratization.

Like almost everything else in contemporary Mexico, however, the process of dispersing political power by granting a degree of autonomy to states and municipalities (*municipios*) and by opening up the political space to the opposition has not been easy. Yet it *has* occurred. The political scenario in Mexico, where after more than sixty years of one-party rule one now finds opposition parties running important city and state governments, is testimony that something has changed; in many respects, these opposition governments may be regarded as representative of Mexico's new political tapestry.

This volume argues that the Mexican government's decentralization efforts in the last fifteen years have been pursued to regain some of the legitimacy and credibility that both the government and the ruling party have lost in the course of the political crisis that began to unfold in the early 1980s. My contention is that, beginning with Miguel de la Madrid's presidency (1982–1988), the Mexican government embarked on a serious effort of political and administrative decentralization as a means of improving its hold on power; paradoxically, it centralized by decentralizing. That effort continued until the end of the administration of Carlos Salinas de Gortari (1988–1994). Since the beginning of Ernesto Zedillo's presidency (1994–2000), however, it has become increasingly clear that the survival of the ruling party and, indeed, the viability of Zedillo's government require a genuine, de facto reduction of centralism. For Zedillo and beyond, decentralization in some guise or other will have to be an ingredient in any recipe for modernization.

Necessarily, the dispersion of power—in political, economic, administrative, social, and geographical terms—forms a crucial part of any analysis of democratization, modernization, and public policy in contemporary Mexico. This book contributes to this analysis in three ways. First, it addresses an area of public policy—decentralization—that has not received the attention it deserves in terms of its relevance for contemporary Mexico's political and administrative system. If the system that has been so widely admired for its stability and its ingenuity in enduring all kinds of domestic and foreign pressures is to survive, then some decentralization of power will have to be a part of the political project. If the changes occurring in Mexico's political scenario are more than cosmetic, which will become more evident as opposition parties continue to gain access to power in both state and local governments, then the importance of decentralization will grow.

Second, this book also sheds new light on another understudied aspect of the Mexican political system, namely, intergovernmental relations. The character of the relations between the center and the periphery has quite clearly affected the design and implementation of decentralization policy. The overall effort to decentralize power away from the center has dictated the pattern of resource allocation among the three levels of government—federal, state, and municipal—and will continue to affect the conduct of their relations. For a system solidly based on the benefits of patronage and clientelism, any attempt at deconcentration of resources affects each level's response to the others.

Finally, this is a study of the exercise of power in Mexico. "Who governs" has always been an important research area in Mexico, and this book offers a contemporary addition to that body of literature by addressing the whole issue of empowerment. In Mexico, decentralization has been the medium for empowering both the lower levels of government and the opposition parties. Indeed, I hope that this study will be of some interest to non-Mexicanist scholars curious about the interplay of politics and public administration, regardless of the cultural context in which the analysis may be conducted. The study of decentralization as an area of public policy, coupled with its political dimensions, is highly illustrative of the struggles inherent in the allocation of power and authority anywhere.

Municipio Libre: A Quickening of Interest

In its broadest sense, decentralization in Mexico has been targeted at strengthening the municipality, the lowest tier in the federal-state-local government hierarchy. After being neglected for decades, in the mid- to late 1980s the municipality suddenly caught the attention of analysts, academics, policymakers, and politicians. By the early 1990s, the study of the Mexican municipality had become highly "fashionable"—in much the same way as Diane Conyers (1983) had earlier described decentralization's becoming "the latest fashion" in the late 1950s among development scholars. Academics and analysts who had studied areas foreign to Mexico's local politics and government suddenly found themselves attracted to the lowest tier of government and expanded their fields of study to incorporate the municipality. Likewise, politicians and policymakers who earlier had shown no interest in the municipality were thrust into numerous forums and public events where they had to speak to the issue and show an interest in it. The relevance of attending and participating in the multitude of *encuentros, reuniones nacionales,* and *foros* (meetings, national conferences, and forums) on the municipality that began in the mid-1980s became evident in the Foro Nacional hacia un Auténtico Federalismo (National Forum for a Genuine Federalism), which took place in Guadalajara in March 1995. The Foro drew presentations and comment from numerous Mexican academics, governors, municipal presidents, and other public officials; President Zedillo, in fact, opened the event with a clarion call.

In a variety of ways, decentralization has become a priority issue throughout the developing world. International organizations like the World Bank and the Ford Foundation have also developed a keen interest in local-level Mexican politics and have generously supported projects in this area. The World Bank has at least one decentralization and regional development project up and running in many less-developed countries; most of these projects are geared to strengthening the localities' productive and administrative capacity. In Mexico, the World Bank began to support decentralization and regional development projects in 1989. These projects were targeted at strengthening municipalities and promoting the development of the poorest rural municipalities in the poorest states. The Ford Foundation in Mexico has supported and avidly promoted the study of municipal government and citizen participation processes since the early 1990s. Indeed, it has developed ambitious projects to compare local government practices in various countries throughout the world (see Wilson and Cramer 1994).

This interest in the study of Mexican municipalities has evolved rapidly. Overwhelmingly, with less than a handful of exceptions (Fagen and Tuohy 1972; Graham 1971), the attention of academics and analysts before the mid-1980s had focused on the macrolevel and emphasized the study of national political processes and institutions. Any attention at the state and local level was directed almost exclusively at political parties and electoral processes—not at governance. Thus, the research on municipal government had to begin virtually from scratch; little was known about how a municipality was organized and how it functioned, and even less about how decisions were made and policies actually implemented. The only issue that was perfectly clear was that municipalities were totally dependent on the higher levels of government.

Thus, academics set out to investigate just how this dependence actually occurred on a day-to-day basis. They analyzed political relationships with higher levels of authority, the formulation and outcomes of their policy agendas, and so on. (See Rodríguez and Ward 1991, 1992, Cabrero 1995, Merino 1994, and Ziccardi 1995; the last three were supported by the Ford Foundation, Mexico Office.)

Although many remain convinced that this dependence has hardly diminished, recent research has begun to suggest that profound changes in intergovernmental relations are occurring. The variety of issues that now occupy the research agenda includes, among other things, more equitable levels of revenue sharing, what constitutes good local government and what practices can be learned, innovations in the management of public finances, citizen participation, representative democracy, modernization of the public administration apparatus, increased responsiveness and accountability, increased efficiency and effectiveness in policy design and implementation, more transparent government practices, privatization of public services, and even, in some cases, the application of Total Quality Management to the public domain.

Why all this sudden interest? The trigger, in my view, was the recognition that democratic opening and greater pluralism in government would extend, necessarily, to the local level. Moreover, the dimensions of the economic crises of 1982, 1986, and 1994, and the inevitability of the ensuing austerity measures, demanded a new era of legitimacy for Mexico's federal government—a legitimacy that needed to bring the states and municipalities "back in." As I argue in this book, the evolution of economic and political events during the last fifteen years has inexorably led to the implementation of a genuine, de facto decentralization that, while not necessarily implying the central government's abdication of power, has benefited, in different ways, both the states and the municipalities.

Note on the Research

Information on how Mexico's political system operates *formally* can be readily found in numerous government documents, periodicals, and scholarly literature and, particularly as a result of the dramatic events occurring in Mexico over the last few years, in virtually all popular journals and the commercial media. For data on how the system functions *informally*, researchers often must rely on conversations with public officials privy to the decision-making process and who have access to key information. By far, these personal contacts and acquaintances with government officials often prove to be the most valuable sources of information.

My principal sources are the written materials produced by a variety of government agencies and numerous interviews conducted with public officials at the federal, state, and local levels during fieldwork. In some cases data were not readily accessible, especially when they concerned budgets and public finance. Some of the data used in this volume I was able to gather only after extensive conversations with public officials who do not wish to be named. The information they provided was from internal, unpublished government documents not readily available to the public. In fact, Mexicans tend to be quite secretive, particularly with regard to budgets; as one public official put it to me, "La cuenta pública no tiene nada de pública" (Public accounts are not public at all). Moreover, at all levels of government two budgets purportedly exist: the one that is more or less accessible to the public, and the "real" one.

Nonetheless, because at present there is a more open climate in Mexico, a number of scholarly publications dealing with intergovernmental finances have begun to appear (see, for example, Aguilar 1994; Cabrero 1995; Merino 1994; Ziccardi 1995). Indeed, at the local level, several governments have adopted the practice of publishing their budgets regularly in local newspapers; yet others display it permanently in the town's plaza. For consistency, most of the federal budgetary figures I use in this book are from official documents: the *Presupuesto de Egresos de la Fed-*

eración (*Federal Expenditures Budget*), the presidential *Informes de Gobierno* (*State of the Nation Addresses*), and the statistical data provided by the Instituto Nacional de Estadística, Geografía e Informática (National Institute for Statistics, Geography and Information, INEGI). Additional documents that I found particularly useful are those collected from the Programa Nacional de Solidaridad (National Solidarity Program, PRONASOL, hereafter Solidarity), the Secretaría de Desarrollo Social (Ministry of Social Development, SEDESOL), the World Bank, and from numerous state and municipal government public finance offices.

The fieldwork for this manuscript spanned more than ten years and was carried out throughout the country. The first phase, from the early to the mid-1980s, centered around my doctoral dissertation and was conducted mostly in Mexico City and in the state of Guanajuato. I followed the Municipal Reform from its inception and assessed some of the preliminary stages of implementation during the first part of the de la Madrid administration. In Mexico City I worked closely with the Centro Nacional de Estudios Municipales (National Center for Municipal Studies, CNEM), the institution created within the Secretaría de Gobernación (Ministry of the Interior) to guide the Reform; in Guanajuato I studied how the Reform was implemented in various localities.

The second stage consisted of my involvement in 1993–1994 as a consultant with a World Bank project on decentralization and regional development in Mexico. This project tried to promote effective development in the poorest rural municipalities of the eight poorest states (Chiapas, Hidalgo, Guerrero, Michoacán, Oaxaca, Puebla, Veracruz, and Zacatecas). One of the principal components of this project was municipal strengthening, particularly in the area of intergovernmental finances and local governance. In traveling throughout these states and speaking with numerous municipal presidents, other local officials, state-level officials, and scores of community leaders and residents, I had an exceptional opportunity to assess firsthand the implementation of various Solidarity programs, particularly Fondos Municipales (Municipal Funds). My work on this project also allowed me to meet repeatedly with Secretaría de Hacienda y Crédito Público (Ministry of Finance, SHCP) and SEDESOL officials in Mexico City.

The third and most wide-ranging stage of this research is tied into a larger research project that I have been conducting jointly with Peter M. Ward since 1989. This project, which began as an analysis of what we first referred to as "opposition" governments, has expanded to include state and local governments of all political persuasions. While in its initial stages there were only one state and a handful of localities governed by the opposition, the advances that opposition parties have made in the last few years have increased their number dramatically. In addition, as electoral competition has stiffened, *priísta* (Partido Revolucionario Institucional—Institutional Revolutionary Party, PRI) governments have quickly learned that, in order to win elections, they must govern in a more transparent, effective, and efficient manner; the differences in style that were previously ascribed to the governments of particular parties were thereby narrowed. Thus, as the political space in Mexico has widened, our research has increasingly studied state and local governments qua governments.

In the first stage of our joint project we focused on the 1983–1986 *panista* (Partido Acción Nacional—National Action Party, PAN) municipal governments of Francisco Barrio and Luis H. Alvarez in Ciudad Juárez and Chihuahua, respectively (Rodríguez and Ward 1992). The second phase focused on the state of Baja, California and assessed the municipal government experiences of both the PAN and the PRI in the cities of Mexicali, Tijuana, and Ensenada, but now within the context of the PAN's exercise of power at the state level under the governorship of Ernesto Ruffo Appel, the first opposition party governor ever elected (see Rodríguez and Ward 1994a).

The third phase of the research explored municipal government experiences of other opposition parties, namely, the Partido de la Revolución Democrática (Party of the Democratic Revolution, PRD) in Michoacán and the PAN in Zamora, Michoacán, and San Pedro Garza García, Nuevo León. We also analyzed the experiences of municipal administration in Monterrey, under both PAN and PRI mayors (Rodríguez and Ward 1996).

Since exploring a variety of municipal governments of different parties, sizes, and regions, our joint research has now moved on to analyze an area that, even within the flourishing literature on intergovernmental relations, remains unexplored—the role that *state* governments play within the evolving context of decentralization and a renewed federalism. We are currently investigating the states of Oaxaca, Puebla, Guanajuato, Aguascalientes, Baja California, and Chihuahua. The ways in which New Federalism appears to be shaping up indicate that the states are certain to become critical actors in its implementation, and therefore in the future of decentralization (see Rodríguez and Ward et al. 1996).

Finally, my research benefited greatly from my collaboration with Peter M. Ward during 1994–1995 in a project on administrative and management innovations in local Mexican government, led by Enrique Cabrero at the Centro de Investigación y Docencia Económica (Center for Economic Teaching and Research, CIDE) in Mexico City and under the auspices of the Ford Foundation, Mexico Office. This project studied the municipalities of León, Aguascalientes, Tijuana, Ciudad Guzmán, Naucalpan, and Tlalnepantla (see Cabrero 1996). Once again, these cities' rich variety of political and economic environments and the many ways in which they were changing governing practices at the local level provided an ample forum for assessing the advances of decentralization in Mexico.

Victoria E. Rodríguez

Acknowledgments

Working on a research topic for more than ten years and in three countries often means that the list of people to whom gratitude and appreciation are owed can be dismayingly long. Having worked in the general area of decentralization in Mexico first for my doctoral dissertation and then for this book, I am fortunate enough to find myself in that predicament. In the interim—partly because of the rapidly changing political environment in Mexico in the last decade and partly because of my rapidly changing personal and professional life—this manuscript has gone through several versions. At each stage, many colleagues and friends have encouraged and supported me, the principal of whom I wish to acknowledge here.

The first version of this manuscript was written as a dissertation at the Center for U.S.-Mexican Studies at the University of California, San Diego. While I was a Visiting Research Fellow there I developed some of the most important personal and professional relations of my life. For that opportunity my warmest thanks go to Wayne Cornelius, for making me a part of the Center and for his personal support during my tenure as a postdoctoral President's Fellow. My thanks also to the Center's staff for their support and good cheer, and to the other Research Fellows for the intellectual stimulation. In particular, I wish to thank Joe Foweraker, Larry Herzog, Alan Gilbert, and Peter Smith, all of whom were especially supportive and encouraging.

In Berkeley, David Leonard, David Collier, and Alex Saragoza gave me much of the valuable guidance I required at that stage. I am particularly grateful to David Leonard for his openness and understanding, for keeping the pressure on, and for demanding the best.

Version two was written while I was (blissfully) on leave at the University of Cambridge. In addition to Peter Ward, my most valued colleague and friend, I wish to thank Celia Brading for her friendship and Gareth Jones and David Brading for their interest in my work.

The final version calls for my deepest gratitude to Peter Smith, as manuscript reviewer, and to David Warner, as chair of my tenure committee. In their own ways, they spared no time or effort in my behalf and gave me their advice generously. They have my immense appreciation for their confidence and for ensuring that both the book and the tenure "happened."

At the institutional level, I wish to acknowledge Andrea Silverman of the World Bank for inviting me to join the Bank's Decentralization and Regional Development Project and for providing me with the priceless learning opportunity of being part of the project's missions. I am thankful, also, for her permission to describe some of those experiences and to use some of the project data in this book. My appreciation also to Enrique Cabrero and his team at CIDE for our many discussions on joint research projects and for generously sharing data and information. Thanks also to Debbie Warden for her exceptional and unfailing administrative support, and to Kathy Bork for her outstanding editorial abilities.

Finally, I must thank those closest to my heart, each of whom has supported me and been interested in my work in his or her own way. In addition to being an incomparable companion, my mother instilled in me the value of education and taught me to persevere. Thanks also to my brother, Santiago, for the many times he has given spark to my life; to my sister, Laura, for reminding me that there is more to life than academia; and to my brother-in-law, Luis Manuel Jiménez Lemus, for suggesting that I write on this topic in the first place. During the various periods of fieldwork in Mexico, he made my work easier while my sister made my life more enjoyable. The closeness we developed then will remain with me always. The memory of my father has been with me at every stage of my life. I've always wished he were here to share my accomplishments. From his example I learned the unequivocal value of honesty and hard work. In a very special and personal way, this book was written for all of them—for sharing with me the pains and the triumphs.

And last, but by no means least, I wish to thank my husband, because neither the challenge nor the enjoyment of writing this book would have mattered as much had he not been there. In more ways than I can ever express, I owe this book to my darling Peter.

V.E.R.

Decentralization in Mexico

1

Decentralization in Mexico: The Reconfiguration of Centralization

For the last fifteen years, *descentralización* has been a persistent term in the Mexican political vocabulary. Even in the turbulent first half of the 1990s, when political traditions and institutions were undergoing dramatic and unprecedented change, decentralization consistently remained at the top of the public policy agenda. This book analyzes Mexico's efforts to decentralize political power and administrative decision-making during the 1982–1996 period. While my emphasis is on President Miguel de la Madrid's administration (1982–1988) because it marked the beginning of the most serious effort in modern Mexico to give political and administrative autonomy to the lower tiers of government, I also assess the steps undertaken by the administration of Carlos Salinas de Gortari (1988–1994) and end with an interpretation of what the future has to offer for decentralization under the presidency of Ernesto Zedillo (1994–2000).

Decentralization, as proposed by President de la Madrid and continued under Salinas and Zedillo, has focused on easing mounting political pressures and alleviating some of the administrative problems that have contributed to the erosion of the government's legitimacy and control. The general argument to be developed in the following chapters is that, while some significant advances toward decentralization have been achieved, in general, Mexico remains a highly centralized state. The country's reconfigurations of centralization are the subject of this volume.

I shall use various sets of data gathered during fieldwork to support my arguments, but I rely primarily on the Municipal Reform of 1983 and the Municipal Funds program of the National Solidarity Program to test the effectiveness of decentralization. Both of these cases are particularly useful for assessing the accomplishments of the de la Madrid and Salinas administrations as far as decentralization is concerned. The interpretation of (and speculation about) what the future holds under Zedillo centers around his New Federalism project.

The Municipal Reform of 1983 is critical not only because it provided the foundation on which subsequent decentralization programs have been built, but also because it initiated the development of a "decentralization culture" in Mexico. From the very beginning of de la Madrid's administration, the Reform became the cornerstone of his decentralization policy. On December 6, 1982, only five days after assuming the presidency, de la Madrid presented to the Mexican Senate an initiative to reform Article 115 of the Constitution, which deals with municipal government. The basic purpose of the proposed reform was to guarantee municipalities fixed and untouchable sources of revenue, which would allow them to provide public services and, more important, to strengthen their political independence. The changes in Article 115 took effect on January 1, 1984.[1]

The areas more directly affected by increased municipal autonomy from the federal government included public administration, public services, financial control, and development planning. Politically, the Reform sought to provide for more pluralism in municipal government, especially as opposition parties had become entitled to proportional representation at that level. Administratively, municipal governments were allowed to formulate their own internal governance rules. But by far the most important aspect of the Reform was financial; municipalities were charged with the management of their own finances and became entitled to those revenues that, although technically belonging to them, had been taken over by the state and federal governments (e.g., property taxes). Also, the Reform offered municipalities some protection from a clearly inequitable system of revenue sharing.[2]

By the end of the de la Madrid presidency in 1988, evidence suggested that the financial and political autonomy promised to local governments had not materialized. The Municipal Reform did, however, set a number of goals that, in effect, would be fulfilled through other government programs in successive administrations. Efforts under the Salinas and Zedillo administrations do indeed indicate additional accomplishments. This analysis will look at the Reform from more of a long-term perspective and posit questions within this expanded time frame. After a dozen years of implementation, how effective has the Municipal Reform been? Lingering questions remain about whether it has produced any visible changes in the way political decisions are made at the local level and, more significantly, about whether it has served as a mechanism for actually redistributing power among the different levels of government. In short, to what extent has the center sought to loosen, or simply to reconfigure, its political control?

On taking office, Salinas, like de la Madrid, pledged to focus his efforts to decentralize around the issue of redistributing political and economic power. He also pledged to continue the efforts of his predecessor by invigorating the Municipal Reform and other programs aimed at administrative deconcentration rather than presenting a specific decentralization policy of his own. Even though from the beginning of his administration Salinas spoke much more in terms of solidarity than of decentralization specifically, federalism, regional development, and municipal life were important elements of his administrative program from the very beginning. In fact, many observers saw a commitment to decentralization from the very early stages of Salinas's career, when he was director of regional development at the Secretaría de Programación y Presupuesto (Ministry of Programming and Budget, SPP) and later, when he directed this same ministry under de la Madrid. Thus, although under Salinas decentralization per se did not figure as a core element within his policy agenda, its presence was implicit, particularly in the National Solidarity Program, the all-encompassing program under which most social welfare and regional policies were grouped. A concern with unbalanced regional development, although subsumed under Solidarity, remained on Salinas's agenda; in fact, his whole decentralization discourse seemed to focus on this perspective.

As the Salinas administration came to an end, early evaluations of Solidarity's achievements in terms of redistributing power remained mixed.[3] While some of Salinas's programs did advance municipal autonomy in certain cases, there was no question that much remained to be done and that, indeed, his presidency ended with a retrenchment of centralism. At the very least, however, there appears to be consensus that, if decentralization has not fully materialized, some progress has been made and the plan for long-term change has been laid out. Indeed, decentralization's likely continuation becomes evident not only because of its prominent place in the agenda of the Zedillo administration, but also because of the three 1994 presidential candidates' stands on regional development, revenue sharing, and municipal strengthening as principal issues in their respective campaigns. Toward the end of 1996, policymakers, politicians, and spokespersons for all three political parties had articulated their support for decentralization under some guise or other. While Zedillo and the PRI continually speak of Nuevo Federalismo (New Federalism), the PAN argues for an Auténtico Federalismo (Genuine Federalism), and the PRD for a Federalismo Democrático (Democratic Federalism). What needs to be underscored, then, is that decentralization is no longer a discourse item that needs to be included because it is politically expedient to do so. For reasons that will be developed in the following chapters, decentralization has become a policy issue of primary relevance.

The argument offered in this book is that, beginning in the early 1980s and continuing into the late 1990s, the Mexican government embarked on an extensive program of decentralization as a means of holding on to political power and bolstering its faltering legitimacy. The principle of decentralizing in order to retain overall political control (and indeed, to *strengthen* it) seemed to be particularly salient during the Salinas administration. For Zedillo, a genuine, de facto decentralization has become an imperative that cannot be postponed if his party is to survive and retain control of the central government. This apparent paradox—to retain power you must give it away, or at least *appear* to give it away—provides the background for understanding the intergovernmental distribution of power in contemporary Mexico. The underlying purpose of Mexico's decentralization policy—to centralize by decentralizing—guides the argument of this book.

The Centralization/Decentralization Dilemma

An examination of the decentralization literature repeatedly reveals that decentralization is designed to relieve the administrative congestion that burdens centralized systems. The argument is that eliminating central overload is important because it allows the center to think and act in terms of strategy, rather than dealing with day-to-day bureaucratic operations.

In essence, the fundamental disjuncture between centralization and decentralization is that "some functions of the state are inherently better handled by the center while others are inherently better resolved by a deconcentrated structure" (Cohen et al. 1981: 34). Thus, once a government decides, for whatever reason, to decentralize, the next issue is deciding *what* to decentralize. In an effort to retain as much control as possible, and because most decentralization efforts (at least in the initial stages) tend to be rather tentative and halfhearted, most frequently governments opt for decentralizing the more *routine* tasks to subordinate units, while the *strategic* tasks remain under the center's control. From both an administrative and a political point of view, deciding which functions are to be handled where and by whom forms the central issue at hand.[4]

Yet many practical reasons explain centralization (see Oates 1990). In precolonial Latin America, for example, geographic conditions dictated the formation of a number of sparsely populated communities throughout the territory; these were almost inevitably controlled by strong city-capitals.[5] After independence, several Latin American countries recognized that the only way to coordinate the development of infrastructure and to establish a governmental administrative system was by creating a strong central state (Borja 1989; Graham 1990).

The advantages of a decentralized system can be illustrated best with concrete examples that also show the close correlation between decentralization and development, even though decentralization is a relatively recent phenomenon. In the nineteenth century, centralization meant stringent governmental control of the economy. As industrialization advanced, this governmental control decreased (giving way, also, to more political decentralization) and led to rapid economic growth. This was the case in Great Britain and Japan, which were much more localist and developed more rapidly than, for instance, France and China, which had inherited strong imperial bureaucracies. The same circumstances favored the development of Germany, which showed higher rates of industrial growth before 1850, when its system was more fragmented (Teune 1982: 98).

But as industrial development continued, pressures for change mounted. It became increasingly necessary for the state to intervene to deal with such issues as cyclical recessions, to stimulate growth, and to solve the social problems caused by capitalist development (Olloqui 1983). Thus, governmental centralization evolved into something that was accepted and even desired in most countries, at least until the middle of the twentieth century. Mexico certainly fit into this pattern.

Several factors developed toward the second half of the twentieth century that required reconsideration of the advantages of centralization. Probably the most important of these was the effect of demographic growth on the economy. The unprecedented growth of the larger cities produced not only higher costs and more administrative difficulty, but also the more common urban problems (declining standard of living, unemployment, insufficient housing, inadequate public services, etc.). In some countries (Poland and the former Soviet Union, for instance), the migration from the countryside to the cities had a disastrous effect on the agricultural sector, made the country dependent on foreign trade, caused innumerable social problems, and affected the very process of industrial growth.

Excessive centralization also made decision making and bureaucratic procedures slower and more rigid. Some countries began to show large regional inequalities because the prevailing system could not take effective advantage of the country's resources; not only did some areas develop more rapidly than others, but overall national development suffered. The centrally planned economies became increasingly associated with inflexibility, lack of incentives for development outside the primary metropolitan areas, and an almost stagnant administrative system.

At the same time, the means of communication developed rapidly. Progress in the communications field facilitated decentralization because it became increasingly easier to maintain coordination from a distance. The former Yugoslavia, for instance, was a pioneer in implementing a massive program to decentralize from 1952 to 1955. It was so successful that the government intensified its efforts starting in 1965. In fact, the success of this decentralization effort gave the country one of the highest growth rates in the world (Teune 1982: 95). Austria also experimented successfully with decentralization, although its program was not planned but, rather, forced on the country as a response to the Nazi invasion and then the Allies' occupation. The program had such a positive effect on the country's development, however, that since 1955 Austria has been one of the European leaders in per capita growth. The excessive centralization inherited from the imperial bureaucracy has also practically disappeared (Keefe 1976).

Many industrial nations have experienced an important shift in their production patterns under late capitalism. Industrial production has become more "footloose" and has shifted toward high-amenity areas (e.g., the U.S. sunbelt) or to lower-labor-cost regions in the national and global peripheries. At the national level this has stimulated a process of counterurbanization with a corresponding decline in the older established industrial and urban centers (Short 1984). In some developing countries a similar shift has been observed recently, as their formerly highly concentrated urban patterns demonstrate a "polarization reversal" (Townroe and Keen 1984).

In short, by the 1970s most industrialized countries had adopted policies to harness the decentralization process to their economies and their public administration apparatuses. In fact, during this decade most countries embarked on ambitious decentralization programs of one type or another.[6] It is significant that the majority of these programs were also related to the overall objective of increasing political participation (Teune 1982: 102).

In Latin America, though, from independence on, political factors tended to support a more centralized state, which could control whatever conflicts arose among local and regional caciques. As Graham (1990) argues, decentralization of power and relaxation of control would have equaled disintegration of the newly created national institutions.

Into the 1980s, however, as shown in Chapter 3, massive foreign debt and related economic problems demanded that more emphasis be placed on economy and efficiency by cutting down on the state apparatus. The unpopularity of the International Monetary Fund's austerity plans forced the discussion to turn to modernization of the state, and it was in this context that decentralization became a critical element—not least for alleviating the congestion of the centralized state (Graham 1990).

As will be discussed in the chapters that follow, a strong centralist tradition has prevailed in Mexico since the pre-Hispanic period, although, as Benson (1958) showed, federalism did indeed exist under Spanish rule and for a short period after Mexico obtained its independence. The restoration of the republic led to the need to unify the country by means of political and economic centralization, first under the dictatorship of Porfirio Díaz (1877–1911) and, more intensely, after the Revolution of 1910. As the country attempted to regain control of its resources, the bureaucratic apparatus expanded considerably, and economic activity and decision making were increasingly concentrated in the capital city, for both political and economic reasons.

Beginning in the early 1930s, political power was consolidated in the highly centralized and hierarchical structure of the Partido Nacional Revolucionario (which later became the PRI), based, of course, in Mexico City. This was to be the beginning of more than sixty years of hegemony. Economically, too, this political concentration planted the seeds for economic growth—the miracle of the 1940s—built around the project of import-substituting industrialization, which privileged the principal metropolitan areas and, most of all, Mexico City itself (Hansen 1974).

Thus, as elsewhere, developmental criteria dictated the need for a centralized state for Mexico, which emerged with two incontrovertible characteristics: first, as an extremely weak federal system reflected in the local governments' lack of autonomy and the strong domination of a single political party; and second, as a massive concentration of economic power, population, and governmental activity in the metropolitan area of Mexico City.

A Framework for Analyzing the Mexican Case

Given that no single, specific paradigm or theoretical model guides the process of successful decentralization, the particular route toward decentralization that a country follows is determined by that country's needs and, more concretely, by the characteristics of its political system. In other words, national and local political conditions determine the center's ability to control the periphery. Therefore, the national political system provides the framework in which organizations function and in which all policies, including decentralization, will be carried out. An analysis of the Mexican political system is thus indispensable for enabling us to better understand the contemporary attempts to decentralize, and will be provided in the chapters that follow.

Because Mexico's contemporary decentralization policy appears to have been designed for a mixture of administrative and political reasons, its study underlines the importance of the political context for policy design and implementation. The political tone of decentralization is evident in one of President de la Madrid's most cited statements: "Descentralizar es democratizar y democratizar es descentralizar" (To decentralize is to democratize and to democratize is to decentralize). President Salinas repeated the identical sentence several times and pushed it further: "La modernización de México avanzará por el camino de la descentralización. La fortaleceremos . . . para ampliar la democracia" (Mexico's modernization will advance by means of decentralization. We shall strengthen it in order to increase democracy). President Zedillo has called for a renewed federalism to support "una economía sana, una democracia limpia y una justicia transparente" (a healthy economy, a clean democracy, and a transparent system of justice).[7] As is the case in most national contexts, decentralization in Mexico may be perceived as mainly administrative, but it is deeply embedded with political overtones. As in other parts of the world, decentralization in Mexico obeys simultaneously administrative *and* political imperatives.

In an effort to sustain its power base and to regain its credibility, the Mexican government has increasingly experimented with reallocating power, not least by giving more autonomy to local governments and by recognizing the electoral victories of opposition parties at both the state and the local levels. But at least in its early stages, the reallocation of power in no way signaled any intention to loosen central control. Indeed, as Bailey (1994) argues, instead of a decentralization process, we have witnessed an increase in centralized power and presidential control, particularly under the Salinas administration. As Peter Smith (1979) emphasized earlier, the question was one of limited pluralism; the limits needed to be extended, but without sacrificing control over legitimacy. Under Zedillo, however, things may take a different twist. Having assumed the presidency in the midst of the worst political and economic crisis Mexico has experienced in modern times, Zedillo has had little choice but to effectively make an effort to redistribute political power. Paradoxically, by doing so, he has weakened the institution of the presidency and loosened the center's grip.

Thus, one has to keep in mind the relevance of the political context when analyzing decentralization. Many other rationales are cited when studying and advocating decentralization, most frequently, the need to relieve administrative overload, reduce demographic pressures, increase the bureaucracy's effectiveness and efficiency, improve the spatial distribution of economic activities and social benefits, and so on. But by and large, none of these perfectly good reasons can be detached from politics. The central government, after all, decides why, where, what, and how to de-centralize. I shall argue that, in the Mexican case, it has done so for an overarching political reason—namely, to sustain political control, rather than to improve the efficiency of governance.

Mexico is no exception in this respect. Indeed, as a case study, it fits comfortably within the parameters established in the literature in the sense that most attempts at administrative reorganization have political implications. The Mexican case is therefore useful for assessing the impact of decentralization in a broader comparative context. In fact, most administrative decentralization programs throughout the world are so heavily conditioned by political factors that they can seldom be considered as cases of pure administrative deconcentration. What is most interesting and relevant about these programs of administrative decentralization is that they not only are often designed for evidently political reasons, but they also are expected to have significant political consequences:

> Any evaluation of the consequences of decentralization for administrative reasons must take into account the general motivations underlying the central government's actions. . . . Most often, it is adopted with the ultimate aim of permitting the center to operate more effectively and efficiently. Secondly, administrative reasons for decentralization do not necessarily imply an administrative solution (i.e., deconcentration of the central bureaucracy). . . . Third, even administrative solutions are not politically neutral. Shifting the locus of power and authority over resources down the administrative line has major political consequences as it affects the ability of various social groups to influence the allocation of those resources. (Cohen et al. 1981: 35)

Hence, there are numerous ways in which decentralization can be analyzed, but some limits must be imposed. My primary theoretical concept is *devolution*, which I contrast with *deconcentration* as I emphasize how the linkages between superior and subordinate entities affect policy implementation. Devolution shifts control from the center to the localities. The main issue to be explored here concerns whether there has actually been a shift of power from the center to local governments, that is, whether municipalities in Mexico have achieved greater autonomy from the higher levels of government. In brief, as far as Mexican municipalities are concerned, the question is whether the center has promoted and pursued any devolution at all.

The Concept of Decentralization

Although decentralization may be rather simplistically defined as the opposite of centralization, in reality, the concept is far more complex, not least because "in the real world perfect decision autonomy and hence pure decentralization do not exist" (Leonard 1982a: 28). Decentralization, then, must be understood as a *process*, rather than as a final goal or objective that can be fully attained in a set period of time. Instead of being something that can be accomplished, it must be regarded as a series of measures that are followed in an attempt to eliminate or at least to reduce overconcentration.

The concept is complicated further by the various meanings assigned it. Some clear-cut distinctions are made in the literature among political, economic, social, and administrative decentralization; between functional and areal decentralization; and among devolution, delegation, and deconcentration.[8] Only when these distinctions are clarified can one begin to draw lines and attach labels that identify a system as being "administratively decentralized," "politically centralized," and so on. For the purposes of this analysis, these distinctions are crucially important because my objective is, precisely, to distinguish between political and administrative decentralization and to analyze how and why they interrelate and overlap, even if potentially they might be contradictory. Using as a framework the different *types* and *modes* of decentralization presented later, I shall assess the ways in which the Mexican government has attempted to decentralize.[9] Certainly, the myriad of programs for administrative decentralization indicates that there has been an intention to disperse administrative decision-making authority from the center to the periphery, but the attempts to decentralize political power—in Mexico and elsewhere—are more complicated, more interesting, and, ultimately, more relevant.

Types of Decentralization

In spite of the conceptual difficulties that the different types and modes of decentralization may pose, what is important here is that in academic debate centralization usually has negative connotations and is referred to as something that must be undone.[10] In essence, as will be illustrated, all types of decentralization are only variations of the same phenomenon: the dispersion of functions and power from the center to the periphery.

Political Decentralization

When political decentralization materializes to its full extent, it is equated with democratization, citizen participation, and representative government. In essence, it gives more political power by granting citizens and their elected representatives autonomy in decision making and resource control.

Spatial Decentralization

The general goal of spatial decentralization is to seek a more balanced pattern of urban development by "diffusing urban population and economic activities geographically among settlements of different sizes to prevent or reverse high levels of concentration in one or two large metropolitan areas" (Rondinelli 1990: 9; see also Gilbert 1989). The expected outcome is to build the capacity of public and private organizations in secondary cities to raise their own revenues in order to acquire and provide the services, facilities, and productive activities required for economic development.

Administrative Decentralization

Administrative decentralization is the weakest, broadest, and relatively easiest type of decentralization to implement; it is also usually the first step highly centralized governments take toward decentralization. It entails "the transfer of responsibility for planning, management, and the raising and allocation of resources from the central government and its agencies to field units of government agencies, subordinate units or levels of government, semiautonomous public authorities or corporations, areawide, regional or functional authorities, or nongovernmental organizations" (Rondinelli and Nellis 1986: 5). Administrative decentralization and spatial decentralization almost necessarily reinforce one another, given that the need for effective local government increases as a city's urban management becomes more complex; however, decentralization of administration does not necessarily imply expanded political participation. Indeed, central political control in centralized systems is often maintained by means of administrative decentralization.

Market Decentralization and Privatization

Market decentralization is "a process of creating conditions in which goods and services are provided by market mechanisms primarily though the revealed preferences of individuals" (Rondinelli 1990: 13). This type of decentralization is usually accomplished through policies of economic liberalization, such as the deregulation of the private sector. Deregulation reduces the legal constraints on private participation in the provision of services and allows private suppliers to compete for services that have been public monopolies. Often, private organizations provide services that local governments cannot offer efficiently and effectively on their own, although ownership remains public. Privatization ranges widely in scope, which allows private enterprises to offer services and facilities that were previously provided by the public sector, contract for the management and operation of public services and facilities, and create public-private partnerships.[11]

Modes of Decentralization

Although "decentralization" has become an overarching term that includes a variety of processes and administrative structures, there are three general forms that are most frequently differentiated in the literature: deconcentration, delegation, and devolution.[12] The distinction between them is important because, although all three concepts are *forms* of decentralization, they are often confused or are separated by a very fine line. The most commonly accepted distinction among them is that one grants autonomy while the others do not. "Devolution" refers to the creation of an independent entity or the transfer of decision-making powers to autonomous regional and local organizations. "Deconcentration" and "delegation" imply a certain transfer of functions, which remain under the supervision and control of the central organization. Hence, the basic difference between them is one of degree: while devolution gives autonomy to the decentralized unit, deconcentration and delegation do not.

Deconcentration

Deconcentration is generally understood as a transfer of functions, powers, and resources to the state offices of central (federal) agencies. Broadly speaking, the center executes normative functions, as well as those of supervision and control, general programming and budgeting, and coordination of regional operations. The states are responsible for the operation of services and programs and for the specific programming of resource utilization in the state agency, but the ultimate authority resides in the center. In short, deconcentration means

> a shift of administrative authority, but along a central administrative line. This can mean a simple shift in place; the government sets up branches outside the capital, or dispatches some arm of the administration to a provincial location. This process can involve considerable transfer of authority and power or none at all. . . . Deconcentration is also sometimes used to mean a thinning-out of activity at any one place. In this case, no transfer of power is intended, though some might take place. What is important to note about deconcentration is that it is an administrative action and does not alter the flow of command in the system. In contrast, devolution may involve some change in the loci of control. (Cohen et al. 1981: 19)

Official Mexican sources cite deconcentration and the delegation of functions when the head of a public agency transfers specific authority, and hence responsibilities, to a subordinate person or administrative unit. The possibility of the superior's stepping in and taking over the delegated functions is always present, however. The center provides normative guidance and also plans, controls, and evaluates the activities of the deconcentrated unit; it also has the right to revise or annul the resolutions adopted by the subordinate unit or person at any time. Thus, even if the subordinate or the deconcentrated administrative unit has a certain autonomy, the hierarchical lines with the center are neither broken nor weakened substantially (see, for example, Beltrán and Portilla 1986; Pardo 1986; Secretaría de Salud 1985; SPP 1985, 1988).

Delegation

"Through delegation, central ministries transfer responsibility for decision making and administration to semiautonomous organizations not wholly controlled by the central government, but ultimately accountable to it" (Rondinelli 1990: 11; see also Cheema and Rondinelli 1983). Delegation also occurs when parastatals are assigned responsibility for implementing programs or maintaining sector investments, primarily in the energy, communications, and transport sectors (Silverman 1992: 1). Thus, delegation implies the creation of public enterprises and corporations that can provide services more effectively and efficiently than can central bureaucracies and, simultaneously, provides a mechanism for expanding services requiring large capital investments (Bennett 1990; Oates 1990).

Devolution

In its broadest sense, devolution strengthens the relations among the federal, state, and municipal governments. In principle, this implies autonomy for the states and municipalities and therefore is illustrative of a federal system. When there is devolution, important elements that enhance the center's control are transferred to the lower levels of government (Cheema and Rondinelli 1983; Conyers 1983; Sherwood 1969). Thus, devolution transfers responsibilities to municipalities that elect their own officials, raise their own revenue, and have independent expenditure authority, which distinguishes a local *government* with independent status from a local *administration*.

From the central government's perspective, the granting of authority for decision making (and, consequently, the granting of autonomy) is the largest problem with devolution. In most cases, if not all, the center tends to be reluctant to lessen its control over the subordinate units and moves swiftly toward dissolution—rather than devolution. This seems particularly true with regard to political autonomy, and Mexico has proved to be no exception. Indeed, because "the essence of devolution is discretionary authority" (Silverman 1992: 1), Mexico's principal efforts at decentralization have been held to administrative deconcentration rather than full devolution.

Mexico's use of devolution, while somewhat confusing because it is equated with decentralization, is twofold: (1) functional, when specific powers are transferred to a decentralized organization; and (2) territorial, when programs and resources are transferred to the state and municipal levels. Thus, when the federal government decentralizes through devolution, it transfers authority, functions, programs, and resources and thereby grants the decentralized organization comprehensive autonomy; consequently, all strict hierarchical lines of power are weakened (Beltrán and Portilla 1986: 92; Pardo 1986; Secretaría de Salud 1985; SPP 1988). In a strict sense, however, this is not pure devolution, given that the Mexican interpretation uses devolution and decentralization interchangeably. Moreover, there is no accurate translation of the word into Spanish; while one might be inclined to use *devolver* or *devolución*, these do not convey the real meaning of devolution. *Devolver* means to give something back; devolution means granting full autonomy.[13]

Organizational Linkages

The extent of autonomy granted to the decentralized unit depends on the type of organizational linkages between the superior and the subordinate entities. "Linkages are the mechanisms by which one organization is tied to or attempts to influence another" (Leonard 1982a: 6); they include financial aid, technical assistance, regulation, representation, and informal influence (Leonard and Marshall 1982). All these types of linkages are built in different ways and for different reasons, but, broadly speaking, all linkages either control or assist:

> The purpose of control linkages is to enable one organization to determine some aspect of another's performance. . . . All regulation and most monitoring devices are control linkages. Technical and personnel assistance . . . may also be designed to gain influence over the aided organization. All of these linkages are used by central organizations to control intermediate and local ones. (Leonard 1982a: 36)

The purpose of assistance linkages, as the term itself implies,

> is to provide assistance. Finance, service, and most technical and personnel assistance have this facilitative function. A central organization then facilitates the program by filling the gap. In principle, assistance can be provided without control; in practice, this rarely is the case. Inter-governmental assistance virtually always has some degree of control attached to it. (Leonard 1982a: 36)

The amount and mix of control and assistance linkages varies according to the characteristics of the organizations being linked. Broadly speaking, assistance linkages are more important than control linkages because in most decentralized units assistance from the superior organization is necessary to overcome financial and administrative deficiencies. Assistance linkages, however, are seldom provided without some attached measure of control. If the center furnishes something, it will usually expect something in return.

Decentralized units do reciprocate, and thus the linkages go both ways. As Marshall (1982: 41) indicates, these "downward and upward linkage mechanisms" provide the basis for the development of a relationship of mutual dependence between the center and the localities. The center may have greater administrative and technical capacity, and assistance linkages may be necessary for the survival of a local organization or program, but localities implement policies and programs and thus can influence how much effective control is attached to such assistance. Hence, local organizations can bargain with the center for some autonomy in decision making; if local organizations deliver the services and implement the policies, their bargaining position and ability to apply pressure to the center is enhanced.

By and large, however, the most effective pressure that a decentralized unit can exert on the center is of a political nature. While the center may apply stringent linkage mechanisms in an attempt to control the subordinate units politically, the localities are not impotent and may refuse to accept such control by applying political pressure on the center. Thus, local political conditions affect the center's ability to control the localities. The best example is the allocation of funds for policy implementation from the center to the periphery: the center allocates the monies and demands that policy be implemented according to the guidelines that it sets, otherwise funding will be cut; but the subordinate entity may insist on autonomy and claim that, if it cannot implement the policy according to its own guidelines and its own preferences, it will refuse to cooperate or resort to measures such as public denouncement of central control.

The pattern of linkages that emerges from most examples drawn from the Mexican case is one of clear-cut subordination. Traditionally, in practice, municipal governments have enjoyed very little autonomy and remained subordinate to the federal and state governments. While assistance linkages often serve as a measure of control, and such control can be very stringent, in some cases, state and municipal entities do enjoy substantial autonomy in decision making and have a certain degree of control over their resources, whether these are allocated by the center or generated locally. In some instances, moreover, assistance linkages come without control, or with very low levels of control. A comprehensive assessment of the types of linkage mechanisms that have evolved with the implementation of decentralization in Mexico in the last fifteen years will be explored throughout the book.

Overview of the Book

Chapter 2 discusses the nature of federalism in Mexico and how the political system has evolved into one of extreme centralization. It assesses the system of intergovernmental relations in Mexico, emphasizing how, historically, Mexican municipalities have evolved as entities subordinate to federal and state government, even though the Constitution grants municipalities full autonomy. If we understand this historical subordination, we can better understand the decentralization efforts of the past fifteen years. To better evaluate the political and financial dependence of the lowest tier of government, Chapter 2 also analyzes the organizational and political structure of a typical Mexican municipality.

Chapter 3 sets the background for understanding the imperatives of decentralization. Against the backdrop of the worst political and economic crises Mexico had ever experienced, the de la Madrid government found itself confronted with more problems than it appeared able to handle; at the end of 1994, the Zedillo government was faced with a similar (or perhaps worse) situation. Chapter 3 describes and analyzes the political and economic crises of the 1980s and the 1990s and the alternatives proposed to deal with them, including a series of electoral reforms beginning in the 1970s, growing recognition of opposition victories, and effective plans to decentralize.

Chapter 4 follows on the discussion of the need to decentralize political and economic power away from Mexico City and provides an overview of the efforts to decentralize undertaken during the last five presidential administrations. In some way or other, since the 1970s, successive Mexican governments have tried to deal with this enormous concentration in the capital by formulating plans and policies designed to counteract its dominance, but concentration has persisted. Chapter 4 emphasizes the efforts of President de la Madrid's administration (1982–1988) and then turns to describing decentralization under President Salinas (1988–1994). For de la Madrid, decentralization consisted of a Municipal Reform that sought to grant some measure of autonomy to municipalities; for Salinas, decentralization was subsumed under the National Solidarity Program, the all-encompassing social welfare program that became the trademark of his administration. Both policies are discussed in detail, as well as the principal tenets of President Zedillo's New Federalism.

Chapter 5 explores how the character of intergovernmental relations has affected the implementation of decentralization specifically in terms of intergovernmental finances. This chapter analyzes in depth Mexico's intergovernmental fiscal system in order to better understand Mexican revenue-sharing theory and practice. It offers a detailed description and analysis of the implementation of the Ley de Coordinación Fiscal (Fiscal Coordination Law, LCF), the distribution formulas for revenue sharing, changes in fiscal policy, and the principal impact of Solidarity investments at the state and local levels. Finally, and as a critical component of this assessment of Mexico's fiscal federalism, Chapter 5 demonstrates how state governors have "hijacked" decentralization, thus making the states, not the municipalities, the true beneficiaries of change.

Chapter 6 offers a detailed analysis of the financial structure of a typical municipality and analyzes the implementation of the plans, programs, and institutions created as a result of decentralization (e.g., the Municipal Reform, Solidarity, revenue sharing, and the increased generation of revenues at the municipal level). Although an early evaluation of the Municipal Reform showed that the financial autonomy it promised had not materialized, things began to change with the implementation of Solidarity at the local level and, more important, with the need for local governments to generate their own revenues in order to fulfill the responsibilities that decentralization thrust on them. Although the Reform had little impact on the distribution of federal resources to the lower levels of government, the advent of Solidarity (particularly one specific program, Municipal Funds), did provide municipalities with fresh investment resources. Also, the generation of revenues at the local level through a variety of mechanisms (e.g., efficient collection of property taxes and of fees for public services) reduced somewhat the municipalities' traditional dependence on the higher levels of government. The data analyzed in Chapter 6 come from a variety of municipalities throughout the country.

Chapter 7 presents my conclusions and assesses the prospects of decentralization. Although the vast majority of municipalities remain financially subordinate—not only because their largest source of revenue is from federal allocations, but also because the higher levels of government (most notably, the state level) still determine the amounts that are funneled down—the advances undertaken in the past few years have set the path for consolidation under President Zedillo's New Federalism. Chapter 7 concludes that the de la Madrid and Salinas efforts to decentralize, and the prospects under Zedillo, point unequivocally to the reconfiguration paradox mentioned earlier: to hold on to power, the regime must give some of it away. As the current political climate has dictated, and if the regime is to survive, the Zedillo administration must move quickly to offer some reassurance that the reallocation of power currently under way will continue to include the opposition; but more important, it must be unequivocal in demonstrating that power will be *genuinely* shared not only vertically, with the various levels of government, but also horizontally, with the other branches of government.

2

Federalism *a la Mexicana*

In this chapter I propose to analyze Mexico's special brand of federalism and to assess, in historical perspective, the patterns of intergovernmental relations that have developed there. I shall devote a substantial part of the chapter to the political and administrative aspects of the municipality, the lowest level in the government hierarchy. Given the well-known centralized nature of the Mexican governmental system, my purpose is to determine whether *any* degree of decision-making discretion exists at the local level. The principal issue I will address is the extent to which the system is as centralized as commonly perceived. The question of whether decentralization as a policy has made a difference in providing local governments with some discretion in decision making will be taken up in other chapters.

Mexican Federalism: A Historical Overview

Although Mexico is officially recognized as a federal system organized in a similar fashion to the U.S. system, no one can dispute the extreme centralization of governmental powers in Mexico City. Since the Revolution of 1910 power has concentrated progressively in the executive branch—more specifically, in the president himself (Bailey 1994; Carpizo 1978; Garrido 1989; Meyer 1986). Power within Mexico has been channeled to the office of the president through a host of structures—including the official party, the PRI—and the influence of checks and balances as understood in the United States has been minimal. As summarized by Acosta Romero,

> the theory of our federalism may run deeply, but the practical realities are such that the powers of the political and policy processes have become increasingly centralized in the republic's federal executive . . . Mexican federalism is an aspiration punctuated by the reality of an undeniable centralism which is characterized by an increasingly pervasive presidency. (1982: 401–402)

Thus, while the structure of the Mexican government, on paper at least, is very similar to that of the U.S. government—with three autonomous branches of government (executive, legislative, and judicial), with checks and balances, and with a federal system with considerable autonomy at the local level—in practice, they are far apart. Unlike in the United States, decision making in Mexico is highly centralized, and the executive has almost unrestrained authority over the legislative and judicial branches. Until recently, both houses of Congress were overwhelmingly dominated by PRI members, and members of the opposition recognized that their points of view would not be decisive in shaping legislation. The domination of the federal executive has also extended to the lower levels of government, making state governors dependent on presidential initiatives and placing the municipality at the bottom of the federal-state-local pyramid in all matters concerning its own governance.

Thus, despite theoretical and official statements to the contrary, federalism in Mexico is extremely limited. Indeed, over half a century ago, Lloyd Mecham stated that "federalism has never existed in fact in Mexico. It is an indisputable commonplace that the Mexican nation is now and always has been federal in theory only; actually it has always been centralistic" (1938: 164). Therefore, in seeking to understand federalism in Mexico, one should not try to understand it as it functions in the United States, for it operates in an entirely different way in Mexico. Local self-government and the fear of centralized power are U.S. traditions that have no parallel in the Mexican context.

The special brand of federalism that has developed in Mexico dates from the pre-Hispanic period. The Aztec center maintained firm control over the country's other regions, and it was only after the Conquest, particularly during the colonial period, that federalism began to emerge, albeit within the confines of centralism.[1] Mexico owes much of its centralist tradition to Castile, which combined a system of central control with local autonomy and bequeathed this tradition to its colonies in New Spain.[2] Although "the trend toward decentralization of Spanish North America began practically with the conquest of the area" (Benson 1958: 90), the tradition of central control imposed on Mexico during the colonial period is of critical importance because it provided the basic framework for the future organization and functioning of the political system as a federation.

Nettie Lee Benson was the first scholar to call attention to the fact that Mexico's federalist system originated in Spain, rather than in the United States, and was informed by a need to unify what were increasingly becoming autonomous provinces: "Contrary to the common belief that federalism was suddenly forced upon a unified country, impractically splitting it asunder, it was adopted in Mexico in 1823 because it was the only possible way to unite and solidify a country which, under the influence of a Spanish institution, had broken up into independent provinces that were verging on becoming independent states or nations" (Benson 1958: 90). Beginning in 1810, one deputy from each of the (then) twenty-two provinces participated in the Spanish Cortes. Each province was an independent political division governed by a political chief, an intendant, and a provincial deputation, who were responsible only to the Cortes in Spain; the political chief in Mexico City had no control whatsoever over the political chiefs of the other provinces (Benson 1958: 92; see also J. Rodríguez 1992).

This was the setting surrounding a debate that began initially in the Spanish Cortes and continued in the provinces themselves, and that lasted more than a decade. The debate focused during the early years on the powers that these new provincial governments should assume, and later on the nature of any confederation between the provinces and the role of the Congress (Benson 1958; Gortari 1994; J. Rodríguez 1992). The tension was between the two opposing political traditions of executive power versus legislative supremacy (J. Rodríguez 1994) and of central control versus provincial independence.[3]

The first president who tried to make the federation work was Guadalupe Victoria (1824–1829), but his efforts proved fruitless. Federalism was reinvigorated during the Juárez period (1867–1872), when, in addition to the center's battle with local and regional bosses, the struggle between the executive and the legislative became stronger. The infighting ended with the unquestioned dominance of the executive over the legislative and judicial branches, as well as over the states, during the dictatorship of Porfirio Díaz (1877–1911). As Jaime Rodríguez succinctly puts it, the outcome of the conflict was that "the great liberals Benito Juárez and Porfirio Díaz imposed *presidencialismo* upon the country" (1994: 132).

In addition to federal executive control, the Díaz regime also solidified its regional control by sharing the country's newly acquired wealth with local regional bosses. Most of these bosses were happy to exchange local autonomy for a share of the revenues brought on by the modernization of the country's economy and by its political stability (Benson 1958; Meyer 1986; J. Rodríguez 1992, 1994).

Following the Revolution of 1910 a new political and economic system was established—not surprisingly, centralist again. The new state slowly but firmly took over control of local governance and, to support this control, created a series of institutions. The most important of these, by far, was the Partido Nacional Revolucionario (National Revolutionary Party, PNR), created in 1929. It later became the PRI and has governed Mexico uninterruptedly at the federal level ever since. Although the PNR was created as a mechanism to counteract the power of local bosses, it soon controlled with an iron hand the "revolutionary family" of the new regime. According to Lorenzo Meyer, it was a party that was born not to fight for power, but to administer it without sharing it (1986: 31).

The postrevolutionary centralization of power crystallized during the presidency of Lázaro Cárdenas (1934–1940), and by the end of his administration the authoritarian features of the state had been firmly established. This authoritarianism, however moderate, acknowledged local interests and autonomy only to the extent that they did not interfere with the interests of the central power. During the 1940s it was an established fact of political life that no state governor or local political boss could go against the president's wishes. Neither could the military. Neither could the powerful private industrial groups. And into the 1990s, little had changed.

Presidencialismo: Executive Power
Versus Legislative Supremacy

Although the Mexican federalist system is formally enshrined in the 1917 Constitution, political power has been concentrated at the central level, particularly in the hands of the president (Carpizo 1978). Mexico's political system is a highly centralized one in which although, ostensibly, paramountcy is given to the states and municipalities (*municipio libre*, "free municipality"), in practice power is given up to the center, particularly to the executive branch. While some federalist systems have developed a system of checks and balances to ensure that paramountcy is accorded to the local level (i.e., to ensure *vertical* decentralization), or to create checks and balances to regulate the *horizontal* separation of powers of the three branches of government, that is not the Mexican case. The United States, for example, has tended toward both, although administrations vary in the degree to which they emphasize local responsibilities (i.e., "new federalism" versus greater federal intervention) and in the extent to which the separate powers work effectively with one another or become gridlocked. Neither of these features of federalism, however, has yet emerged in Mexico to any significant extent, although I shall demonstrate that they are indeed beginning to appear.

The centralized nature of the Mexican political system is well known and widely researched. In his work on *presidencialismo* (presidentialism) in Mexico, Garrido argues that in addition to prescribed constitutional powers, the Mexican president also exercises a series of "metaconstitutional" powers. These powers are the unwritten norms of the Mexican political system (Garrido 1989: 422; see also González Oropeza 1983). The Mexican president has the power to act as a constituent power with the authority to amend the Constitution, to act as chief legislator, to establish himself as the ultimate authority in electoral matters, to assume jurisdiction in judicial matters, and to remove governors, municipal presidents, and legislators at the federal and state levels (Garrido 1989: 424). This combination of constitutional and metaconstitutional powers has made the Mexican president one of the most powerful chief executives in any democracy. The great degree of centralization at the federal level, particularly in the hands of the president, reduces dramatically the ability of the separation of powers to act as a system of checks and balances.[4]

While it can be argued that in recent years Congress has become more active in initiating legislation and more autonomous from the executive branch, by and large, the Mexican political system continues to be dominated by the president. Although major interest groups (traditionally organized around sectors and represented in Congress) have had some influence on public policy, the existence of an "official" party whose orthodoxy is all-pervasive and whose behavior is guided by the executive, means that Congress's role in actively shaping the political process has been minimal—dominated as it has traditionally been by the PRI. Many observers of the Mexican political system have pointed to the relatively weak role of the national legislative body. Indeed, in the early 1970s one author argued that the role of the legislature was "minor and basically ceremonial and technical" (Needler 1971: 43). Most analysts agree that this must change if the process of democratization is to intensify in Mexico and elsewhere in Latin America (Graham 1993: 187). While the focus may be primarily on the executive branch during regime transition, it is the strengthening of the legislative branch that is critical for the institutionalization of democratic processes.

If Congress has historically been weak, so too have state legislatures, although they have sometimes demonstrated some vibrancy vis-à-vis the governor (particularly in the 1920s and the 1930s). Governors (and presidents, for that matter) are likely to find it more difficult to control their legislature under conditions of interparty competition, or where the governor (or municipal president) is imposed on the dominant faction of the official party at the local level, and when that same group disobeys official party discipline by not falling into line with the imposition.[5] Concurring with Fagen and Tuohy (1972), however, most authors have noted that each successive layer of government is substantially weaker, less autonomous, and more impoverished than the level above it. Although it may be an exaggeration to say that state legislatures have automatically approved initiatives coming from the governor, they have not been, in the main, active influences on executive power. This pattern is also found at the municipal level, as *cabildos* (municipal councils) have been largely dominated by municipal presidents. If legislative bodies at the state and municipal levels are dominated by their executives, and interparty competition does not operate as a constraint, then the application of checks and balances limiting the concentration of power is unlikely, if not impossible. In effect, the only check on the concentration of power is the no-reelection clause. As will be described, individual elective power bases cannot be constructed; one's political future depends largely on party higher-ups.

As mentioned earlier, the president's metaconstitutional powers grant him influence in the judicial as well as the legislative branch. As in the U.S. system, Mexico's president may appoint Supreme Court justices with the advice and consent of the Senate. Although the Supreme Court is the highest in the land, however, the federal government includes several special jurisdictions in electoral, administrative, tax, and agrarian matters that are headed by "autonomous courts." These autonomous courts, in practice, are closely related to the executive (Puertas Gómez 1993: 8). As with legislative power, judicial power dissipates as it moves to lower levels. On the state level, tribunals are bound by national law, regardless of any local constitutional or statutory provisions to the contrary (Puertas Gómez 1993: 8). Although state tribunals are responsible for determining the constitutionality of legislation, the Supreme Court has ruled that no such controversies can be tried by local authorities.

In sum, although in theory a system of checks and balances exists in Mexico, in practice it is overridden by an overpowering presidency, born of the control that the official party has traditionally exercised over all branches. Prior to the wave of opposition victories at the state level in the first half of the 1990s, the only place where the mold appeared to have been broken was in the state of Baja California, where presidential control was weakened as a result of having an opposition governor.[6] Moreover, within Baja California itself, we can observe the emerging exercise of these separate powers, informed as they are by inter- and intraparty conflict (see Rodríguez and Ward 1994a). These conflicts, in turn, provide checks on the responsiveness of each of the three branches in state government, and greater monitoring and debate within the local government (*ayuntamiento*). In our work on Baja California (Rodríguez and Ward 1994a) we argue that in the area of *intra*-governmental relations, change has occurred in Baja California under PAN governance. Although the process is just beginning, the exercise of a separation of powers at both the state and the municipal levels can be observed. On the state level, we argue that the checks and balances offered by genuine electoral competition are beginning to lead to a growing separation of powers as mandated in the Constitution. On the municipal level, we discuss how an increasing amount of debate and independence between municipal presidents and *cabildo* members (often born of inter- and intraparty strife) has also allowed an incipient system of checks and balances to emerge. Separation of powers in state government and a more active review and monitoring system of policy making are only now being activated in ways that we regard as conducive to the emergence of more democratic systems of government and to the practice of federalism.

Intergovernmental Relations

Intergovernmental relations are an understudied aspect of the Mexican political system. For the most part, over the last seventy years relations between the different levels of government have been determined by the highly centralized nature of Mexico's political system, and have become as stable as the system itself. After Graham's (1971) and Fagen and Tuohy's (1972) seminal work studied and defined how relations between the center and local governments were conducted in the early 1970s, little more was written, as virtually nothing changed. Since the system's centralization served as one of the major determining forces for this stability, one could hardly expect any changes in the field of intergovernmental relations. This lack of change explains why research on the interaction among different levels of government has not constituted a substantial part of the voluminous literature on Mexico. It was only in the early 1990s that the general theme of intergovernmental relations in Mexico acquired renewed importance (see, for example, Aguilar 1994; Cabrero 1995; Merino 1994; Ziccardi 1995).

With only a few exceptions, scholars have concerned themselves more with policy formulation at the national level and disregarded the other governmental units. This seems especially true in the case of Mexico. But the study of intergovernmental relations has begun to gain importance in the United States, Europe, and even Latin America because the local level is the point at which policies are implemented and where their success or failure can be assessed. Moreover, the study of the relationship of the center and subnational units, while still relatively neglected, is now considered a critical element in the process of democratization; as a host of countries are becoming incipient democracies, the interrelationship between democracy and autonomy at the local level has acquired new strength (see Resler and Kanet 1993). In the case of Mexico, the decentralization efforts of the last decade have all been expected to change the character of intergovernmental relations fundamentally.

Former U.S. House Speaker Tip O'Neill once commented that in the United States "all politics is local politics," and although this is probably an exaggeration, the contrast with Mexico is nonetheless striking. In Mexico, one can unequivocally say that all serious politics is federal politics. As pointed out earlier, because of the extremely centralized nature of the system, most policy decisions that concern local governments are made in Mexico City and, sometimes, in the state capitals. In such a system of policy making, the few decisions made at the local level are made by those who hold political or economic power, who also remain in close touch with the federal and state elites.

But how does all this bargaining and centralized decision making impinge on local government in Mexico? Studies in community decision making are concerned with identifying the locus of the decision-making process and the mechanisms for securing positive outcomes to demands. The question of "who governs" is of special interest because the power structure is inevitably reflected in policy outputs and determines who benefits from public policy. In terms of who governs and who benefits in the Mexican intergovernmental system, centralism goes hand in hand with clientelism.

Clientelism

The most important mentor in the Mexican clientelistic structure is the president, whose control over state government is based on a wide variety of formal and informal powers. Article 89 of the Constitution, for example, permits the president to step in and declare the powers of a state government null and void, and Article 76 allows the president to remove a governor and replace him or her with a provisional one (with Senate approval). In addition to these constitutional provisions, the president can use a host of informal powers, including control of the police and the military, the PRI party structure, and the finances allocated to the states in the form of larger development projects. All of these powers, as discussed earlier, make up the constitutional and metaconstitutional powers of the presidency. Moreover, since final decisions are made in Mexico City, interest groups often circumvent the governor and go directly to the president to achieve their goals.

This clientelistic structure with the president at the apex extends all the way down the hierarchy. Governors appoint and remove officials at the state and municipal levels, and municipal presidents do the same locally. But the need for removal seldom occurs, given that both state and local appointees remain grateful to their appointers and show their gratitude by following their mentors' policy initiatives without questioning. Thus, presidential preferences are firmly supported at all levels of government, since most state and local officials owe their loyalty to the governor who appointed them, and the governors' loyalty, in turn, is owed to the president (not to the constituency who elected them). In brief, as Cornelius and Craig note, "all but a few officeholders in Mexico serve at the pleasure of the president" (1984: 428).[7] Although matters are now beginning to change as a result of internal party reforms and personal dissatisfaction with *presidencialismo*, by and large, the few officeholders who prove to be the exception tend to belong to the opposition.

The clientelistic structure of the system not only allows for extending the *camarilla* system all the way from the presidency to the local level, it also allows the selective distribution of government benefits.[8] Thus, for instance, clientelism has been instrumental in determining the benefits that each state government receives from Mexico City. While the system of revenue sharing determines by formula the exact amount that each state is to receive, and the formula is rigidly adhered to, there are a variety of ways of circumventing the formula-driven share, particularly in the form of the so-called *proyectos especiales* (special projects), such as a major highway, a dam, or an electrification plant. As I will demonstrate in Chapter 5, the politically favored states tend to receive these special projects from the federal government. The central-state pattern is then duplicated at the state-municipality level; that is, the politically favored municipalities end up getting the largest allocations from the states. Thus, the "who governs—who benefits" question comprises a linked distribution of benefits that extends from Mexico City all the way down to the smallest municipality.

This preferential distribution of benefits at the state level, tied into clientelism, is best illustrated by the fact that the state capital overwhelmingly takes the largest share of the federal funds allocated to each state, not only because it happens to be the seat of state government and the place where the governor resides, but because most favors dispensed by governors and their top officials tend to be concentrated in the state capital. In some states the capital keeps up to 80 percent of the federal funds allocated to the entire state, while some of the smaller municipalities, at the end of the federal-state-municipal chain, get virtually nothing.

In the more traditional communities, the responsibility for the distribution of goods and services is often given to individual patrons, who sometimes perform functions roughly equivalent to those of the U.S. lobbyist. For example, to have as a patron someone from one's town working in a federal agency will help that community to get funds allocated and projects funded locally, and the patron will receive all due credit. Likewise, if a community does not receive the expected services, it is because the patron in the state capital has not done his or her job properly, or because the community itself has not cultivated the right patron in the right agency—what Evelyn Stevens calls "the myth of the right connection" (1974: 94). Such reasoning serves the system well because it helps limit the people's frustration with poor government performance, since the blame for policy implementation failures falls directly on specific patrons rather than on the system as a whole. This deflection of criticism serves local officials particularly well because it allows them to detach themselves from the responsibility for policy failures by placing the blame on a higher level of government or on some state or federal agency.[9]

State Governors: The Modern Viceroys

Gubernatorial loyalty to the president has led observers to perceive governors and other state officials as little more than political brokers acting as the local representatives of federal power. Indeed, in the opinion of many, the governor's primary role is mostly ceremonial (e.g., dedicating projects or attending state functions); those who truly govern are in Mexico City. As Graham describes the role of the governor, it is, essentially, one of an "elected prefect" (1971: 5). In fact, it has been argued that administrative agencies proceed with their daily business with little or no concern for the governor's office (Graham 1984: 4), and that administrative officials owe greater allegiance to their superiors in Mexico City than to their immediate political bosses in the state capital.

But since the mid-1980s, particularly through the implementation of the Municipal Reform, it has become evident that the power of governors and state officials is much more substantial than previously believed. As will be discussed in detail in chapter 5, federal funds are allocated to municipalities through the state government, which allows the governor and other state authorities to ultimately decide which municipality will receive which and how much funding. This seems particularly true for local projects. The president may allocate the funds, but the governor decides who gets them and who does not; the governor may be obliged to follow broad presidential policy outlines, but he or she decides how and where to implement them. All of this illustrates that governors do have real political power; in fact, as it was described to me, "un gobernador es el virrey de su estado" (a governor is the viceroy of his state). Particularly from the perspective of the municipality, the dominant power is the state rather than the central government in Mexico City (see González Oropeza 1986: 502).

Yet the function of the governor is mostly political in nature, rather than administrative. In fact, it is so political that, as long as a governor can keep his or her state socially calm and, increasingly, in line electorally, he or she will not be overly bothered by Mexico City. But if a governor is not proving adept at regaining support for the PRI or falls foul of the president for some reason, then he or she is likely to be replaced, as happened to Oscar Ornelas in Chihuahua and Enrique Velasco Ibarra in Guanajuato in the mid-1980s under President de la Madrid. Both were removed from office for reasons that were clearly political and that had nothing to do with administrative matters. Ornelas was removed because he had "allowed" too many PAN victories in his state; Velasco Ibarra was removed because he supported the wrong candidate to succeed him as governor and openly opposed the party.

Under Salinas, more governors fell foul of the president than at any time since Cárdenas. No fewer than sixteen constitutionally elected governors stood down during his mandate for a variety of reasons. Some (Patrocinio González Blanco from

Chiapas and Genaro Borrego from Zacatecas) were promoted to top-level positions in the government or the party; some (Salvador Neme Castillo from Tabasco and Mario Ramón Beteta from the state of Mexico) were forced to resign because of a perceived lack of loyalty to the president and the party; others (Ramón Aguirre in Guanajuato; Luis Martínez Villicaña in Michoacán; Fausto Zapata in San Luis Potosí) were punished for electoral "improprieties" or because postelectoral conflict had made their positions untenable.

Part of the problem was not simply the need to remove governors who could not be relied on; the president also needed to circumvent any political opposition that they might otherwise present to presidential policies, specifically those associated with electoral opening and with Solidarity (PRONASOL) expenditures. During PRONASOL's first two years (1989–1991), many governors strongly resented the way in which major lines of funding were bypassing them and going straight to local community groups over which they had traditionally held control. Part of the reason for this program's being run out of the president's office, as will be discussed later, was precisely because Salinas did not trust those governors to dispense resources in ways that would cushion and forestall the social unrest that might arise from his macroeconomic policies.

Until the recent electoral defeats suffered by the PRI at the state level (Baja California in 1989 and 1995, Chihuahua in 1992, and Jalisco and Guanajuato in 1995), and the negotiated PAN interim governorship of Guanajuato in 1991, political custom had it that, through the official party, the PRI, the Mexican president directly appointed state governors and they, in turn, appointed municipal presidents and officials to higher positions.[10] Then they were all officially elected by the people and ratified by the legislature. Matters may have changed somewhat now that opposition candidates pose a serious challenge, but it appears that candidate selection methods have not changed a great deal for PRI candidates, who seem basically to follow the same procedures of the past. This may change soon, however, because one of the most significant issues within party ranks involves candidate selection procedures. Part of the challenge for the PRI's internal reform relates to the development of a candidate selection process in tune with the party's alleged efforts at internal democratization, one that satisfies the party's rank and file and presents credible candidates to the local electorate.

For now, the traditional pattern of federal control over potential PRI candidates for municipal-level political office continues unaltered. As with other appointments to the highest state positions, which are made concurrently by the president, high-ranking party officials, and the governor, the selection of each municipal president also occurs within the higher levels of the PRI and state government. In the past, it was common for each *diputado federal* (member of Congress), also from the PRI, to propose the nominees for the mayoralty of his or her district and present the list to the governor. The list of selected candidates was then submitted to the local PRI committee, which presented them as official party candidates. All of this occurred through extensive bargaining, and loyalty was owed to the nominating patron(s), with the governor acting as supreme patron. Not surprisingly, this was a source of conflict within municipalities, particularly because municipal presidents chosen by the incumbent governor or by outside party leaders were often unpopular with the general public, local politicians, and members of the *ayuntamiento* for their inept handling of local problems (Cornelius and Craig 1991: 26). Local PRI leaders (especially the party's municipal secretary), however, generally expected to have the most say in selecting candidates for *regidores* (aldermen) and *síndicos* (trustees) listed on the ballot on the same *planilla* (slate) as the municipal president.

This is one way in which the governor and the local party sought to constrain the municipal executive, since, once elected, the municipal president has almost total control over the appointment of municipal officers—treasurer, secretary, public works chief, and so on. These appointed officials constitute the executive wing of the *ayuntamiento*, and within the guidelines laid down by the municipal president (at whose pleasure they serve), they enjoy considerable autonomy over their agendas and programs. Not surprisingly, some would-be municipal presidents who have some independent political "weight" and are, therefore, in a position to negotiate, insist on nominating their own people to the slate in order to avoid possible problems farther down the line.[11] As will be discussed later, the *cabildo* monitors the municipal president and his or her officers' activities and periodically approves budgets, but usually the municipal president is able to negotiate programs by means of the *cabildo* meetings. In fact, one of the principal tasks of the municipal president is to negotiate his or her policy agenda, particularly when the opposition *regidores* close party ranks and refuse to support the municipal president (Rodríguez and Ward 1994a, 1996).

Local Government in Comparative Perspective

The Mexican municipality is approximately equivalent to the U.S. county. A brief comparative analysis of the Mexican and U.S. counterparts is useful if one is to assess the importance and functions of the former. Both constitute important types of local government; both provide the basis for the states' territorial division; and both cover rural as well as urban areas.

County government in the United States varies in importance. In New England, for instance, counties are subordinated to the cities and towns and have minimal or virtually no functions at all. In the South and in many western states, the county is the dominant form of local government. In other areas, city and county government are concurrent; that is, their responsibilities are so closely related that they are run by the same government. Denver and San Francisco, for example, are both a city and a county.

There is no uniformity in county government in the United States, although in most of the states each county has a county board to run its affairs. Board members are elected and are called supervisors, county commissioners, or justices of the peace. The county board has only those powers granted to it by the state constitution and the legislature, and these powers vary from state to state. Besides the members of the county board, other county officials are the sheriff, the prosecuting attorney, the coroner, the assessor, the auditor, the recorder or registrar of deeds, the county clerk, the county superintendent of schools, and the treasurer. Depending on local laws, these officials may be either elected or appointed (Steinberg 1984: 386).

Under the federal and state constitutions, municipal governments in Mexico are uniformly organized and structured. As is the case in the United States, however, their size, and therefore their importance, varies greatly. The variation among Mexican municipalities is so large that it would be impossible to attempt any generalization. Baja California Sur covers 73,475 square kilometers (28,380 square miles) and is divided into only three municipalities, for example, while the state of Puebla comprises 33,902 square kilometers (13,095 square miles) and is divided into 217 municipalities. Divergences in population density are even larger: the Federal District has a population density of 6,337.6 residents per square kilometer, while in Quintana Roo population density is 4.2 (CNEM 1985b: 474, 479–539). A similar pattern can be found in the United States, where counties vary in size from San Bernardino County in California, which is bigger than the states of Vermont, Delaware, and Rhode Island combined, to New York County (Manhattan), which is only 57 square kilometers (22 square miles). Densities, too, vary markedly: Los Angeles County in California has about 7 million residents, while several of the state's rural counties have only a few hundred widely scattered residents.

What is important is that, in spite of the vast differences among Mexico's 2,412 municipalities, their governmental structures are consistently similar. Every municipality is governed by the *ayuntamiento*, which is made up of both elected and appointed officials. The municipality is legally regulated by the Mexican Constitution, the state constitution, urban development laws, fiscal laws, municipal laws, and the rules and regulations issued by the *ayuntamiento*. There are no elected city administrations above the level of the municipality, however. Whereas in the United States individual city and county governments not only vary but may also coincide (e.g., the cases of Denver and San Francisco), in Mexico, large cities may embrace several adjacent municipalities (e.g., the metropolitan areas of Mexico City, Guadalajara, and Monterrey), but each one of these municipalities has its own independent government.

Another similarity between Mexico and the United States is that the Mexican municipality resembles in its functions and organization the mayor–city council form of government employed in many major U.S. cities, particularly the "strong mayor" plan. And just as the municipality is governed by a series of laws, rules, and regulations, U.S. cities are ruled by city charters. Both the U.S. city council and the Mexican *ayuntamiento* have the power to pass local ordinances, collect taxes, and vote expenditures, although they are subject to limitations imposed by state constitutions and laws, as well as by the leadership and initiative exercised by a strong executive. The most important similarity between the U.S. mayor-council government and the Mexican *ayuntamiento* is their internal organization, particularly their tendency to centralize power in the mayor and the municipal president, that is, the tendency toward strong executives.

It is often said that the municipality is the "basic cell" of Mexico's political and administrative organization and that as such it is relatively autonomous, since it is best informed about local needs and the availability of resources and is also in charge of administering the territory's goods and services. As a cell, however, it is part of a larger body, which makes it interdependent with other municipalities and with the other levels of government. Article 115 of the Constitution formally constitutes the Mexican municipality as an autonomous administrative unit—the *municipio libre* (free municipality). In practice, however, municipalities are not always as independent of the larger political body as their legal definition might imply. The pattern of intergovernmental relations in Mexico, characterized by the heavy dominance of the higher levels of government and the almost complete dependence of the lower ones, does not easily allow for municipal autonomy. The following sections describe how a typical municipality is organized and the functions performed by municipal officials.

Internal Organization of the Mexican Municipality

The most important institution in the Mexican municipality is the *ayuntamiento*. It is responsible for the municipality's overall administration, and there are no intermediate authorities between it and state government. Although slight variations exist from one state to another in terms of how their municipal structures are organized, those described here may be considered representative. Some of the details will vary (e.g., the role of *regidores* or the number of *síndicos*), but the basic structure as laid down in the federal Constitution is common.

The *ayuntamiento* comprises a municipal president (mayor)*, síndicos, regidores,* and other public officials, assisted by professionals, technicians, and administrative personnel. The municipal president*, síndicos,* and *regidores* are elected for a three-year term (*trienio*), and cannot be reelected for two consecutive terms. All other senior public officials and top-level administrators are appointed by the municipal president. Of these appointed officials, the most important are the *secretario* (secretary), the *tesorero* (treasurer), and the *oficial mayor* (chief of staff) and, following them, the head of public works and the police chief. All of them report directly to the municipal president. Each *ayuntamiento*, depending on its administrative organization, economic resources, size, and local needs, decides the number of high-level public officials it requires. The municipal president, in conjunction with the municipality's top-ranking officials, also appoints all other (lower-rank) municipal administrative employees, that is, the support and clerical staff. This staff tends to retain its positions from one municipal administration to the next, and therefore these employees are the only ones who provide some continuity between administrations. The *ayuntamiento* as a whole, or one or more of its members, may be suspended or removed from office, providing the proposition to do so receives at least a two-thirds majority in the state legislature.

The Municipal President

The municipal president is the executive power in the municipality, in addition to serving as the *ayuntamiento*'s legal and administrative representative. The municipal president's role in the municipality, like the governor's in the state, is more political than administrative in nature, since the primary function of the office is to maintain social tranquillity by negotiating and conciliating between economic and political pressure groups; in fact, municipal presidents, unequivocally, describe their principal role as "*conciliador de intereses*" (conciliator of interests). Because political functions absorb the largest part of the mayor's time, there has been some discussion and debate in Mexico about the advisability of having an official designated for administrative duties (somewhat like the city manager in the United States), thus relieving the municipal president of the administration and allowing him or her to concentrate on the political role.

Traditionally, in *priísta* municipalities the mayor's responsibilities have included preparing, organizing, and monitoring the electoral process, with federal and state support (if the governor is also a *priísta*). In these instances, the municipal president tends to work closely with the local PRI structure, also supported by the higher levels of the party and by the local political bosses.[12] The PRI's Municipal Committee, in fact, is likely to be an important element in a mayor's governing team, particularly since the municipal president is closely involved in the appointment of the party's Municipal Committee members. The local party leader is usually selected by state and federal party officials shortly after the municipal president assumes power. Thus, the party's Municipal Committee changes every three years, with the swearing in of a new *ayuntamiento*.

The selection of the local party committee is important because it provides the municipal president with strong political support, and therefore must have as members people who can "work" with him or her. Nonetheless, the municipal president does not have a free hand in the selection process, as the higher levels of the party also select their own representatives; these representatives are charged with checking on the municipal president and keeping the administration in line with the party.

Opposition municipal presidents, by and large, seem to be less openly involved with their respective party structures and operation. In most cases, this is not necessarily because this is what they want, but, rather, because their party apparatus is less experienced and poorly organized and there is little tradition of converting governance into political and electoral support (although that may change). Nonetheless, in some cases, the policies and programs that they endorse tend to be defined along partisan lines, which makes them differ little from *priísta* municipal governments. If *priístas* tend to espouse projects that favor the poor and lower middle classes because that is where their most important base of support has traditionally come from, *panistas*, for example, will endorse projects that benefit the urban middle class, because that is where their core of sympathizers is found. In general terms, however, research indicates that opposition municipal presidents across the board seem to be more concerned with effective government than with building up their party base; in fact, many of these municipal presidents have been criticized for not using the opportunity while in office to build party support.

There are other significant parallels that can be drawn between the municipal presidents of the "official" party and those of the opposition; one is particularly worth mentioning. Generally speaking, opposition municipal presidents tend to be more involved in the *administrative* aspect of their administration, while PRI municipal presidents have traditionally seemed to be more engaged in the *political* aspect.[13] Particularly in some northern municipalities, however, this seems to be changing. By and large, PRI municipal presidents there are equally concerned with effective and efficient government and shun political and partisan pressures (see Rodríguez and Ward 1996). This new style of governing among PRI municipal presidents is very much a consequence of opening the political space at the local level (at present, about 20 percent of municipalities, including several large cities, are governed by the opposition) and of making elections more competitive. Those running for office at the local level now know that much of their campaign success will ride on the past performance of their party while in office (Ward 1996).

In brief, in spite of the fact that research has shown that the goals and objectives, as well as the background and experience, that *panista* and *priísta* officials bring to office tend to be different, a more efficient, open, and accessible style of management seems to be taking over in local government in Mexico. In fact, one of the principal findings of our research (Rodríguez and Ward 1992, 1994a, 1995, 1996) centers around the changes that have occurred in municipal administration in Mexico during the past decade. Our study of two PAN administrations in Chihuahua in the mid-1980s found that the difference in the background of public officials coming from the two parties was openly reflected in their approach to public policy. While PRI officials focused their efforts on highly visible and costly public works and made no clear effort to change the traditional PRI style of governing, PAN officials went out of their way to make their administrations open and accessible and actually managed to govern in a quite efficient manner. Our 1994 analysis of Monterrey and San Pedro Garza García in the state of Nuevo León, governed by the PRI and the PAN, respectively, showed virtually no differences in the governing style of both cities. Partisan affiliation, for all practical purposes, did not impinge on governance at the local level in these cases; government was dictated by effectiveness and efficiency (see Ward 1996).

The Síndicos and Regidores

Together, the *síndicos* and *regidores* constitute the "legislative branch" of municipal government. In some municipalities the *síndicos* control municipal finances to a large extent and are members of the commission in charge of the municipal treasury. The *síndicos* are also the juridical representatives of the municipality (i.e., any injunctions and criminal or civic proceedings are taken against them). The *regidores* are charged with one or more commissions created to see to the municipality's well-being and development.

In some municipalities there is more than one *síndico*, and the number of *regidores* varies from one municipality to another (usually according to population); the number of *síndicos* and *regidores* is specifically defined in each state's constitution and municipal laws.[14] In the state of Guanajuato, for example, the Ley Orgánica Municipal (the comprehensive legal code that applies to municipalities) stipulates that the state's most important municipalities (Guanajuato, León, Celaya, Irapuato, and Salamanca) must have two *síndicos*; the number of *regidores* varies from eight to twelve. The largest municipalities have twelve *regidores* in charge of the following commissions (named by the municipal president): municipal finances; government, rules and regulations, urban ordinances; public security, traffic, fire fighting; public health, water supply, drainage; social assistance, education, recreation; public works, streets, paving, street naming; street lighting, street cleaning and garbage collection, parks and gardens; markets, supply centers, slaughterhouses; municipal goods, public parking lots, graveyards; promotion of agriculture, cattle raising, industry, tourism, and rural areas; and sports. Thus, each *regidor* has responsibility for a particular administrative aspect.

Regidores are elected by getting their names on each party's slate. The name of each party's candidate for municipal president is followed by the names of the candidate(s) for *síndico* and then by the list of candidates for *regidor*. Thus, each vote that is cast for a party automatically elects an entire team; that is, one cannot cross party lines to vote for municipal president and *regidor*. In other instances, the number of *regidores* who actually get into office is directly proportional to the party's vote, and come into office in the order in which they appear on the ballot. The remaining *regidores* are taken from the losing slates, also in proportion to the vote for each party and also in the order in which they appear on the ballot. In yet other cases, one of the less important *regidor* positions is assigned to each one of the losing political parties that participated in the election.[15]

Naturally, mayoral candidates negotiate with their parties to have at the top of their slate the names of their closest collaborators, which will ensure that, if elected, the municipal president will have a working majority in the government. As might be anticipated, the municipal president will assign the most important *regidor* commissions (especially finances and governance) to members of his or her slate; the party/constituency representatives from whom the municipal president can anticipate the staunchest opposition will become *regidores* in the least important areas (e.g., sports and recreation).

The Cabildo

When the members of the *ayuntamiento* meet for a working session, they constitute the *cabildo*, the collegial body that makes the municipal government's decisions. It is presided over by the municipal president. In the *cabildo*, the *ayuntamiento*'s highest authority, all policies, plans, programs, and projects are voted on and the municipal budget is approved. All *elected* members of the *ayuntamiento* have voting rights and cast a vote on each issue, with the municipal president having the tie-breaking vote. The municipal secretary and other appointed officials may also attend the meetings, but do not have voting privileges. In addition to deciding policies and budgets, the *cabildo* also has the authority to approve and issue the rules, regulations, and administrative dispositions that govern the municipality.

Thus, the political life of Mexico's municipalities centers around the *cabildo*, where all interests are represented and where all policy decisions affecting the community are reached. The various pressure groups and constituencies within the community will naturally seek to have their interests met by having a spokesperson sitting on the *cabildo*. Typically, each group has someone who will represent its interests on the various party slates. Given that in most municipalities all political parties are represented on the *cabildo* (albeit only one will be in control), most groups can expect to have someone speaking on their behalf. In this fashion, the *cabildo* may act as a check and balance for the municipal president and his or her appointed officials, who will have the majority. Strictly speaking, of course, one cannot talk of a true separation of powers, since the *cabildo* is a collegial body elected on the same slate as the municipal president and today also embraces some degree of minority party participation. It functions as both legislature and "watchdog" (Ochoa Campos 1986), and the exercise of both functions should be observable if real democratization is occurring within city hall—the level at which government most directly affects people's daily lives.[16] Checks and balances may be measured by examining the amount of debate within the *ayuntamiento* and by the degree to which the municipal president and his or her appointed executive officers are made accountable to elected *cabildo* members.

As opposition parties have made inroads and gained more access to *regidor* positions within the *ayuntamientos*, one finds more instances in which a *regidor* may firmly oppose the municipal president or be openly critical of policies and programs. For example, under opposition government in Ensenada (since 1983) and in Tijuana (since 1989), *regidores* have assumed a more active role in challenging municipal presidents; the same was the case in Mexicali while the PRI dominated municipal government (Rodríguez and Ward 1994a). Moreover, there are several cases where *regidores* from the mayor's party have turned against him and created partisan factions within the *cabildo* (Tijuana under the 1989–1992 PAN administration; see Rodríguez and Ward 1994a for a full account). In these cases, and particularly where partisanship may help determine the position adopted by each *regidor*, the *cabildo* may become extremely divided and conflictual. In the last instance, it may seek to overthrow the municipal president, but this can be done legally only by the state legislatures. More frequently, overall conflict will make governing extremely difficult and lead, in a much more indirect fashion, to the municipal president's total loss of control over his or her *ayuntamiento*.

On a more positive note, these inter- and intraparty differences have turned *cabildos* into the arenas of debate they were meant to be, where local governance decisions are made as a result of discussion and interest representation. To the extent that there is increasing debate and independence between municipal presidents and *cabildo* members, it appears that this would be indicative of greater democracy in local government (Rodríguez and Ward 1994a, 1996).

Typically, the *cabildo* meets twice a month in ordinary sessions. The municipal president or a majority of the members of the *ayuntamiento* can call a special session to discuss a specific issue at any time. During a meeting, each member is entitled to speak for approximately ten minutes and on only two occasions about the same subject, except when he or she is the chief proponent of the issue being discussed. All meetings are open to the public, except when a confidential issue will be discussed. If a *síndico* or *regidor* fails to attend the meetings for two months, he or she can be removed from office. The municipal president cannot be absent for more than two weeks, and the secretary of the *ayuntamiento* acts as the mayor's substitute during an absence. These rules serve to prevent members of the *cabildo* from "sneaking in" policies in the absence of their opposition; in a way, this also serves to insulate local government from partisanship.

Thus, the authority and obligations of municipal government are determined by federal and state legislation and by the rules and regulations set forth by the *ayuntamiento* itself through the *cabildo*. In most states, municipal administrative structures are organized according to the specific guidelines dictated by the state's Municipal Code, the Ley Orgánica Municipal (under various names, each state has its own Municipal Code). With the 1984 reforms to Article 115, *ayuntamientos* have been empowered to issue the Bando de Policía y Buen Gobierno, as well as various internal decrees within their respective jurisdictions. The Bando de Policía y Buen Gobierno provides the basic set of rules and regulations for municipal public administration, that is, the municipality's internal bylaws. It also contains the dispositions that govern the provision of public services and all other matters pertaining to community life, including the citizenry's obligations toward their community. All of these regulations combined provide the basis for the functions performed by municipal government.

Municipal Dependence

Although in principle the Mexican municipality is *the* governmental unit for local administrative purposes, in reality the *ayuntamiento*'s powers have traditionally been limited by state and federal government. Although the 1917 Constitution stipulates that municipalities are to be autonomous, it does not state specifically *how* this autonomy is to be exercised. Hence, the key question concerning the evolving role of states and municipalities in the Mexican federal system relates to the degree of autonomy they have wrested from Mexico City. There is virtual agreement that very little autonomy has actually resulted (Martínez Assad and Ziccardi 1989; Merino 1994; Cabrero 1995) and that, by and large, the states have remained under the control of the central government while municipalities have remained under the control of state governors. Describing intergovernmental relations in Mexico in the early 1970s (and not much has changed since) Fagen and Tuohy write:

Each successive level of government is weaker, more dependent, and more impoverished than the level above. Since the municipality is at the bottom of the federal-state-
local chain, it is in reality—despite its official designation as the *municipio libre* (free
municipality)—the least autonomous unit of government in the republic. An ayuntamiento or municipal government is normally constituted at the pleasure of the state
authorities, is in control of very few funds, and is limited juridically and politically to
caretaker and administrative functions. (1972: 20–21)

Municipal political dependence on federal and state government has always been
directly related to economic dependence. Formerly, municipalities could not collect
property or income taxes, and thus all revenues went to the state and federal governments. Little money was left for locally initiated projects, and local governments
had to resort to other sources of revenue, such as market fees, slaughterhouse fees, or
licensing fees for business establishments (Purcell 1973: 51). Municipal dependence
increased as the federal government assumed responsibility for providing communities with basic public services such as housing, education, and health care. Thus, the
number of houses, schools, and clinics in every community depended on the decision of some official in Mexico City. Furthermore, to make up for municipal deficiencies and improve the standard of living at the local level, the federal government
took responsibility for paving and maintaining roads, providing water and a sewage
service system, and building electrification projects. For example, the number of
dwellings without electricity decreased nationally from 41 percent to 25 percent and
the number without piped-in water decreased from 61 percent to 50 percent between 1970 and 1980 (Ward 1986: 88). Not surprisingly, these and other services
were supplied to urban areas first. But even in rural areas the federal government
also actively intervened, through programs such as the Programa de Inversiones para
el Desarrollo Rural (Program of Public Investments for Rural Development,
PIDER) and a wide range of housing and regularization agencies under President
Echeverría, and through major initiatives such as the IMSS-COPLAMAR extension
of social welfare facilities to peripheral and marginal regions beginning in 1978
(Ward 1986). In short, in the 1970s, it was practically impossible to find a municipality in Mexico where the presence of the federal government was not evident in
some degree or another; as Fagen and Tuohy described it, "even a routine (although
important) decision concerning electrification or drainage in the municipio will often be out of the hands of local authorities and located, for political or economic
reasons, in some state or federal office less sensitive to community needs and more
insulated from local pressures" (1972: 22).

What does this pattern of intergovernmental relations mean for the policy
process in Mexico? Public policy under such a system becomes isolated from those
who are supposed to receive the benefits of governmental actions. As Grindle noted
in the late 1970s—and little seems to have changed since—"policy making . . . is
the exclusive prerogative of a small elite and is characterized by limited informa-
tional inputs, behind-the-scenes bargaining and accommodation, and low levels of

public discussion and debate" (1977: 5). Moreover, the fact that the distribution of services derives from policy initiatives in Mexico City leaves ample room to question whether local needs ever enter the discussion when formulating policy, or whether these plans develop more as a response to national political needs and pressures as perceived in Mexico City. Nonetheless, even if the local community has little input in policy decisions, this does not necessarily imply that its needs can be ignored; there are times when public demands and demonstrations get out of hand and, in this respect, social protest does play an important role in policy making.[17]

The personalities, interests, and ambitions of the public officials involved in making decisions about local policies also play a critical role. All too often the public's interests have clashed with some officials' personal interests—mainly those affecting career advancement—and important projects have been dropped. In other cases, the public actually does benefit from the personal interests of officials. For example, in the state of Guanajuato in the mid-1980s, a top-ranking state government official who had openly expressed his ambitions for the governorship also happened to own a construction company and embarked on an intense campaign to get the streets paved throughout the state. In fairness, however, this was a rather unusual case because it was done so openly; although it may be common for Mexican politicians to take as much personal advantage of the system as possible, it is usually done more discreetly, particularly when material wealth is to be gained. Nonetheless, the construction of public works for purposes of career advancement is commonplace throughout Mexico; Fagen and Tuohy refer to these as *plazismo*, an enthusiasm for showy public works projects symbolized by improvements to the town's central square, or plaza:

> The attractions of such projects to cautious officeholders are legion: they are physically and politically visible; they can be completed in a relatively short time and thus accrue wholly to the reputational capital of the incumbent; they are for all the people and thus require no hard choices as to what sector or project should receive scarce resources; they are uncontroversial in the tradition of "good works"; they can often be partially funded through the donations of others eager to have their names associated with civic improvements. (1972: 26)

In addition to seeking career advancement or personal gain of another sort when designing and implementing policy, state and local public officials, like their counterparts in the federal government, must operate under the time limitations set by the *sexenio* system.[18] The governor's term also functions in six-year cycles, and therefore most state and local officials must accomplish (personally and otherwise) as much as possible during their term in office. Political turnover at the local level is even greater than at the state and national levels, for *ayuntamientos* change every three years. This rotation complicates public policy further because it renders unlikely any long-range planning and any stand on public policy issues, even more so than at the federal level. Indeed, the lack of continuity from one administration to the next caused by turnover has led to much discussion of increasing the three-year municipal term to at least four years.

However defective and inefficient policies may be, the fact remains that at least some services and assistance are provided (see Cabrero 1995 for some landmark cases), and in the recent past municipalities have become stronger. As will be discussed later, this became increasingly true in the Salinas administration, as citizens and communities became involved in the construction of public works funded by the various Solidarity programs. Municipal Committees also form the principal vehicle for Zedillo's Superación de a la Pobreza (Overcoming Poverty).

Conclusion

Although Mexico's Constitution and legal codes emphasize the *municipio libre* and its autonomy over its own affairs, Mexico's highly centralized political system has historically prevented municipalities from exercising the freedom and independence promised them by the Constitution. As stated at the beginning of this chapter, the commonly held perception of the overwhelming centralization of Mexico's system cannot be refuted; as we have seen, the clientelistic structure of the system extends from the president all the way to the lower ranks of municipal government. This asymmetrical but reciprocal exchange of favors for political support has cemented the political system for decades—for centuries, in fact, since the profound legacy of patron-client ties dates from the colonial period. Like other Latin American nations, Mexico has been dominated by a strong center, but it is a center significantly reinforced by its clients in the periphery. That is, it is a system that provides opportunities for local political elites to have an effect on the decisions made at the center. Particularly during politically difficult times, the elites in the center cannot afford to ignore the needs and demands of the periphery and simply impose their will. With the regime's legitimacy at stake, federal elites have become increasingly aware that the true focus of control needs to be directed toward the local level, because, ultimately, that is where their support comes from. For over sixty years, the PRI was able to control elective offices at all levels of government, and the party's patronage was oriented, precisely, at maintaining this control. Yet as this chapter has argued on a descriptive basis, and as I will seek to demonstrate in the remaining chapters, this does not presuppose that local government, whether in the hands of the PRI or of the opposition, has no discretionary powers whatsoever. Chapter 3 discusses how the localities have advanced on the path toward autonomy, even though this advancement has been conditioned by two important decisions made at the center: deciding to open the political space, and deciding to decentralize.

3

Responding to Crisis:
Opening the Political Space and
Deciding to Decentralize

The rich scholarly literature on Mexico's political system offers a variety of interpretations on the degree of authoritarianism and the nature of the country's democracy. As discussed in Chapter 2, however, there are certain elements of the system about which there is little disagreement: it is highly centralist, with enormous power vested in the presidency, and the level of pluralism has been extremely limited.[1] Since its emergence in the 1930s, and until the historic 1988 election, the PRI ensured that almost all of its presidential candidates regularly won 85 percent of the total vote. This changed in 1988, when Carlos Salinas de Gortari won with (a highly questioned) 51 percent of the vote; in 1994 Ernesto Zedillo's margin of victory was even smaller (20 percent). Nevertheless, Mexico's *priísta* presidents have ruled virtually unchallenged in regular but nonrenewable six-year cycles (*sexenios*). Also, until 1988, the transition of power from one administration to the next occurred relatively smoothly—something worth noting on a continent where coups and countercoups have occurred with great regularity.

The concentration of power in the figure of the president discussed in Chapter 2 is symbolic of the high degree of centralization that permeates the entire system and dictates the country's social, political, and economic activity. While the last decade has seen major efforts and some significant advances toward decentralization, by and large, centralization has persisted. Indeed, policies designed to decentralize fiscally, politically, and administratively have in effect led to more centralization (Bailey 1994). This is particularly the case for the relations among the three levels of government; in spite of all the constitutional and legal provisions for municipal autonomy, local governments have remained subordinate to the state and federal hierarchies.

In this chapter I shall explore some of the political and economic consequences of such centralization. These became manifest in the most serious political and economic crises Mexico has confronted in modern times: first in the early 1980s, and then at the end of 1994, shortly after Ernesto Zedillo was sworn in as president. First I discuss in broad terms the unfolding of events that led to the economic crises and, in each case, the political crises that were engendered. In the second section I will explore how, *sexenio* by *sexenio*, successive Mexican governments have cautiously searched for solutions to these crises by using economic and political liberalization. The political opening (*apertura*) can be more significantly observed in three specific areas, which will be analyzed in the third part of this chapter: (1) a series of electoral reforms, starting in the late 1970s; (2) the recognition of opposition victories, beginning in the mid-1980s; and (3) decentralization. The interplay between economic crisis and political change has brought to the fore new political forces and practices in government, principally from the opposition parties, which have further intensified the presence of decentralization as a key element within the national agenda.

The Economic Crisis

Anyone who visited Mexico in late 1982 found a country living under a set of conditions that Cornelius and Craig vividly describe as follows:

> a virtually bankrupt government, running an unprecedented budget deficit; a financial system severely shaken by the recent nationalization of all private banks; a central bank with its reserves wiped out; investment paralyzed by the flight in the preceding year of more than $23 billion in private capital to other countries; a crushing foreign debt of more than $82 billion, and funds insufficient even to pay the interest due on these loans; a currency that had been devalued by more than 80 percent against the dollar in less than a year; inflation running at more than 100 percent; an economic growth rate of minus 0.2 percent, with a year of even greater economic contraction ahead; more than 20 million people—over half the nation's work force—either unemployed or drastically underemployed; a population stunned by the abrupt turn of economic events, and deeply distrustful of public authorities. (1984: 411)

This was the scenario Miguel de la Madrid faced when he assumed the presidency on December 1, 1982. In his inaugural address he acknowledged the seriousness of the crisis and vehemently stated, "I will not allow the country to come apart in my hands!"

What events precipitated the crisis of the 1980s? What happened to the Mexican political system, which had always been referred to as the most stable regime in Latin America? What happened to the "Mexican miracle," which was expected to continue indefinitely?[2] The crisis began to unfold in the 1970s, when Mexico became one of the largest suppliers of oil to the world market. As the price of oil quadrupled in 1973–1974 and then tripled again in 1980–1981, the international community promptly took notice of Mexico, particularly as it was the world's tenth-largest nation in terms of GDP. At the same time, U.S. bankers found themselves with billions of petrodollars, and Mexico appeared to be an almost risk-free borrower—it had enormous amounts of oil and ambitious modernization plans. It seemed logical for international bankers to make loans at attractive interest rates and for Mexicans happily to accept them. Although for a while everything went well, all of a sudden the bubble burst—the world oil market collapsed, and so did Mexico's economy. In September 1982 then-president José López Portillo nationalized Mexico's privately owned banks, and Mexico found itself on the verge of default. What triggered all of this?

The two main causes of Mexico's debt were the huge increases in public spending undertaken by the López Portillo administration after 1978, and the decision to keep the Mexican peso overvalued in order to dampen the inflationary effect of all that spending. The money went for construction, mining, electricity generation, and manufacturing. Also, corruption was especially rampant at that time. Under de la Madrid it seemed to subside as attempts were made at "moral renovation," but it proved very hard to change long-held habits. Under President Salinas corruption appeared somewhat more discreet, but as a series of scandals showed at the end of his administration and in subsequent months, it is still a major problem—and it infects the lowest to the highest of government employees.[3]

By the mid-1980s, inflation raged at over 100 percent, capital flight seemed unstoppable, high interest rates pushed up the amount of the debt, and the world recession made it increasingly difficult for these debts to be repaid. Interest payments on Mexico's debt amounted to about ten billion dollars annually and devoured almost three of every four dollars that the country earned from its exports and the tourist trade. Sometimes the money borrowed in the United States did not even leave the country because Mexico had to pay it right back.

To complicate matters even further, it seemed as though almost everything that could go wrong in Mexico did. The devastating earthquakes of September 1985 killed almost twenty thousand people and left tens of thousands living in tents and temporary shacks.[4] In May 1986, American officials appearing before a U.S. Senate subcommittee publicly condemned Mexican officials for corruption and complicity in drug smuggling. A further decline in the price of oil stripped the already weak economy of a substantial amount of projected foreign exchange. The peso, which was worth twenty-six to the dollar in 1982, fell to over one thousand by the end of de la Madrid's *sexenio*. Inflation continued at over 100 percent, and purchasing power dropped to the levels of twenty-five years earlier. Unemployment and underemployment reached the highest levels ever. In Mexico City one could see signs posted everywhere that read "No a la deuda" (No to the debt), which really meant "Let's default." The Mexican people were tired of hardship. But even so, Mexico did not want to become a pariah among Western countries, and it steadfastly refused to default on its US$100 billion debt.

The largest problem for Mexico's ruling elite at that time was that the country's policy decisions as well as the outcome of its economic and political strategies depended on external factors that were beyond Mexico's ability to control. The most important of these factors were the price of oil in the world market and the interest rates of U.S. and world money markets. Time and again it was pointed out that for every dollar per barrel the price of oil dropped, Mexico lost US$500 million in revenues, and every time interest rates went up or down one percent elsewhere, Mexico lost or saved approximately US$700 million in interest payments on its foreign debt.

With Carlos Salinas de Gortari as his secretary of programming and budget, President de la Madrid set out to pull the country together by rebuilding the economy.[5] A series of important economic measures were taken, starting with an austerity package called the Programa Inmediato de Recuperación Económica (Program for Immediate Economic Recovery, PIRE), which included adjusting the exchange rate, increasing non-oil exports, and closing down inefficient parastatals. Continued decreases in income, however, worsening economic conditions internationally, real decreases in the price of oil, and increases in interest rates destroyed domestic demand. To provide just one example, the real monetary base in 1988 was less than one third that of 1977, and one sixth the 1982 figure (Jones 1991). But rather than relax the austerity measures, as had been the custom in the final year of a *sexenio*, the de la Madrid administration toughened the state's economic policy. In December 1987, the controlled exchange rate, on which all business and debt interest is calculated, was devalued by 22 percent to bring it into line with the floating rate. The price of government goods, especially those aimed at the middle class, was also increased: gasoline rose by 85 percent; electricity, by 84 percent; air travel, by 20 percent; and fertilizer, by 82.9 percent (Banco de México 1988). This paved the way for de la Madrid's Pacto de Solidaridad Económica (Economic Solidarity Pact, PSE) between the government, the employers' federation, the Congreso del Trabajo (Labor Congress), and the Confederación Nacional Campesina (National Peasant Union).

In addition to the obvious political considerations—it was less than a year until an election and inflation was at 150 percent—the PSE had concrete aims: to reduce inflation; to bring public finances into current account surplus; to limit demand through credit control; and to open the economy to international competition. For three months, therefore, prices, wages, and foreign exchange were frozen. Monthly inflation, which had been 15.5 percent in January 1988, fell to just over one percent by August.

One of the major successes of President Salinas's administration was to further consolidate control over inflation and to reduce it to single figures by the end of his term. He extended the PSE by recasting it in his Pacto para la Estabilidad y el Crecimiento Económico (Economic Stability and Growth Pact, PECE) (Mexico 1989b). This was a clear signal to the business community and to the middle classes that this particular changeover of political power (unlike the previous two transitions) would see a continuity of policy and personality. The reward for the efforts made during the 1980s, therefore, was not economic growth, but economic and financial stability.

Briefly, the Salinas project appears to have had three parts: first, to reform the Mexican economy; second, to attain a high level of economic growth and regain the standard of living attained during the 1970s; and third, to restructure the political system in order to provide both immediate legitimacy and assured future hegemony.

It was, in short, fast-track restructuring, slow-track political reform. As Lorenzo Meyer put it, "Aquí en México, Perestroika sin Glasnost" (Here in Mexico, Perestroika without Glasnost).

Central to Salinas's restructuring strategy was the creation of international confidence in an invigorated Mexican economy. To meet this goal, he removed most restrictions on foreign ownership; he attacked and destroyed the power base of several entrenched leaders in key unions; he began to offer some of the major parastatals for privatization in order to attract foreign investment and to generate major "windfall" government revenues for projects elsewhere; and, in conjunction with the United States, Mexico participated in the Brady Plan debt renegotiations, which freed up a further US$20 billion for public expenditure in Mexico. On the financial services front, his aim was to make Mexico a major financial center for the rest of Latin America, and the share flotation of several profitable public companies as part of the privatization project gave the Mexican Bolsa (stock exchange) several "star" performers, such as TELMEX (Teléfonos de México, the telephone company). Subsequent flotations of steel plants, airlines, insurance, telecommunications, and trucking concessions are estimated to have brought in a further US$20–25 billion (*The Guardian*, June 25, 1991).

Foreign investment was also attracted to Mexico through the issue of treasury bonds, which offered a high rate of return, guaranteed liquidation in dollars rather than pesos, and short rollover periods. As we now know, although the strategy was very successful in attracting foreign capital and investment, it exacerbated the "dollarization" of the Mexican economy and made it highly vulnerable to sudden withdrawals brought on by any significant loss of confidence.

As long as Salinas was in office, however, that confidence did not seem likely to ebb. Quite the contrary; the very fact of Mexico's being willing to negotiate a free trade agreement among Canada, Mexico, and the United States demonstrated the country's clear intention to intensify the tearing down of protective tariff barriers initiated under de la Madrid, when Mexico entered the General Agreement on Tariffs and Trade (GATT) in 1986. Once the North American Free Trade Agreement (NAFTA) was secured, there was no stepping back from free trade, even if the *sexenio* or ideology changed—which usually frightened would-be foreign investors. NAFTA also enhanced Mexico's attractiveness to foreign investors.

In order to offset some of the inevitable hardships that Mexican producers would face, especially in the agrarian sector, Salinas created a heavily financed support program, the Programa de Apoyos Directos al Campo (Program in Support of the Countryside, PROCAMPO), designed to facilitate restructuring and to cushion small producers in the early stages (although under NAFTA many of the price supports and protective tariffs that exist for staples will be the last to be removed). The agrarian sector notwithstanding, an assessment of NAFTA clearly indicates that the benefits of the agreement were expected to fall especially in Mexico's direction by promoting major new growth, job creation in the productive export sector, and rising real incomes.

Certainly, economic prospects were "bullish" during the Salinas period: financial services became a leading economic sector (with 28 percent of the total share in 1991 versus 22.6 percent for manufacturing), and manufacturing intensified the trend after 1985 as the leading export earner (with 55 percent of export earnings versus 30 percent for petroleum). Not everything went smoothly for Salinas, however. Both the trade and current account balances moved sharply into deficit after 1988. As Lustig (1992: 59) points out, the economic recovery in part was predicated on an upsurge in imports, which increased 17 percent in 1991. Although exports were increasing 5.5 percent per annum (with non-oil exports increasing at more than double that rate), a growing trade deficit was emerging. While this was partly covered by large inflows from the IMF and the World Bank, which strengthened Mexico's foreign reserves, the signals were clear. As Lustig (1992) argues, a possible silver lining to this particular dark cloud was that the highest increase in imports was not in consumer goods, but in capital goods, these being essential for raising productivity. Nevertheless, these indicators, and insecurity about whether NAFTA would pass in the U.S. Congress, made investors jittery about Mexico in 1993, to the point that occasional sharp slides in the value of stocks on the Bolsa were not uncommon.

Politically, of course, 1994 was in a number of respects a very bad year for President Salinas, with the Chiapas uprising timed to coincide with the implementation of NAFTA, and with the assassination of his designated successor, Luis Donaldo Colosio in March. Not surprisingly, these events made the market even more jittery, and with elections looming in August, the Salinas government did everything it could to keep the ship steady. While the president's popularity remained very high and many argue that he "won" a good victory for the PRI's replacement candidate, Ernesto Zedillo, concern was mounting about the overvalued peso and the possibility and timing of a devaluation. There were also concerns about the growing trade deficit, and about the decline in national foreign exchange reserves. Politically, too, the PRI appeared to be in danger of imploding, as a further assassination—this time of the party's general secretary—appeared to be the responsibility of one of its internal factions.

Notwithstanding these concerns, it was a surprise when the economic tapestry flew off the loom in such dramatic fashion immediately after President Zedillo assumed office on December 1, 1994. Instead of experiencing the expected continuity in macroeconomic policy, Mexico was thrown into its most severe economic crisis ever, one that, overnight, effectively destroyed Salinas's reputation, but, more important, one that threatened to have the most severe consequences for Mexico's short- and medium-term economic future and, as a concomitant, for the political future of the PRI.

The reasons for the December financial crisis are fairly straightforward and were quite succinctly reported on by President Zedillo himself during his first State of the Nation Address on September 1, 1995: a dangerously low level of foreign reserves and high vulnerability to withdrawal of foreign investment, a high proportion of which was in short-term, dollar-guaranteed treasury bonds. The missing element was a trigger for a dramatic loss of confidence. That trigger was provided by a badly mismanaged devaluation attempt on December 15, which offered too little and, more important, was not managed in such a way as to stem the hemorrhage in confidence. The uncontrolled tailspin that occurred throughout December and early January, and the almost total depletion of foreign reserves, threatened to place Mexico in bankruptcy with the immediate prospect of having to renege on guarantees to those investors wishing to cash in their treasury bonds as these rolled over. There seemed to be little that President Zedillo could do to reassure those investors. His government's handling of the devaluation was widely criticized, and there appeared to be little effective leadership from Los Pinos (Mexico's equivalent of the White House). In short, unlike any previous presidential transition, his government was beleaguered almost before it got into office.

The economic lifeline was to come from the United States, initially, it was expected, from a US$40 billion bailout of loan guarantees by Congress. This guarantee would have two major functions: first, it would restore international confidence and, it was hoped, stem the withdrawal of foreign investment from Mexico; second, it would ensure payment to those investors who chose to withdraw anyway. The initiative stalled in Congress, but President Clinton authorized the maximum line of credit that he was able to without congressional approval—US$20 billion—and the remainder came from the IMF, the World Bank, and other sources, for a total of almost US$50 billion. The Zedillo government cut public spending dramatically and initiated a new period of austerity with major price increases in gasoline, electricity, and the value-added tax (VAT; *impuesto al valor agregado*, or IVA).

The economic impacts on the Mexican population have been severe. Although prices were frozen on basic foodstuffs, the low-income population (most Mexicans) has had to confront a doubling in the level of open unemployment and, equally important, major reductions in family earnings due to lower demand for goods and services. At a stroke, President Zedillo's principal election slogan, "Bienestar para tu familia" (Well-being for your family), was in tatters. Those eligible for credit (largely middle- and upper-income groups) in the form of mortgages, loans, and credit cards were confronted with interest rates approaching, in some cases, more than 100 percent, so that massive defaulting was almost impossible to avoid. The middle classes, then, were no fonder of the incoming government than were the lower classes. Thus, the administration has had to act on a number of fronts to shore up private banks and to create refinancing packages and arrangements that will offset widespread defaulting. By early 1996, the government was attempting to "talk up" some level of recovery, but it was not until the third quarter of 1996 that significant growth began to be observed.

The implications of these financial and economic crises in 1982, 1987–1988, and, above all, in 1994–1996 extend far beyond economics. More specifically, as we shall observe, the most recent crisis has in many ways accelerated the prospects for reform and for the implementation of Zedillo's New Federalism. All three crises gravely harmed the ruling party. Opposition victories beginning in the mid-1980s, the poor showing of the PRI in the presidential election of 1988, and, perhaps even more significant, the loss of the first governorship ever in 1989, demonstrated the first effects of the crisis on the PRI. Since 1988, as a result of continued internal and external dissatisfaction, the party has had to revamp itself in an attempt to become more of a political party and in order to confront the real possibility of losing an increasing number of elections.

But what is important here are the implications of the political and economic crises for federal, state, and local government relations. The crises have meant that intergovernmental revenue transfers must be viewed in another light, given that local governments have depended heavily on these transfers since the "miracle" years. With less money to be distributed, this dependence was threatened and opened new possibilities for the opposition, which it promptly took advantage of. In 1988, Cuauhtémoc Cárdenas, Manuel Clouthier, and every other opposition presidential candidate campaigned heavily on the hardships caused by the debt, and in 1994, again, both Cárdenas and Diego Fernández de Cevallos made intergovernmental revenue sharing an important element of their respective campaign platforms. The two candidates demanded reform of the existing fiscal laws and a substantial increase in the amounts allocated to states and municipalities through intergovernmental transfers. For the PRI candidate, Ernesto Zedillo, changes in fiscal policy and decentralization of powers to the other levels and branches of government became principal elements of his campaign discourse. Indeed, Luis Donaldo Colosio had earlier emphasized these elements as critical issues in his own platform as presidential candidate.

The issue to analyze, then, is the manner in which the crises altered the patterns of decision making, and how the responses to crisis (e.g., political liberalization) have changed the character of local politics and, consequently, of intergovernmental relations. Indeed, the critical question is whether there was a resuscitation of state and local politics.

It appears that a new division of intergovernmental authority began to take shape as the much-touted split between the politicians of the PRI and the technocrats of the bureaucracy penetrated the local level. Arguably, the chasm was originally caused by the administrative agencies' focus on technical concerns, which undermined the PRI's political base and thereby led to serious political challenges to its hegemony (Centeno 1994; Centeno and Maxfield 1992; Sanderson 1983). The subsequent division of authority resulted in the technocrats' becoming responsible for solving economic problems at the national level while the state- and municipal-level politicians were expected to manage political problems locally. One can speculate that the whole issue of municipal reform was at least in part directed at regaining the PRI's weakened hegemony by recasting the political role of municipalities. By offering the local level greater opportunity for political autonomy, as we shall see, the center at the same time offered new ways for the PRI to become involved in local government and thereby to regain the ground it had lost throughout the crisis.

Simultaneously, it offered an opportunity for narrowing the technocrat-politician split.

Both the economic crises and the process of reconstruction—begun in 1982 and accelerated with Mexico's entry into GATT in 1986 and the prospects of entry into NAFTA in 1994—led to important changes in the regionalization of Mexico's economy. The North and the Center together formed the new vanguard of Mexico's entry into the global economy, but the South was in danger of being left behind. This led to a marked strengthening of the opposition, not only in its national legislative presence, but also in its presence in state and local government. In the North, in particular, former economic elites and entrepreneurs (many of them disenchanted with the bank nationalization in 1982) began to get directly involved in politics through the conservative PAN. By the mid-1980s, the North was becoming a consolidated stronghold for the opposition. In the South, although it was far less consolidated than the Right was in the North, the Left was making substantial headway among peasant groups and was beginning to win elections. The response was similarly regionalized. The federal government seemed to react more fiercely to all leftist victories.

There is no doubt that the various crises have placed unprecedented stress on the country's political and economic system and raised questions about how the resulting social tensions can be handled. Cornelius and Craig asked in the 1980s what could be done "to convince the average citizen to expect something more from his government than corruption, currency devaluations, rising prices, austerity budgets, and declining employment opportunities in the years ahead" (1984: 413). This has been the challenge for the de la Madrid, Salinas, and Zedillo administrations: to *simultaneously* rebuild political legitimacy, modernize administrative structures, and resolve a monumental economic crisis.

The Political Crisis

Having provided an overview of the economic crises during the last two decades, I now want to review the stages of the political crises that emerged during that same period. At various times, the centralization described in Chapter 2 has directly allowed authoritarianism to take hold unchallenged; many observers believe, indeed, that political repression and intimidation have been widespread and systemic since the 1960s (Bartra et al. 1975; Cockroft 1983; Harvey 1989; Schers 1972). Periodically, however, there were upwellings of dissent, such as erupted in the student disturbances in 1968, the rural guerrilla movements during the early 1970s, and other urban social movement disturbances. Some of the labor unions in Mexico, too, occasionally set themselves against the official union structure and, particularly since the 1970s, there have been strong pressures within several of these organizations to break away and form unions with more independent, democratic, and representative structures (Middlebrook 1991). Community organizations have also asserted themselves through coordinated urban social movements (Foweraker and Craig

1990; Ramírez Saiz 1986), and since the early 1980s local leaders have tended to be far more representative of their followers than formerly (Harvey 1989; Montaño 1976; Ward 1993). In the past, dissent also manifested itself in the occasional victory of an opposition party at the municipal level, but prior to the 1980s this was likely to occur only if popular dissatisfaction with the PRI or with a local power elite had become intolerable (see Bezdek 1995, for example, on the case of San Luis Potosí).

By the late 1960s, there were widespread pressures for change that went beyond these upwellings of unrest. Most significantly, within the PRI itself, some senior leaders recognized the need for internal democratic reform; they found a vehicle for voicing their discontent in Carlos Madrazo, who, for a short period during the 1960s, until his untimely death in an airplane accident, was president of the PRI. Much of the discontent of these PRI members stemmed from their recognition that the system had to become more pluralistic. Until the 1960s only one party, the Partido Acción Nacional (PAN), at the right of the political spectrum, had provided any significant electoral opposition, although its share of the national vote never exceeded 20 percent. Those parties on the left of the spectrum were either outlawed altogether or their existence and fortunes were stage-managed by the PRI in order to ensure the semblance of electoral competition (González Casanova 1970; Molinar 1991). Until 1979, elections were often rigged—not so much to prevent opposition parties from winning as to reduce abstentionism to a level that would not undermine the legitimacy of the regime and of *priísta* victories (Camp 1993; Hansen 1974; Smith 1979).[6]

By the 1980s, the façade of Mexican democracy had deteriorated so badly that the entire political system was in dire need of a facelift. Juan Molinar (1986, 1991) characterizes the changes that have occurred since the early stages of the political crisis as a shift from PRI monopoly to hegemony to limited competition. While some significant advances were made in the elections of 1983—when several important opposition victories were recognized in critical cities (including five state capitals)— these trends were reversed in the state and local elections of 1986. The de la Madrid government gave in to pressure from certain powerful sectors of the PRI's inner ranks, which refused to give space to the opposition, and once again the PRI resorted to any measures to secure victory. There is little doubt, in fact, that widespread fraud occurred in the 1985 and 1986 elections (Aziz 1987; Bezdek 1995; Guadarrama 1987). These events, coupled with stringent austerity measures, led to great disillusionment among many PRI members (especially the young), who recognized that the need to reform the system had to come from within the party's own ranks.

This was the background for the creation of the *corriente democrática* (democratic current), the movement formed within the PRI under the direction of several very senior and influential party members. The movement was to mark the beginning of the sea change that resulted from the presidential election of 1988. A group of PRI members, strongly dissatisfied with the internal system of candidate designation (largely, perhaps, because it stifled their own political ambitions) and seeking internal democratic reform, banded behind the leadership of three prominent party members: Porfirio Muñoz Ledo, Cuauhtémoc Cárdenas, and Ifigenia Martínez, all of whom had occupied senior elected and appointed positions within the party and the government. Supported by other left-wing parties, the movement hastily formed the Frente Democrático Nacional (National Democratic Front, FDN) to contest the presidential election and proposed Cuauhtémoc Cárdenas as its candidate against the PRI's Carlos Salinas de Gortari and the PAN's Manuel Clouthier.[7]

The 1988 election has been extensively documented and analyzed (Barberán et al. 1988; Cornelius, Gentleman, and Smith 1989; Molinar 1991). In short, Cárdenas did so well that some analyses insist that he won the election. Certainly the evidence seems to indicate that the results were "adjusted" in order to ensure a majority for Salinas, as the officially declared vote gave him a bare 51 percent majority. Cárdenas received 31 percent of the vote, and Clouthier got 17 percent, the typical percentage for the PAN in a presidential election (Camp 1993: 152). But even though some analyses also suggest that Salinas actually did win, albeit perhaps with a smaller percentage than was declared, the point to emphasize is that this election marked the beginning of a new era in Mexico's electoral politics. For the first time the PRI's candidate was genuinely challenged, as voters expressed their dissatisfaction with government performance and sought to cast their vote for change. Perhaps the votes that went to Cárdenas and Clouthier were much more anti-PRI than supportive of the PAN or the FDN, but what matters is that, as Salinas himself acknowledged the day after the election, "the era of the virtual one-party system has ended, giving way to a period of intense political competition" (Cornelius and Craig 1991: 1).

In the aftermath of the 1988 election, electoral politics has moved to center stage. No longer are electoral results easily predicted, particularly as the opposition has learned to intervene actively by monitoring elections, conducting quick counts, and contesting electoral results, often having them reversed in its favor. Indeed, although in most cases relatively peaceful acts of civil disobedience will suffice to overturn the results, in other instances there has been violence and even death. Sometimes protest is unnecessary, as opposition wins are recognized outright. While several examples will be discussed in more detail later, the point I wish to emphasize here is that, as a result of 1988, the PRI was obliged to undertake a series of internal reforms in order to gain credibility when electoral results were announced.

The reforms quickly paid off; in the 1991 and 1992 elections the PRI did relatively well, especially in certain regions of the country where it had done poorly in 1988, and had sometimes been defeated by both the PRD and the PAN. The 1991 congressional election, in particular, showed a major swing back to the PRI. Whether by fair or foul means, and in large part because of the political decisiveness with which President Salinas acted, by late 1993 both the PRI and the government indeed appeared to have regained much of their lost legitimacy.

There has also been an opening up of civic culture and process since 1988. Clientelistic relations between community and labor groups and PRI politicians and gov-

ernment officials have declined and been replaced by more systematic and rou-
tinized patterns of interaction (Ward 1993), although some would argue that Salinas's Solidarity Program turned the clock back, toward populism and clientelism
(Dresser 1991, but cf. Cornelius, Craig, and Fox 1994). Powerful bosses in major labor unions, such as PEMEX's and the teachers' union (Sindicato Nacional de Trabajadores de la Educación, National Union of Education Workers—SNTE), were either removed or undermined by President Salinas, and, generally speaking, unions
today seem to offer more democratic representation (Cook 1990, 1996; Foweraker
1993). Residents' associations and community organizations are also more likely to
be led by democratically elected leaders or individuals (Foweraker and Craig 1990).
There has also been an opening of the press, particularly in the realm of national
weekly or monthly publications, such as *Este País* and *Voz y Voto*, and through more
independent dailies, like *Reforma*. Also, since 1988, the media have been much
more open in publicizing the results of opinion polls conducted by a growing number of partisan and nonpartisan organizations. Indeed, public opinion polls became
one of the major foci of attention in the 1994 presidential election and have played
an important role in subsequent elections.

Most important of all, several national movements—Alianza Cívica (Civic Alliance), the Convergencia para la Democracia (Democratic Convergence), and the
Movimiento Ciudadano Democrático (Citizen's Democratic Movement) born in
San Luis Potosí and extending to the national level—have emerged to monitor and
protect the vote at elections, defend the democratic advances that have been won,
and denounce any attempt by the regime to interfere with these advances.[8] NGOs
and informal associations only rarely are overtly tied to a political party, although
most tend to be broadly supportive of the opposition. This is because they do not
wish to lose credibility by being tied to a party whose fortunes may fluctuate. Nor
do they wish to be co-opted by a partisan orthodoxy that would drive them away
from *civic*-oriented processes and goals.

Finally, there has been a growing concern over the protection of civil rights. In
1989, President Salinas created the Comisión Nacional de Derechos Humanos (National Human Rights Commission), which appeared to make some progress in reducing human rights abuses nationwide. At the very least, today almost every state
has its own statewide civil rights commission, the first of which was created, interestingly, by an opposition government, the PAN, in Baja California.

The August 1994 presidential election, however, provided the acid test of the extent of democratization. The credibility regained by late 1993 has undeniably been
affected by a string of events that badly shook the nation, particularly the uprising
in Chiapas in January 1994, the assassination of the PRI's presidential candidate,
Luis Donaldo Colosio, in March 1994, and then the assassination of the PRI's general secretary, José Francisco Ruiz Massieu, in September of the same year. These
events, and a series of other unprecedented events in Mexico—kidnappings, car
bombings, open drug wars, allegations of PRI involvement in drug cartels and politically motivated assassinations—have shattered the Mexican people's confidence in

the system that claimed to be leading them out of the crisis. All this, followed by the December 1994 economic crisis at the start of the *sexenio*, presents Zedillo and his party with the major (and also unprecedented) challenge of how to maintain his party in control of the government.

The Institutionalization of Political Reform

Mexico's political background clearly has been both a cause and an effect of electoral politics. In order to undertake the revitalization required to sustain the PRI's credibility and legitimacy and that of prospective *priísta* governments, electoral reform initiatives were undertaken beginning in 1963, extended in 1973 and 1977, again in 1986, and most recently, in 1993 and 1994.[9] Significantly, this process is always referred to as *apertura política* (political opening), but never as *apertura democrática* (democratic opening)—perhaps, unwittingly, because, although there may have been a willingness to make space for the opposition, the party's intention was never to allow it to become too powerful.

From the mid-1960s to the mid-1970s, the opposition averaged about 17 percent of the seats in the lower house, the Chamber of Deputies (Camp 1993: 147).[10] The 1973 reform allowed for a wider range of political parties, particularly those on the left (including the Communist Party). Most important of all was the 1977 Ley de Organizaciones Políticas y Procesos Electorales (Law of Political Organizations and Electoral Processes, LOPPE). This law set aside one quarter of all seats in the lower house to be divided among the opposition parties on the basis of proportional representation.[11] Thus, although their legislative power remained highly constrained, especially since the PRI never let its internal divisions carry over into split votes, opposition parties now had their foot in the door.[12] Both the amount and the quality of debate in the Chamber of Deputies improved, and members no longer blindly supported legislation initiated by the PRI or the president (Middlebrook 1986).

The important point to recognize is that the fundamental purpose of the reform was not to weaken the authority and the role of the PRI, but, rather, to enhance and sustain it. In essence, the political reforms of 1977 were introduced as a needed change in the political system. As Middlebrook (1986) and others argue, these reforms were a regime-sponsored effort to retain stability and reflected declining support for the system. Reduced support of the regime and lessened political legitimacy, which were exposed by the Tlatelolco massacre of students in 1968, became steadily more evident in public opinion polls, in the decline of voter participation, and in the emergence of several new opposition parties. Perhaps more important, it was clear that the decline in the PRI's fortunes meant a rising incapacity to fulfill its primary functions of delivering the vote and achieving social control over the poorest segments of the population (Hansen 1974).

Briefly, the objective of the reforms was to strengthen the PRI by encouraging a more credible (but carefully constrained) opposition. Indeed, although the initiation of a *plurinominal* deputy system encouraged opposition parties, their representation proportion between 1979 and 1985 remained roughly stable, suggesting that, in Congress at least, there was little evidence of growth (Camp 1993: 148). Moreover, the reforms turned out to be problematic not only because they failed to give the opposition a real opportunity to participate, but also because they were opposed by state governors and local political bosses, who believed that their own power depended on the PRI's total domination of state and local government.

President de la Madrid introduced a reform in 1986 intended to enhance the opposition's opportunities for adequate representation. This reform prevented the winning or majority party from holding more than 70 percent of the seats in the lower chamber. It increased the number of seats in Congress to 500, with 300 of those reserved for those elected by relative majority in their congressional districts, and 200 allotted for proportional representation. The party winning the greatest number of the 300 majority seats got some additional proportional representation seats, which allowed one political party to gain an overall majority in Congress. Thus, while the opposition's representation was raised to a minimum 30 percent of the now-enlarged legislature (i.e., 150 of the 500 seats), the PRI managed virtually to guarantee its hold on Congress by extending *plurinominal* seats to any party receiving fewer than 50 percent of the legislative seats. Once again, what should be underscored here is that the increased opposition party presence was allocated by the government rather than earned by those parties, and that the PRI was willing to make space for the opposition only to the extent that its own majority position in the Chamber of Deputies was not threatened.

The 1988 elections were historic not only because the PRI presidential candidate's victory was dubious, but also because for the first time opposition parties acquired sufficient strength in the lower house to shape the policy process, particularly when a two-thirds majority vote to change the Constitution was required. By 1989 opposition parties had acquired close to 50 percent of the seats in the Chamber of Deputies, suggesting the first true alteration in the PRI's power within that body. With PRI representation dropping to a bare majority, and well below the 66 percent majority required for constitutional changes, the party had to seek coalition partners for any constitutional amendments.

This does not mean, however, that opposition parties were satisfied with their gains, particularly in light of the PRI's significant electoral success in 1991. Since 1989 the opposition has pressed hard for major constitutional changes and for improvements in electoral processes by means of the Código Federal de Instituciones y Procedimientos Electorales (Federal Code for Electoral Procedures and Institutions, COFIPE).[13] In 1989 the Instituto Federal Electoral (Federal Electoral Institute, IFE) was also created as an independent entity to organize and monitor elections in a manner above suspicion. The credibility of the IFE's predecessor, the Federal Electoral Commission, was suspect at best. Since its creation, the IFE has spared no effort to make a reputation as an autonomous and transparent institution. It has bent over backwards to accommodate the demands of all political parties, but particularly opposition parties. In preparation for the 1994 presidential election, the IFE boasted of having one of the more accurate voter registration lists (the *padrón electoral*) in the world (47.5 million registered out of 50 million qualified to vote) and opened it to audit and inspection by both national and international organizations. Also in preparation for this election, the IFE spent over US$730 million to update and revise the voter registration lists and produce a voter ID card that has more anti-tampering devices than, as an IFE official put it to me, "the ID of a NASA engineer wishing to board a rocket."

But in spite of the expenditure of so much money and effort on the 1994 election, there were still allegations of fraud and complaints about electoral procedures. The final verdict was that the election, overall, was clean but not fair.[14] The fraud, many contend, was committed by the PRI *before* the actual election, through its unfair access to campaign finance resources, virtually unlimited access to the media, and so on. Irregularities were also reported throughout the country, such as running out of ballots early in the voting at the *casillas especiales* (e.g., voting places set up at the border so that Mexicans living in the United States could vote there). Reported irregularities led to the overturning of results in some cases, for example, in the election for the municipal presidency of Monterrey, where the PRI victory was annulled in favor of the PAN.

Congressional debate on electoral reform had reached a stalemate by 1993, and although the PRI could easily have built the necessary two-thirds majority to push through some innocuous reforms, it was reluctant to do so. President Salinas wanted the COFIPE passed with the support of at least the PAN in order to provide greater legitimacy for the 1994 elections. In effect, this meant that the COFIPE had to pass by August 1993. At the last minute, in order to win *panista* support, the PRI offered major concessions. The most important of these was that after 1994 each state would have four senators, three of whom would be elected directly and the fourth allocated to the party coming in second.[15] Other concessions related to greater equity of access to the media during campaigns; the imposition of campaign spending limits; the removal of the so-called governability clause, which had ensured a working majority in Congress for the PRI since 1989,[16] and the turning over to local electoral councils and to the IFE the process whereby incoming Congresses voted to approve their own election (*autocalificación*). Also, the voter registration list was to be verified by an independent body. The opposition was unsuccessful in two other significant areas they had fought for: first, that there be limits on the direct participation of public functionaries in campaigns; and second, that no party be allowed to use the colors of the national flag as their own. [17]

Thus, it seemed certain that the process of amplifying and bolstering an opposition party presence in the two houses of Congress would continue. The reforms of the past thirty years underscored the fact that, while the precedent was one of creating a plurality, it was also one that was heavily constrained and that ultimately assured the PRI's dominance in Congress, albeit on terms that were less favorable from its point of view than in the past. The rules under which Congress was to be constructed provided the framework for state legislatures, and even municipal governments, to begin thinking about proportional representation at the local level.[18]

Events in late 1996 and early 1997, however—specifically, the political reform, the marginal majority that any one party may have in Congress, and the rising fortunes of the opposition—threaten to severely undermine any guarantee of PRI domination of Congress. Although one of the opposition parties has yet to win a majority in Congress, the days in which the PRI sought to ensure a minority opposition party presence are numbered.

The Rise of Opposition Governments at the State and Local Levels

It is not only within Congress that there has been an expansion of pluralist representation. Beginning in 1982, a significant number of city governments have been won by opposition parties. The de la Madrid administration took the first steps in applying the principles embodied in the political reform when in 1983 it recognized several outright opposition victories at the municipal level, including some in major cities. No fewer than five of these were state capitals (Chihuahua, Durango, Hermosillo, Guanajuato, and San Luis Potosí) and another one was in a large border city (Ciudad Juárez). The PRI hoped that this political opening would help alleviate some of the frustrations caused by the economic crisis.

But for many, giving in to the opposition seemed too high a price, and the moves toward greater pluralism were subsequently reversed, often by means of electoral fraud. In southern Mexico, for instance, the Left won in the municipality of Juchitán, but was never allowed to take power; the case was heavily publicized and brought the administration's commitment to political liberalization seriously into question. As mentioned earlier, the PRI seemed more threatened by electoral losses in southern rural areas, where it had traditionally enjoyed *carro completo* (clean sweep) victories, than in major northern cities, where its near monopoly had long since been eroded. Indeed, some opposition victories, such as that of the Partido Demócrata Mexicano (Mexican Democratic Party, PDM) in Guanajuato and the Partido Socialista de los Trabajadores (Workers' Socialist Party, PST) in Ensenada, both in 1983, appear to have been orchestrated by the PRI itself in order to promote a semblance of democracy (Rodríguez and Ward 1995). Others occurred when splits within the PRI led to so much disagreement over candidate selection that the door was left open for an opposition victory. Also in 1983, in cities such as Durango, Ciudad Juárez, and Chihuahua, the PRI seems to have been caught off guard by the massive swing to the PAN.

The ambivalence caused by liberalization, on the one hand, and the retention of absolute political control, on the other, resurfaced with a vengeance in the midterm elections of 1986. There seems little doubt that the opposition, specifically the

PAN, won major victories in many municipalities, particularly in the North, where it had been so successful in 1983. The PRI, however, resorted to its timeworn practices of intimidation, vote rigging, and ballot stuffing to contrive victories in these electoral districts (Cornelius, Gentleman, and Smith 1989), even though these electoral irregularities were widely condemned at home and abroad, especially in the United States. In retrospect, it seems almost certain that de la Madrid was obliged to sacrifice his willingness to move toward political liberalization in order to sustain his hard-nosed monetarist policies of austerity and economic control.

Since the presidential election of 1988, in every subsequent election opposition victories have multiplied. At the state level, the first major breakthrough was the PAN's victory in the gubernatorial elections in Baja California in 1989, followed by Chihuahua in 1992 and then by Jalisco, Guanajuato, and Baja California (again) in 1995. Indeed, when in the 1989 elections in Baja California the PAN became the first opposition party to win a state governorship, it was suggested that Salinas might have deliberately let the opposition win in this northern state—or at least let the PRI lose—as part of his own political project. The 1992 elections in Chihuahua appeared to be less suspect. While not wishing to discredit in any way the PAN victory in Chihuahua, however, many analysts believe that this win was also negotiated at higher levels.[19] How and when and between whom these negotiations take place is most difficult to ascertain, but it does seem clear that negotiations over electoral results have become a crucial factor in today's electoral process.

The process does not, however, apply equally to all parties. While it has evidently worked well for the PAN, this is certainly not the case with the PRD. Not all opposition parties are treated equally. To a large extent, President Salinas's democratization project was a process of negotiation, but because of the PRD's origins (i.e., as the party born from the democratic current that caused the debacle of 1988), any negotiation between the PRD and the government was virtually impossible. Once again the 1992 election serves to illustrate the point: while the PAN's gubernatorial victory was readily recognized in Chihuahua, the PRI claimed victory in the state of Michoacán and hung tough, despite the case's being widely publicized as electoral results were hotly contested by the PRD. Although in the end Salinas had to give in, he did so only partially; the sworn-in *priísta* governor was obliged to take a "leave of absence" and was replaced by an interim governor—but one from the PRI, not the PRD. As of 1994, Baja California and Chihuahua remained the only two states to have been won by the opposition in the history of contemporary Mexico.[20] A major wave of opposition victories at the state level in 1995, however, brought the PAN the governorships of Jalisco and Guanajuato and, perhaps even more significant, the governorship of Baja California for the second time.

At the municipal level opposition wins have not stopped; indeed, in some cases the same municipality has been won consecutively by an opposition party—for example, San Luis Potosí, Zamora, León, San Pedro Garza García, Ensenada, and Tijuana. As the data in Table 3.1 indicate, the number of municipal governments con-

TABLE 3.1 Municipal Governments, by Party and State, 1996

State	No. of Municipalities	Controlled by PRI	Controlled by PAN	Controlled by PRD	Controlled by Others[1]
Aguascalientes	11	7	4	0	0
Baja California	5	3	2	0	0
Baja California Sur	5	5	0	0	0
Campeche	9	9	0	0	0
Coahuila	38	35	1	1	1
Colima	10	9	1	0	0
Chiapas	111	84	5	18	4
Chihuahua	67	55	10	1	1
Durango	39	21	12	2	4
Guanajuato	46	37	5	2	2
Guerrero	76	68	0	6	2
Hidalgo	84	83	0	1	0
Jalisco	124	63	53	6	2
México	122	108	6	4	4
Michoacán	113	43	14	54	2
Morelos	33	32	0	1	0
Nayarit	20	19	1	0	0
Nuevo León	51	45	6	0	0
Oaxaca	570	111	11	35	413
Puebla	217	186	23	7	1
Querétaro	18	17	1	0	0
Quintana Roo	8	8	0	0	0
San Luis Potosí	58	49	6	0	3
Sinaloa	18	12	5	1	0
Sonora	70	62	6	1	1
Tabasco	17	13	0	4	0
Tamaulipas	43	34	6	3	0
Tlaxcala	60	50	5	4	1
Veracruz	207	148	19	27	13
Yucatán	106	93	12	1	0
Zacatecas	56	42	11	2	1
Total	2,412	1,551	225	181	455

[1]"Others" includes PT, PFCRN, PPS, PARM, PDM, and CM. 412 municipalities of Oaxaca in this column were elected by *usos y costumbres*. *Usos y costumbres* is the governance structure whereby indigenous groups of a given community elect their civic leaders according to traditional practices and criteria (*usos y costumbres*). These leaders are recognized as municipal government officials by the state electoral authorities.

SOURCE: Based on information from the Centro de Servicios Municipales "Heriberto Jara," Mexico City.

trolled by the opposition has grown considerably. In 1994, 238 municipalities were governed by the opposition, and although this number may be considered relatively small (there were 2,392 municipalities in Mexico at that time), what is relevant is that many of these were critically important cities, not small rural communities. This number has increased further as a result of the widespread opposition victories of both the PAN and the PRD in the states of Veracruz and Tabasco late in 1994, and, of course, scores of others in 1995, including Aguascalientes, Guadalajara, and in large cities such as Tijuana, León, and Ciudad Juárez. By 1996, 449 municipalities were governed by a party other than the PRI; the PAN alone controlled 225 municipalities and the PRD, 181. Thus, key cities such as Ciudad Juárez, Chihuahua, Mérida, Durango, and Morelia have at various times been governed by the opposition in the past ten years—not to mention that the country's second and third most important cities, Guadalajara and Monterrey, as well as a host of state capitals (Oaxaca, Puebla, Mexicali, Tuxtla Gutiérrez, Aguascalientes, Saltillo, Mérida) are now also governed by the PAN. Indeed, in the 1988 election, had Mexico City had a constitution that allowed for the election of its local officers, the opposition parties (especially the Frente Democrático Nacional, FDN) would have swept the board (Ward 1990a).

The relative closeness of the 1988 election, together with the major advances of opposition parties and the hotly contested 1994 presidential election, have raised, probably for the first time, the possibility of non-PRI or coalition governments. The presidential appointment of a *panista*—Antonio Lozano—to a key position in the federal government—attorney general—can be interpreted as a first, critical, move in this direction, not withstanding his dismissal in late 1996.

Although I do not wish to undermine the significance of Lozano's appointment, the most significant sign of change lies, in my opinion, in the opposition victories at the *state* level, not least because they took place in critically important states: Guanajuato, Jalisco, and Baja California. Guanajuato, the *"cuna de la Independencia"* (cradle of independence), has been the PAN's bedrock; it is now governed by the controversial Vicente Fox, who, having "lost" in 1991, won an easy victory after a successful campaign characterized by the slogan "Ahora sí" (This time we will win). In the other most conservative state with a strong labor union tradition, Jalisco, the PAN swept the state, taking not only the governorship but also the legislature and most municipalities, including the second most important metropolitan region in the country, Guadalajara. In Baja California, in what many anticipated would be an extremely close election on the basis of the results of the 1994 presidential election, the PAN also managed by a considerable margin to retain the governorship, control of the state legislature and the city of Tijuana, and to win, for the first time, the state capital, Mexicali.

More recently, both the PAN and the PRD have won important victories in the South, not just in small municipalities, but in state capitals. In addition to Puebla and Veracruz, both Oaxaca and Tuxtla Gutiérrez were won by the PAN in 1995, while the PRD continued to expand its presence in the smaller municipalities. All of these victories add up to the fact that, as of late 1996, approximately one third of Mexico's population was governed by "the opposition."

Decentralization

The political and economic crisis that first began to unfold in the 1980s had an iterative effect on decentralization. As a policy it became one of the regime's responses to regional economic and political imbalances, which were becoming a threat to stability. The practice of decentralization, and particularly the advances of the opposition, further intensified the pressures for devolution. Broadly speaking, the decentralization policy of both de la Madrid and Salinas pursued the general premise that, by strengthening government (and the party) at the lower levels, the stability of the system could be preserved. They continued to refer to decentralization as a key element in the democratization process. The main issue to explore here, then, is the extent to which decentralization entered into the so-called democratization project and played a meaningful role.

Any attempt to address this issue, however, is highly subjective. While one can argue that all of the processes just described—political liberalization, growing pluralism, greater civic involvement—indicate an important opening in the political space, some might contend that these processes do not necessarily add up to democratization. The period since 1968 has been characterized by many authors as one of "transition," as Mexico has moved away from the traditional political and social order built around revolutionary principles (Aguilar Camín and Meyer 1993; Barros, Hurtado, and Pérez 1991). But does this *political* transition also constitute a *democratic* transition? Although on taking office both Presidents de la Madrid and Salinas very quickly indicated their commitment to change—not least in their preparedness to recognize more opposition victories at both the state and the local levels—in many respects, they found economic change easier than political reform (where resistance is more entrenched) to accomplish.

Could decentralization have been conceived as an alternative to genuine democratization? In light of the extremely high costs involved in promoting full-fledged political change, it does not seem unreasonable to suggest that a policy that claimed to be aimed at redistributing political power might, at the very least, indicate that both de la Madrid and Salinas were moving toward democratization. Their general claim to want to decentralize served their purposes because they could argue that decentralization represented the first step in that direction. It is no small coincidence that Miguel de la Madrid claimed to have designed his decentralization policy in response to pressure exerted by municipal and state officials, and by the public at large, during various popular consultations (*consultas populares*) while he campaigned for the presidency. In addition, academics and political analysts had argued repeatedly that the strain caused by overcentralization could no longer be ignored. As will be discussed more fully in Chapter 4, decentralization under de la Madrid took the shape of a municipal reform designed to grant autonomy to the municipalities, almost all of which at that time were held by the PRI. The evidence suggests, however, that although to a certain extent the reform "pacified" municipal desires for political and financial autonomy, municipalities were never actually granted the independence they craved. Instead, they were asked to take on further responsibility and to ease the burden on the center brought about by the 1982 economic crisis.

This newly asserted independence for municipalities, by and large, would have fit comfortably within a political system "in democratic transition." De la Madrid had attempted to begin that transition by recognizing various opposition victories in 1983 (only one year into his administration), but, as noted earlier, the political cost was too high and his efforts at political opening were reversed in 1985–1986. In light of this backtracking, and as a result of the political pressure exerted on the president from within the party and by senior administration officials, it seems likely that decentralization surfaced as a more attractive alternative than democratization. Although the Municipal Reform was designed to fundamentally change the character of intergovernmental relations in Mexico, it was a reform that was far less risky politically because it could be implemented selectively. It was, in fact, rather inoffensive politically because, while it granted some power to the lower levels of government, it did not sacrifice the power and control of the higher ones. It promised financial autonomy to the municipality, for example, but did not increase the percentage of revenue-sharing allocations. This tactic satisfied the federal government because it did not imply any additional cost. Neither was the promise of municipal financial autonomy threatening to the state governments because the reform did not require the states to specify the criteria used for distributing federal funds among their municipalities. Thus, while appearing to give municipalities the autonomy they demanded, top officials within the party and in state and federal government could be reassured that decentralization, in reality, was a rather inexpensive and safe policy—and much preferable to democratization.

At the same time, the Municipal Reform allowed President de la Madrid to claim that his decentralization policy was truly reformist. In the sense that it had the potential to fundamentally change the role of the municipality in the federal system, it was, indeed, a reformist policy, but the extent to which it was successfully implemented, as will be discussed in the following chapters, makes it appear as a much more modest reform.

Nonetheless, while it represented a less bold change than rapid democratization, the reform did mark the beginning of an era in which the municipality would come to occupy a primary place within the framework of national political priorities. Although the municipality was largely ignored in the past, a general interest in it has quickened in the last ten years, not least within the federal executive branch itself. President de la Madrid's successors have also given high priority to municipal and regional development.

Although under President Salinas decentralization per se did not figure as a core element in his political project or his policy agenda, its presence was implicit. Power was dispersed essentially on two fronts: in the modernization of the PRI; and in providing some support and relative autonomy (through Solidarity's municipal programs) to local governments. While the process of modernizing and revamping the party still has a considerable way to go, there is no doubt that the changes set in train during the Salinas presidency paved the way for future reform; although these changes may have been overshadowed by the events of the last part of his *sexenio*, they represent the first steps taken to turn the PRI into a real political party (Rodríguez and Ward 1994b). Thus, if two of the main objectives of Salinas's decentralization project were to restore the legitimacy of the Mexican governmental system and to modernize the party and the administrative apparatus—both of which he saw as imperative if the PRI's fortunes were ultimately to be restored and its electoral losses reversed, and if economic restructuring and modernization were to proceed—then, once again, a claim to decentralize served his purposes. The reforms of the PRI were in large measure designed to meet the rank and file's demands to be better informed and to participate more in the decision-making process, particularly in candidate selection. The elimination of the party's sectoral organization could potentially also lead to greater decentralization.

As far as the dispersion of power to local governments, clearly, this was only marginally accomplished. Nonetheless, as will be discussed in the chapters that follow, some increases in municipal autonomy did occur. Moreover, Mexico's changing political landscape demanded that this autonomy be granted not only to local PRI governments, but also to those of opposition parties. Thus, the vertical dispersion of power to the lower levels of government was accompanied by a decentralization process that was also wider in scope in that it embraced the opposition.

There is still a question about how far this *implicit* decentralization led to *genuine* decentralization. While some scholars (Bailey 1994, for example) argue that under Salinas we witnessed a strengthening of centralization, other evidence (to be analyzed in the following chapters) points in the opposite direction. The Salinas administration, therefore, presents something of a paradox. On the one hand, we saw measures leading to decentralization, municipal autonomy, greater pluralism, and the targeting of resources directly to marginalized rural and urban areas through Solidarity. On the other hand, there is also considerable evidence that on balance his administration generated more centralism. In fiscal terms, the federation strengthened its control over revenues and showed no willingness to increase the amounts transferred to the states and municipalities. In political terms, as we have seen, there was a sharp increase in the number of times the president chose to exercise his metaconstitutional powers, not least by removing half of the country's governors for one reason or other. Also, unlike any other president before him, Salinas was obliged to undertake two *dedazos*[21] (Colosio and Zedillo) and to keep a tight rein on the party. Moreover, his national and international popularity and stature inevitably strengthened the institution of the presidency in Mexico. Faced with this increased centralism, Zedillo needed to find ways in which effective decentralization could be undertaken and presidential powers diluted—but without losing power for his party.

Conclusion

In this chapter I have argued that the process of opening up the political space by means of electoral reforms and the recognition of opposition victories at the state and local levels has been pursued in a piecemeal fashion in order to suit the center's interests. To the extent that opening the political space implies a decentralization of power, both Presidents de la Madrid and Salinas had to juggle letting go and pulling back. In this context, a decision to decentralize surfaces as a much "safer" and promising alternative and, as I shall argue in Chapter 4, has been the rationale behind the efforts to decentralize during the last decade. The major problem with the decisions to decentralize and to open the political space, however, is that they were made in a context that not only reinforced centralization, but also questioned the entire "democratization" process.

Evidently, there are major problems associated with this construction of a plurality from above. It demonstrates that presidentialism and centralism continue to be entrenched within the Mexican political system and, ultimately, that, unless dramatic changes occur, the consolidation of democracy will advance only as far as the PRI—and the president—are prepared to let it go.

4

Centralizing Politics Versus
Decentralizing Policies, 1970–1995

Mexico City is unquestionably the political, financial, and cultural center of the country. In an area of 1,200 square kilometers (464 square miles) it concentrates the principal seat of government, one fourth of the country's total population, and roughly half of the entire industrial production, commerce, services, and communications (Ward 1990a: 19–20). This ever-increasing centralization of political and economic power in the country's capital caused by the massive concentration of goods and services, and of industry and population, has concerned virtually every analyst and government official for the past twenty-five years. The four most recent presidential administrations—of Luis Echeverría (1970–1976), José López Portillo (1976–1982), Miguel de la Madrid (1982–1988), and Carlos Salinas de Gortari (1988–1994)—have all expressed great concern with the country's overwhelming centralization and made an attempt to counteract it through various programs and policies. Although their success is questionable, the decentralization policy of the de la Madrid administration, in particular, must be regarded as the most forceful effort of the past twenty-five years because it provided the turning point for a de facto decentralization to begin in earnest.

The host of decentralization programs developed since the early 1970s demonstrates the concern with overcentralization in the capital. In this chapter I will discuss how and why Mexico became so overcentralized and then, focusing primarily on the formal efforts of the de la Madrid and Salinas administrations, review efforts to decentralize economic and political power during the last four presidential terms.

Before 1982, most attempts at decentralization were primarily administrative or regional development programs that sought to address the imbalances caused by Mexico City's dominance. Although political factors were also important, fundamentally, reform and change were driven by objective criteria. Perhaps for that reason alone, these efforts carried relatively little weight and were subordinated to economic and political imperatives. As this and following chapters will demonstrate, however, from de la Madrid's Municipal Reform to Zedillo's New Federalism, decentralization has been the policy product of politically induced change, albeit often in the guise of an essentially administrative reform.

Mexico City's Demographic Explosion

Any assessment of Mexico's decentralization policies has to consider the country's urbanization process, which since the boom of the 1940s has led to an overwhelming concentration in metropolitan areas, especially in Mexico City itself (see Garza 1986; Ward 1990a). In 1990 the metropolitan area of Mexico City had a population of just over sixteen million; in 1995 it was home to an estimated nineteen million; and it continues to grow by between one half and three quarters of a million each year. Other Mexican cities, such as Guadalajara and Monterrey, and the border cities of Tijuana, Mexicali, and Ciudad Juárez, have also experienced rapid growth.

With the demographic concentration has come an increasing concentration of wealth in these urban areas—again, especially in Mexico City. Slightly over 50 percent of all industry is located in the Valley of Mexico. This has caused not only an enormous concentration of economic power but also a dramatic deterioration of the urban environment. In fact, the environmental degradation of this once beautiful city may very well be one of the reasons why Mexican political decision makers and intellectuals concluded that something had to be done about centralization.

This picture is nothing new. By the beginning of the nineteenth century, Mexico City had become the largest city in the Western Hemisphere (Hayner 1945: 298) and had developed as the country's most important political, military, and commercial center. The city maintained its primacy in the nineteenth century, and by 1910 had consolidated its position as the seat of economic and political power; it had also become the most important provider of goods and labor and absorbed the largest percentage of the government's budget.

After the Revolution of 1910, the process of concentration increased. As the country's industrialization accelerated, postrevolutionary leaders instituted a policy of industrial incentives that favored the capital city. Mexico City was also the hub of the new road and highway system, the electrical system, communications, water works, educational services, and a host of other urban services.

This concentration had been engineered, basically, to beef up the country's economic development and had some very successful outcomes. Nonetheless, the modernization process also had some major negative consequences: it made the country dependent on foreign capital, produced a largely inequitable distribution of income, and concentrated heavily in Mexico City—which in turn caused large regional inequalities that retarded the development of many regions and, consequently, of the country as a whole.

This concentration of goods and services in the capital brought an almost inevitable concentration of industry. In 1930, Mexico City had a 28.5 percent share of the country's total manufacturing production; in 1940, 32.1 percent; in 1950, 40.0 percent; in 1960, 46.0 percent; in 1970, 46.8 percent; and in 1980, 48.0 percent (Ward 1990a: 20). The population of the metropolitan area grew at a similar rate: in 1930 the city's population was barely over one million; in 1940, 1.64 million; in 1950, 3.14 million; in 1960, 5.4 million; in 1970, 9.2 million; in 1980,

14.4 million; and an estimated 19 million in 1990 (Ward 1990a: 35) (the 1990 census subsequently pegged the estimate back to 16 million, raising doubts about the accuracy of the count). This concentration of industry and population in the capital generated a further concentration of commercial activities, services, and transportation.

The creation of this vicious circle, in short, determined the city's urban explosion. Housing shortages, unemployment and marginalization, insufficient services and infrastructure, inadequate transportation and communications, pollution, and crime are only some of the urban problems that have grown from Mexico City's economic and demographic agglomerations. In a halfhearted attempt to deal with these problems, from 1940 to 1970 the federal government formulated policies that were designed to stimulate the growth and development of various regions and to attempt a deconcentration of industry away from Mexico City. But none of them worked; the concentration in the capital continued to grow uninterruptedly, and urban problems remained unsolved (Unikel and Lavell 1979).

In recognition of Mexico City's becoming unlivable and becoming even more so in future, Mexican planners began to call for decentralization. Since the Echeverría administration, important, but largely unsuccessful, efforts have been made to produce structural changes aimed at decentralizing both economic and political power. What has resulted is a series of national plans, each of which has included provisions for decentralization of one kind or another. Many of the forecasts in these plans are overwhelmingly alarming; by the end of the century, Mexico City was expected to be one of the world's most important industrial cities and, definitely, the world's most populated metropolitan area. Needless to say, this scenario of objective conditions demanded a truly forceful decentralization policy. Yet this notwithstanding, no serious decentralization effort has been undertaken.

It was the Echeverría administration that showed the first interest in changing the patterns of concentration and produced a host of programs and plans to counteract it. But by 1977, only one year into the López Portillo administration, the country's agricultural sector's contribution had fallen to roughly 10 percent of the overall national product, which reflected the increasing importance of the urban-industrial sector. The new administration responded by producing an impressive number of plans and programs, most important, the Plan Nacional de Desarrollo Urbano (National Urban Development Plan), which aimed to restrict future growth and to control and reorganize the capital's urban structure. In addition, a Federal District urban development plan was adopted in 1980. Overall growth rates in the metropolitan area declined considerably during the 1970s and the 1980s, but mostly as an outcome of the reduction in the rates of natural increase achieved through the intervention of the Consejo Nacional de Población (National Population Council, CONAPO). Mexico City continued to grow, however, and the levels of economic activity hardly changed at all.

The de la Madrid administration received the inevitable legacy of Mexico City's concentration problems and showed a marked interest in alleviating them, although this interest soon waned. As the country fell deeper into the economic crisis and the government had to deal with other immediate and more pressing problems—inflation, unemployment, debt payment—the capital's problems were put on hold. The emphasis on decentralization did not appear to be translated into urban-regional spatial policy, although the National Development Plan and seven of its programs did partially relate to urban-regional problems. The issue of spatial and population deconcentration away from the Federal District was forcefully thrust onto the agenda by the September 1985 earthquakes but, as we shall see, the political imperatives of the day prevented any serious attempt at urban decentralization.

In his presidential campaign discourse, Carlos Salinas de Gortari emphasized the urgency of dealing with the massive urban problems of the capital city (see, for example, *Perfiles del Programa de Gobierno* 1988a). He also emphasized the need to enhance regional development programs as a way to reduce concentration in Mexico City. Once in power, however, his administration did little explicitly to tackle these problems in the metropolitan area—probably because there was little that he *could* do. During the Salinas *sexenio*, Federal District policy focused primarily on ecology and security. Indeed, with the exception of the southern area of the Federal District (which remained a conflict zone for incoming population and settlement), the principal problem faced by Manuel Camacho as *regente* (the mayor of Mexico City) was one of reorganizing and restructuring existing land use. Thus, the emphasis of Federal District policy was firmly ecological: to prevent further growth and loss of woodlands and agricultural land in the south, and to reduce contamination levels, particularly those associated with private transportation, by means of the *hoy no circula* strategy of banning automobile usage one day a week on a revolving basis according to license plate numbers. Since the 1970s, growth in the metropolitan area has largely been an issue for the state of Mexico, since it is the municipalities adjacent to the Federal District that have experienced the most dramatic growth (Ward 1990a).

In order to confront the continuing rapid expansion of the metropolitan area in the state of Mexico and the intense social problems associated with that growth (much of it irregular settlement), the Salinas administration acted on two broad fronts. First, it worked to deflect in-migration away from Mexico City and to reinforce the role and growth of intermediate-sized cities nationally, most notably through the Cien Ciudades (One Hundred Cities) program.[1] Second, after 1990, several State of Mexico municipalities—especially the rapidly expanding eastern municipality of Chalco, which had emerged during the 1980s as the "new Netzahualcóyotl"[2]—were privileged with abundant Solidarity funds and programs when other areas were bypassed. Although he had made innumerable visits to Chalco to monitor the introduction of Solidarity programs, Salinas chose to visit this municipality on the last day of his mandate as one of his last official acts, and certainly as a closure to his Solidarity site visits.

In spite of all the efforts of the past twenty-five years, the latest population and industrial censuses show persistent problems of inefficient growth, regional dispari-

ties, and population concentration in Mexico City and the three other largest metropolitan zones—Guadalajara, Monterrey, and Puebla—notwithstanding the fact
that the proportion of the national population residing in these cities declined from
51.3 percent in 1980 to 47 percent in 1990 (Poder Ejecutivo Federal 1995: 107).

Through his New Federalism project, an important part of the challenge for President Zedillo will be to intensify urban policies that will lead to population decentralization and more equitable and homogeneous regional development. This he
proposes to do in four principal ways: first, by consolidating the urban development
of the middle-sized cities included in the Cien Ciudades program; second, by supporting local authorities in promoting urban development plans that will attract
economic investment and population; third, by promoting citizen participation in
the elaboration and implementation of those plans; and finally, by achieving an or-
derly consolidation of the productive role that the major metropolitan areas play
within their regional hinterlands (Poder Ejecutivo Federal 1995). In short, the
Zedillo administration recognizes the strategic role that Mexico City must continue
to play in the nation's economic future, but it is simultaneously seeking to reinforce
the linkages between democratic opening, citizen participation, local government,
and a better regulated and ordered urban growth.

Mexico's Decentralization Policies, 1970–1995

Although former presidents Echeverría and López Portillo showcased decentralization as an important policy issue, it was not a central element of their time in office.
It was not until the early 1980s, when Miguel de la Madrid assumed the presidency,
that decentralization would become a key issue on the presidential policy agenda.
Starting with de la Madrid's campaign in 1981, the nation's problems were grouped
into seven large categories, one of which was "decentralization of national life." Salinas followed, essentially, the de la Madrid line, and indeed one of the basic points
around which his governmental plan was organized was decentralization. By the end
of his *sexenio*, although subsumed under the umbrella of Solidarity, it remained as a
key issue. Under Zedillo's New Federalism, decentralization has climbed to the top
of the government's policy agenda. The following section offers an assessment of the
formal policy efforts to decentralize enacted during the last five presidential administrations.

The Echeverría and López Portillo Administrations

At least partially, centralization in Mexico derived from the fact that beginning in
the 1940s the government became the most important contributor to the country's
economic development. The boom that began in the 1940s and lasted for the next
thirty years was evident in massive state investment in infrastructure, cheap credit,
and countless subsidies, all of which placed Mexico's productive capacity near the
top in Latin America. Even in the 1970s, Mexico went through a period of extraor-

dinary growth, mainly based on its oil-driven economy. But as the number of federal programs increased, so did the federal government's penetration of the states and municipalities; more important, this growth accelerated the already rapid concentration of resources in the center.

The administration of President Luis Echeverría dramatically sought to change the old development strategy of "stabilizing development" (*desarrollo estabilizador*) to one of "shared development" (*desarrollo compartido*). The objectives of this strategy included correcting problems of income distribution and unemployment, raising the population's standard of living, reducing external dependence, controlling foreign investment, stimulating national industry, and increasing international trade (Teichman 1988), all of which required more balanced territorial development.

Throughout the Echeverría *sexenio* many measures were designed for the industrial and agricultural sectors, as well as for the administrative sector, in an attempt at decentralizing both industry and population away from the Valley of Mexico. One of the most important strategies for more balanced regional development was to decentralize the economic activities of the larger cities via the creation of the so-called *polos de desarrollo*. These development poles were designed to alleviate the growing problems of the larger metropolitan areas (unemployment and underemployment, pollution, scarcity of public services, high cost of infrastructure, etc.) and to offer new employment opportunities that would raise the standard of living in the poorer areas; they were also intended to deflect the rural migrating population toward areas other than the huge urban agglomerations.

Thus, the primary focus of a series of programs aimed at alleviating rural and urban problems was to be on regional development rather than on decentralization per se. The most important rural program was the Programa de Inversiones para el Desarrollo Rural (Program of Public Investments for Rural Development, PIDER). Among the urban programs, the most noteworthy were those designed for industrial decentralization, the Lázaro Cárdenas–Las Truchas iron and steel complex, and enlargement of the twin-plant manufacturing program along the U.S.-Mexico border. The regional development programs reflected a holistic vision that included both the agricultural-rural and the industrial-urban sectors[3] however, this vision slowly gave way, around 1973, to one in which urban problems were dominant and rural ones left aside. And more important, however ambitious and effective the various programs appeared to be on paper, strong regional vested interests were determined to impede their implementation.

Just prior to the end of the Echeverría *sexenio*, the Ley General de Asentamientos Humanos (General Law on Human Settlements, LGAH) was passed, partly as an outcome of the international conference on human settlements and the administration's marked interest in this matter. The general objective of the law was to coordinate the three levels of government in their regulation of human settlements throughout the country by carefully planning the development of population centers. The law emphasized the need for formulating urban development plans at the national, state, and local levels.[4]

The López Portillo administration took up Echeverría's concern with the problem of urban development coupled with industrial decentralization, and in 1978 the Plan Nacional de Desarrollo Urbano (National Urban Development Plan, PNDU) was promulgated.[5] State and municipal urban development plans were also formulated. The major policies through which the PNDU proposed to achieve its objectives included, among others,

> discouragement of growth in the Mexico City metropolitan area; promotion of the decentralization of industry, public services, and a range of private-sector activities by orienting them toward areas that the PNDU declares to be priority zones; [and] encouragement of the development of cities with regional services and of medium-sized cities with a potential for economic and social progress. (*Comercio Exterior* December 1978: 494)

Thirteen priority zones were established throughout the country to implement the PNDU. The Secretaría de Asentamientos Humanos y Obras Públicas (Ministry of Human Settlements and Public Works, SAHOP) was established as the institution responsible for overseeing the PNDU's implementation.

Two other important programs were designed to facilitate implementation of the PNDU. One of them, Desconcentración de la Administración Pública Federal (Deconcentration of the Federal Government), was established to reduce the number of federal employees and offices in Mexico City, given that, as the head of SAHOP commented,

> 32 percent of the public sector employees . . . 31 percent of its budget . . . and 45 percent of those covered by the ISSSTE [Instituto de Seguridad y Servicios Sociales para los Trabajadores del Estado, Institute of Social Security and Services for State Workers] are concentrated in the Mexico City metropolitan area . . . there is one public employee for every twenty-four inhabitants and more than 20 percent of the population depends on federal public administration. (Pedro Ramírez Vázquez, *El Universal* September 22, 1978)

The other program, Estímulos para la Desconcentración Territorial de las Actividades Industriales (Incentives for the Territorial Deconcentration of Industrial Activities), had as its main objectives reducing industrial concentration in Mexico City and regulating industrial growth in Guadalajara and Monterrey through fiscal, tariff, and credit incentives, all of these essential elements for determining industrial location.

One of the most important urban-rural development programs of the López Portillo administration was the National Plan for Depressed Areas and Marginalized Groups, COPLAMAR. Initially, COPLAMAR competed with Echeverría's PIDER and duplicated many of its services, a common occurrence in successive administrations in Mexico.[6] Other efforts to decentralize encountered similar bureaucratic difficulties, as a number of so-called decentralization programs were formulated as each government reorganized.[7] What all these programs meant in terms of actual policy implementation is difficult to assess adequately, but the overwhelming evidence indicates clearly that, ultimately, they had very little real impact on decentralization away from Mexico City.

The López Portillo administration's most comprehensive plan was the Plan Global de Desarrollo 1980–1982 (Global Development Plan), whose chief architect, incidentally, was then-Secretary of Programming and Budget Miguel de la Madrid.[8] Although the Global Development Plan dealt with virtually every phase of life in Mexico, it was aimed primarily at urbanization problems.[9] Unfortunately, it was barely off the printing press when Mexico was struck by the economic crisis that brought all programs and plans to a grinding halt. At that point it became virtually impossible to sustain any decentralization effort, as all attention and effort focused on dealing with the economy.

Altogether, the Echeverría and López Portillo administrations' programs for regional development and industrial decentralization had almost no impact on the development of states and municipalities, as industry still tended to locate in the Valley of Mexico. The absence of control over the location of industry in Mexico City's metropolitan area can largely be explained by the opposition of the more powerful industrial groups, which reacted by reducing investments significantly when pressured to relocate elsewhere. Matters were complicated further by the economic crisis, since the government could hardly afford to maintain an autonomous and detached position from the transnational industrial investments it needed so badly. Overall, big industry did not sympathize with the government's regional development strategy, and in most cases preferred concentration.[10]

Medium- and small-sized industry presented a somewhat different perspective. Through the Cámara Nacional de la Industria de Transformación (National Chamber of Manufacturing Industry, CANACINTRA), smaller industries had repeatedly pressured the government to decentralize the growing economic concentration of the metropolitan area of Mexico City and to promote industrial expansion in other areas. CANACINTRA's interest in decentralization was prompted because medium and small industry felt more heavily burdened by the growing costs of locating in big cities (higher costs for land, competition for labor, etc.) and could not afford them as well as big industry. To a large extent, this pressure from the medium and small industries explains the government's decentralizing measures, as CANACINTRA was a traditional supporter of the PRI. In addition, the government was trying to reassure medium and small entrepreneurs that it was seriously attempting to solve the problem of industrial concentration.

A general assessment of the Echeverría and López Portillo administrations, however, conclusively shows that the spatial concentration of industry and population went on uninterruptedly from 1970 to 1982, and that the problems of unemployment and unequal income distribution grew in both urban and rural areas.[11] Overall, the results were quite different from the objectives proposed in the multitude of plans and programs, and very little was actually accomplished. By the time López Portillo left office, decentralization, like virtually everything else in his administration (most important, him personally), was badly tarnished. The public's general perception was that during the last two *sexenios* more harm than good had been done.

The de la Madrid Administration

Given that Miguel de la Madrid was the author of López Portillo's Global Development Plan, when he became the PRI's presidential candidate it seemed likely that decentralization would become a major issue in his governmental program. One of the highlights and innovations of his presidential campaign, which has become a standard for his successors, was the practice of holding a series of public meetings throughout the country to discuss a variety of local and national issues. At these *consultas populares* demands for decentralization, particularly in the form of pleas for municipal autonomy, came up repeatedly, and thus decentralization became a major and widely trumpeted plank in his campaign:

> His purpose is to eliminate, or at least minimize . . . excessive central bureaucracy and population concentration, tardiness and inefficiency in some sectors of the federal government, dependency and financial weakness of the municipalities, and so forth. The time has come to "federalize" the "National Life." Each and every aspect of the state's activities which before were forced to centralize, are now obliged to decentralize. (Cantú Segovia et al. 1982: 408)

In his inaugural address de la Madrid renewed his support for decentralization but did so in such a way as to suggest that this was the beginning of a sea change. Specifically, he indicated that, in order to pursue decentralization, he proposed to transfer the health and education sectors to the states; to amend Article 115 of the Constitution in order to strengthen municipal governments; and to strongly oppose any further growth of Mexico City (Madrid 1984: I: 30–31).

The first major decentralization statement of his administration is in the Plan Nacional de Desarrollo 1983–1988 (National Development Plan, PND).[12] In essence, de la Madrid proposed three broad lines of action in order to resolve the problems of centralization: (1) strengthening federalism; (2) promoting regional development; and (3) invigorating municipal life (Madrid 1982: 96). Formal plans and programs were designed to achieve each of these goals.

Federal Government Decentralization. In June 1984 President de la Madrid issued a decree directing all federal agencies to develop a program to decentralize, deconcentrate, or relocate. These programs were formally embodied in the Programa de Descentralización de la Administración Pública Federal (Federal Government Decentralization Program), implemented in January 1985.[13] In formulating their programs, each federal agency was to consider the states' development proposals in order to share with the state governments the responsibilities for implementing these programs. Thus, the decentralization measures contemplated more than a simple transfer of offices and personnel from Mexico City to the states, although, in general, the program did propose to relocate a large group of central agencies outside the Federal District and to create field agencies to ease the burden of the center. The Ministry of Programming and Budget—SPP—took responsibility for the coordination of this program, particularly for overseeing the three specific ways in which it would be carried out: (1) transferring federally administered parastatal organizations to the state governments; (2) transferring to the state governments the responsibility for coordinating the execution of development plans; and (3) deconcentrating administrative functions. In essence, the program sought to support regional development by enlarging and improving regional infrastructures.

In early 1985 the federal government announced the transfer of various programs to the states.[14] The shot in the arm for this part of the program came in 1986, when the first regional centers for decision making were established in Jalisco and Nuevo León and when twelve ministries, the Office of the Attorney General, and two important parastatals transferred a variety of functions to their representatives in those states (SPP 1988: 32). The reorganization that resulted from the September 1985 earthquakes in Mexico City led to some acceleration and enlargement of many of these plans.[15] The relocation of federal employees, for example, was speeded up after the earthquakes; the Comisión Nacional de Reconstrucción (National Reconstruction Commission) reported that in the few months following the tremors seventy thousand federal public employees (15 percent of all federal employees in Mexico City) would be relocated (Presidencia de la República 1986a: 374). Nonetheless, the effect of the earthquakes on the scale of decentralization was probably only slight. By the end of de la Madrid's administration, sixty-two thousand public employees had actually been relocated, which represented 67 percent of the goal proposed for 1988 (SPP 1988: 34). Although these accomplishments are by no means negligible, they are nevertheless secondary to the two most important and widely publicized decentralizing programs in the federal government's plan: education and health.[16]

The program to decentralize education was intended primarily to transfer elementary education and teacher training to the states through a series of agreements between the federal and state governments that facilitated the transfer of material and financial resources and also provided the framework for the administration of federal and state educational services. But in addition to this very valid administrative rationale, the decentralization of education had some major political considerations, the most important of which was that the government's main educational institution for teachers (the Escuela Normal Superior de México) had become heavily politicized. This politicization had taken a markedly leftist inclination, and the teachers trained there were, allegedly, heavily indoctrinated against the government. From the government's perspective, this political activity became a greater cause for concern than the teachers' academic training; decentralization away from Mexico

City seemed to offer a solution, since this would break up the primacy of the center as a locus for teachers training for public education.

Not surprisingly, the program to decentralize education was not uniformly well received, in particular by the large and powerful teachers' union, the Sindicato Nacional de Trabajadores de la Educación (National Union for Education Workers, SNTE). Fearing that decentralization would weaken its national structure, the SNTE strongly opposed the program, although in the end the union's leaders did support it (Cook 1996; Foweraker 1993). By 1987, the creation of the statewide councils to provide for the transfer of elementary and teachers' education to the thirty-one states was complete (SPP 1988). It fell to Salinas's secretary for education—Ernesto Zedillo— to implement the newly decentralized system of education and, once he became president, to embark on the "municipalization" of education as part of his New Federalism project (Rodríguez and Ward et al. 1996).

The most important step taken to facilitate decentralization in the health sector was the reorganization of the Ministry of Health. The president decreed the Ley General de Salud (General Health Law) in 1983, and then in 1984 issued another decree under which all health services of the Secretaría de Salubridad y Asistencia (Ministry of Health, SSA) would be provided by the states. The same decree stipulated that the services provided by the IMSS-COPLAMAR community participation program would now also fall to the states (*Diario Oficial*, March 8, 1984: 6–8). Also, the promulgation in early 1986 of the Ley sobre el Sistema Nacional de Asistencia Social (National System of Social Assistance Law) transferred all the functions of social assistance from the SSA to the DIF (Desarrollo Integral de la Familia, Integrated Family Development), a family social welfare agency (*Diario Oficial*, January 9, 1986: 33–39).[17] Because the SSA no longer provided social assistance, its name changed from the Ministry of Health and Assistance to the Ministry of Health.

Reportedly, the health decentralization program made some significant progress in its initial stages, but in the final analysis it was not as successful as hoped (see González Block 1989). Even though by 1988 the Ministry of Health had signed agreements with approximately half the states, an effective decentralization of these services was carried out by only fourteen states; in the others, IMSS-COPLAMAR continued operating under central directive.

Actions to Promote Regional Development. In the administrative reorganization of the beginning of de la Madrid's presidency, a new Subsecretaría de Desarrollo Regional (Underministry of Regional Development) was created within the Ministry of Programming and Budget as the entity responsible for overseeing the country's regional development and as a liaison with states and municipalities. The relevance given this underministry, coupled with the transfer of many duties that formerly belonged to urban planning departments, showed that for the de la Madrid administration the urban concept was to be displaced by that of region. Chapter 9 of the National Development Plan (PND) referred to the policy for regional development as "the general basis of the decentralization policy" (SPP 1983: 375) and stated among its objectives the achievement of decentralization primarily by redistributing powers and responsibilities among the three levels of government, by relocating productive activities, and by directing economic activities to medium-sized cities. The PND also included provisions for decentralization, which were subsequently built into the daily operations of all ministries and federal agencies, and an elaborate formal mechanism for the implementation of decentralization.

The target of the regional development policy was to foster more comprehensive development in each of the states. The institutional framework that de la Madrid created for this more integrated regional development was the Sistema Nacional de Planeación Democrática (National Democratic Planning System, SNPD), which institutionalized planning into a system that claimed to be more democratic. The SNPD emphasized the importance of coordination among all levels of government and other organized social groups for planning the development programs of each region and of the nation as a whole (see Aguilar 1994; SPP 1982).

The primary mechanism for promoting regional development was the Convenio Único de Desarrollo (Development Agreement, CUD), signed yearly between the president and the governor of each state. The CUD (called Convenio Único de Concertación under López Portillo) provided the framework for a variety of programs through which the federal government could attend the states' needs more effectively.[18] Through the first CUDs, state governments received federal allocations for education and health only, but gradually the allocations grew to encompass all other federal regional development programs.

In addition to the rather complex bureaucratic structure of the CUD, another equally complex set of agencies and programs was established under the Programa de Desarrollo Regional (Regional Development Program, PDR), which was similar to PIDER and overall proved to be relatively successful.[19] The government also targeted specific areas as priority development zones. Partly to assist each state in the formulation and evaluation of their CUDs, the Comités de Planeación para el Desarrollo Estatal (State Development Planning Committees, COPLADEs) were created. The COPLADEs assisted in coordinating the investment priorities of the federal, state, and municipal governments, as well as of the private sector. The SPP, at the federal level, also used the COPLADEs to include state priorities in federal expenditure decisions. As will be discussed in more detail in Chapter 5, the COPLADEs are still critical players in the process of intergovernmental planning and in the allocation of resources.

The primary importance of the CUDs lay in their being formal agreements designed for the transfer of federal resources to the states. From a decentralization perspective, this was an important first step toward more effective federalism. The CUDs were also important because through them the federal and state government promised to strengthen municipal government. Specific provisions dealt with, for instance, the process of strengthening municipal governments by transferring directly to them the resources that in the past the federal government had retained. Federal revenues were to be allocated *directly* to municipalities, bypassing the states (although, as will become apparent, this did not happen). From 1983 to 1988 the total federal investment in the CUDs amounted to 1.8 billion pesos (SPP 1988: 379).

The de la Madrid administration's urban policy focused primarily on promoting the growth of medium-sized cities. This was no longer the responsibility of the Ministry of Human Settlements and Public Works, SAHOP, which had been recast as the Secretaría de Desarrollo Urbano y Ecología (Ministry of Urban Development and Ecology, SEDUE). Perhaps the most important program designed to attend to urban problems was the Programa Nacional de Desarrollo Urbano y Vivienda (National Urban Development and Housing Program) of 1984. In essence, this was a watered-down version of López Portillo's National Urban Development Plan (PNDU). The new program had two main purposes: to change national population growth patterns, and to regulate the growth of larger cities. From a political standpoint, there was little love lost between de la Madrid and the physical planners (who had held considerable influence under his predecessor) because they had allied themselves with the expansionist lobby of the cabinet, which de la Madrid had strongly opposed (Teichman 1988). It is not surprising, therefore, that he had no spatial policy as such and that, instead, his prime concern was with the economic development plan and its implementation at a regional level. In this context he developed the SNPD and the CUDs, which because of their major implications for program implementation in the states *ipso facto* had spatial implications for regional development. As far as rural areas are concerned, de la Madrid's programs reflected a policy aimed at decreasing inequalities between rural and urban areas and at reducing migration to the United States.

The Municipal Reform.   The Municipal Reform of 1984 was the cornerstone of de la Madrid's decentralization policy. In response to the generalized pressure to decentralize brought up during the *consultas populares* held during his campaign, only five days after assuming the presidency de la Madrid sent to Congress an initiative to modify Article 115 of the Constitution, which deals with municipal government. The Iniciativa de Ley de Reformas y Adiciones al Artículo 115 Constitucional (Initiative to Reform Article 115 of the Constitution) outlined the historical, ideological, and juridical justification for the transformation of municipalities and emphasized that "the centralization that in an earlier period allowed the country to accelerate its economic growth and social development has outlived its usefulness and become a serious limitation on the country's national project. . . . Centralization has seized from the municipality the ability and the resources needed for development and, without question, the moment has come to stop this centralizing tendency" (Cámara de Diputados 1983: 8–9). This constitutional reform, approved by Congress on February 3, 1983, to take effect on January 1, 1984, allowed municipalities to become more autonomous. Indeed, its whole purpose was to give them the autonomy to which they were entitled under the Constitution, but which they had never actually enjoyed. It was the first major step toward decentralization and was intended to strengthen the municipalities and, in so doing, to strengthen Mexican federalism by making local government more independent of state and federal government.

Municipal autonomy was de la Madrid's key to decentralization. The president supported his argument for decentralization by emphasizing the deep historical roots of municipal organization in Mexico, from the *calpulli* of the Aztecs to the present.[20] He also emphasized that, although the Constitution of 1917 granted municipalities economic and political autonomy, this autonomy had been respected only in theory and not in practice. His address to Congress indicated that true decentralization demanded a revision of the constitutional arrangement that divided rights and responsibilities among the federal government, the states, and the municipalities, to determine which of these could be redistributed in order to obtain a better equilibrium among the three levels of government. He appeared firmly convinced that this redistribution would begin by devolving to the municipality its basic powers, that is, the direct governance of the community (Cámara de Diputados 1983: 8). The president forcefully stated that the "changes in Article 115 are aimed at strengthening the municipality's finances, its political autonomy, and all those faculties that somehow have constantly been absorbed by the states and the federal government" (Cámara de Diputados 1983: 10).

De la Madrid's proposals also attempted to deal directly with the major problems associated with the uncontrolled growth of Mexico City and other urban areas, as well as with the disparities among various regions. In changing Article 115, he pointed out, special attention was given to social and economic differences among municipalities, their stages of development, and the contrasts among them. One of the major purposes of the Reform, hence, was to understand and respond better to local needs and conditions.[21] As President de la Madrid indicated, the Municipal Reform was meant

> to strengthen the development of municipalities in order to increase regional development, to increase the feeling of belonging in a community and thus to avoid the constant migration from rural to urban areas, and especially to Mexico City, not only to redistribute the national wealth, but also to have governmental decisions made by the municipal government. (Cámara de Diputados 1983: 11)

Variations among regions were also considered in restoring municipal autonomy and making it a national rule:

> In accordance with the constitutional principle regarding the internal regimes of the states, the regulation of municipal communities will be guided by local laws and constitutions so that these will contain the norms that will correspond to the specific geographic, ethnographic, demographic, and economic characteristics that are distinctive to each of the states. (Cámara de Diputados 1983: 12)

The initiative to reform Article 115 is divided in ten sections, seven specifically related to municipal structures, two that are common to states and municipalities, and one (without any modifications to the earlier text) related to the states. The key sections are II, III, IV, and X. The specific provisions of each of the ten sections of the revised Article 115 include the following:

I. Regulates the electoral procedures of the *ayuntamiento* (municipal president, *regidores,* and *síndicos*) and determines the conditions under which a state legislature may dissolve a municipal government;

II. Reinforces municipalities juridically by granting them autonomy in the management of their finances and by enabling them to design their own rules and laws of governance;

III. Deals with the provision of public services (potable water and drainage, street lighting, street cleaning, markets and supply centers, graveyards, slaughterhouses, street paving and maintenance, parks and gardens, public security, and traffic) and defines precisely which services must be provided by the municipalities. These services can be provided with the assistance of state government when necessary. Other public services may be provided by the municipality when state or local legislatures so determine, depending on the municipality's territorial and socioeconomic conditions, as well as on its administrative and financial capabilities. The municipalities of a state may form an association of municipalities in order to provide public services more effectively;

IV. Deals with the management of municipal finances and is the most important part of the reform. It specifically grants municipal governments all revenues collected from property taxes and from the provision of public services;

V and VI. Enable municipalities to design and implement their own urban development plans. Assistance from, and cooperation with, state and federal government is anticipated;

VII. Stipulates that the federal executive and the state governors have control over the police force in those places where they reside;

VIII. Regulates the electoral procedures for governors and members of state legislatures;

IX. Protects state and municipal employees under the terms of the labor laws (especially Article 124 of the Constitution) in order to provide them with some employment security;

X. Enables municipalities to make formal assistance and cooperation agreements with the state and federal government for the efficient delivery of public services and for carrying out public works.

Shortly after Congress and the thirty-one state legislatures approved the reforms to Article 115, the Centro Nacional de Estudios Municipales (National Center for Municipal Studies, CNEM) was created by presidential decree as the institution responsible for guiding the process of municipal reform. The CNEM was housed in the Ministry of the Interior (Gobernación) and its director reported only to the secretary of this ministry and to the president.

From its inception, the CNEM had no true decision-making powers, but, rather, served as an information center where any reform-related issues could be researched and discussed. The CNEM employed about a dozen academic researchers and organized conferences and meetings with governors and municipal presidents to discuss problems and issues associated with the implementation of Article 115 as revised. This quasi-academic orientation sat comfortably with the technocratic tendencies of the de la Madrid administration.

Soon after the creation of the CNEM in May of 1984, each state also created its own Centro Estatal de Estudios Municipales (State Center for Municipal Studies), whose function, like that of the CNEM, was to promote the assumption of the new powers granted to municipalities. These state centers maintained close ties with their state governments; in fact, the state centers' directors were appointed on the governor's "recommendation." The state centers held a relatively influential position because no specific rules were set to guide the reform's implementation; no one knew how to proceed, and thus municipal presidents and other municipal officials sought the centers' guidance. Often, however, the advice they got seemed to favor the interests of state government over those of municipal government, and rarely were hostile or threatening to the governor's personal interests. The main activity of these centers, like that of the CNEM, focused on organizing seminars and meetings for state and municipal officials. Under both the Salinas and the Zedillo administrations, the state centers have continued to operate in more or less the same fashion, although the national center has lost some of its influence.

The CNEM first received a lot of attention from government agencies and ministries when de la Madrid issued the decree directing all government organizations to produce a program to decentralize, since the CNEM assisted in designing those programs and in organizing seminars to discuss implementation. As part of the impetus given to decentralization under de la Madrid, the CNEM was heavily promoted in the mass media; it had a weekly television program entitled *¿Por Qué la Reforma Municipal?* (Why the Municipal Reform?), and a thirty-minute daily radio broadcast entitled *Voz Municipal* (Municipal Voice). Both programs served as a platform for discussing a variety of issues dealing with the municipality and the reforms.

The CNEM still exists at both the federal and the state levels and has increased its level of activity. Still housed within the Ministry of the Interior, nowadays it is called Centro de Información Municipal and continues to serve as a research and information center on Mexico's municipalities.

The Salinas Administration

During the Salinas administration, "solidarity" was the watchword. The National Solidarity Program, PRONASOL, became the all-encompassing program under which the Salinas administration grouped most of its welfare and regional policies. As might be expected, decentralization was one of them. Even though throughout his administration Salinas spoke much more about solidarity than about decentralization specifically, the latter was an important element in his administrative program from the very beginning. During his campaign, too, Salinas repeatedly emphasized the urgency of decentralization, and indeed some of the largest and most important meetings of his campaign dealt with municipal life, federalism, and regional development. Like his predecessor, he held numerous *consultas populares* on these subjects throughout the country.

But rather than presenting a specific decentralization policy of his own, Salinas pledged to continue the decentralization efforts of his predecessor through an invigoration of the Municipal Reform and other programs for administrative deconcentration, most notably in the education and health sectors. He also pledged, like de la Madrid, to center his efforts to decentralize around the issue of redistributing political and economic power and focused his discourse on the link between decentralization and democratization. Like his predecessor, also, he picked up the "Descentralizar es democratizar" (To decentralize is to democratize) slogan and emphasized the democratic principles involved in decentralization. Although a detailed evaluation of the Salinas administration's decentralization accomplishments will be offered in subsequent chapters, for now our concern is to review the main directives of his *sexenio*'s efforts to decentralize. By far, the most important of these was Solidarity.[22]

The National Solidarity Program.   PRONASOL was originally conceived as a program to combat poverty. It was designed for "los que poco o nada tienen" (those who have little or nothing) and soon became, as one public official put it to me, "Salinas's ticket." Indeed, Solidarity began operations on December 2, 1988—one day after Salinas assumed the presidency—and thus became the first formal act of his government. On December 6, 1988, the Diario Oficial published the decree that created the Comisión Nacional del Programa Nacional de Solidaridad (National Solidarity Program Commission) as the organism for coordinating and overseeing all poverty alleviation and regional development programs. Immediately, Solidarity's visibility became overwhelming to anyone visiting any part of the country; indeed, Solidarity slogans and the logo's small flag can still be seen everywhere.

Solidarity's stated objectives were (1) to improve the living conditions of marginalized groups, (2) to promote balanced regional development, and (3) to promote and strengthen the participation of social organizations and of local authorities. Solidarity's main beneficiaries were originally to be the Indian communities and the poorest peasant and urban groups. The program covered improving nutrition, regularizing land titles and housing, providing legal aid, creating and improving educational facilities, improving health, providing electrical service, providing potable water, building agricultural infrastructure, and preserving natural resources (Consejo Consultivo 1990: 15–16). As the program developed, all these programmatic areas were grouped into three principal "areas of action": solidarity for social welfare, solidarity for production, and solidarity for regional development (SEDESOL 1994: 10–11). In time, the PRONASOL umbrella covered a multitude of programs, the more relevant of which are listed on Table 4.1.

For the first two years the program was run directly out of the president's office. In a highly decentralized—but also discretionary—way, Salinas was able to bypass state governors and municipal presidents and allocate funding directly to local community groups and other organizations.[23] At the end of 1991, Salinas tried to consolidate the program on a more constitutionally sound footing by locating it in a new ministry specifically created for this purpose. He reorganized his cabinet by, among other things, consolidating SEDUE and SPP into the Secretaría de Desarrollo Social (Ministry of Social Development, SEDESOL) in 1992.

Throughout the remainder of the *sexenio*, the new ministry's functions were carried out through three main divisions—Regional Development, Urban Development and Infrastructure, and Housing and Real Estate—in addition to its branch agencies and delegations in the states. SEDESOL's state delegates became the principal actors through which federal, state, and municipal programs were articulated. Among the branch agencies the most worthy of mention are Empresas de Solidaridad (Solidarity Enterprises) and the Instituto Nacional de Solidaridad (National Solidarity Institute). The former supported investments in productive projects; the latter was a training organization for potential leaders of Solidarity programs.

In no time, SEDESOL became the most visible ministry of the Salinas cabinet, not least because it appeared to be the ministry through which all major budgetary resources were channeled.[24] The president appointed Luis Donaldo Colosio, then-president of the PRI, as head of the new ministry and Carlos Rojas Gutiérrez as head of Solidarity (which, naturally, was the principal office of the new ministry). Through SEDESOL, and through both Colosio and Rojas—Colosio in particular—Salinas was able to maintain extremely close ties with the program and to continue using it in a personalized fashion.

Essentially, PRONASOL emerged as a community participation program that worked in a rather simple way: any organized group, be it a state or local government, a residents' group, or a local association, approached local Solidarity officials and presented a project for any type of public work. After analysis and negotiation, and once the project was approved, Solidarity put up most of the financial resources required for the project while the group contributed the labor and, whenever possible, local resources.

As will be discussed in more detail in Chapter 6, the benefits of local projects of this sort are legion, and although not new to Mexico, they gained popularity during Salinas's administration as a direct link between government and the people and as a way of eliminating bureaucratic red tape and government inefficiency. Indeed, just as de la Madrid claimed to have designed his decentralization policy in response to popular demand, Salinas pledged during his own campaign to create a program to meet the demands presented to him to do away with government inefficiency and paternalism and to involve community actors more directly in the decision-making processes that affected their daily lives. These promises were embodied in Solidarity.

TABLE 4.1   Programs Included Under the Solidarity Umbrella

Solidaridad para el Bienestar Social (Social Welfare)
Solidaridad en la Educación (Education)
  Infraestructura Educativa (Educational Infrastructure)
  Solidaridad para una Escuela Digna (Adequate School)
  Niños de Solidaridad (Children)
  Apoyo al Servicio Social (Social Service Assistance)
  Maestros Jubilados y Pensionados (Retired Teachers and Pensioners)
  Infraestructura Deportiva (Sports Infrastructure)
Solidaridad en la Salud (Health)
  Infraestructura de Servicios de Salud (Health Services Infrastructure)
  IMSS-Solidaridad (Social Security)
  Hospital Digno (Adequate Hospital)
  Enfermeras en Solidaridad (Nurses)
Solidaridad en los Servicios de Desarrollo Urbano (Urban Development)
  Agua Potable y Alcantarillado (Drinking Water and Sewage Systems)
  Electrificación Rural y Urbana (Rural and Urban Electrification)
  Urbanización (Urbanization)
  Regularización de la Tenencia de la Tierra (Regularization of Land Tenure)
  Vivienda en Solidaridad (Housing)
  Solidaridad Obrera (Workers)
Atención Solidaria a Población Abierta (High-Risk Populations)
  Jóvenes en Solidaridad (Youth)
  Atención y Orientación Jurídica a la Comunidad en Solidaridad (Community Judicial Attention and
    Orientation)
  Alimentación y Abasto (Basic Foodstuffs)

Solidaridad para la Producción (Production)
Apoyo a Comunidades Indígenas (*Support for Indian Communities*)
  Fondos de Solidaridad para el Desarrollo de los Pueblos Indígenas (Development of Indian Commu-
    nities)
  Apoyo a Cafeticultores (Coffee Producers)
  Fondo de Solidaridad para la Promoción del Patrimonio Cultural (Promotion of the Cultural Patri-
    mony)
  Procuración de Justicia INI-Solidaridad (Juridical Assistance INI-Solidarity)
  Jornaleros Agrícolas (Agricultural Day Laborers)
Solidaridad con Campesinos y Grupos Urbano-Populares (Farmworkers and Low-Income Urban Groups)
  Fondos de Solidaridad para la Producción (Production)
  Empresas de Solidaridad (Solidarity Enterprises)
  Cajas Solidarias (Savings and Loans)
  Mujeres en Solidaridad (Women)
Solidaridad y el Desarrollo Sustentable (Sustainable Development)
  Ecología Productiva (Productive Ecology)
  Apoyo a Productores Forestales (Forestry Producers)
  Solidaridad Forestal (Forests)

Solidaridad para el Desarrollo Regional (Regional Development)
Infraestructura Básica para el Desarrollo Regional (Regional Development)
  Fondos Municipales (Municipal Funds)
  Infraestructura Carretera y de Caminos Rurales (Highways and Rural Roads)
  100 Ciudades (100 Cities)
Programas de Desarrollo Regional (Regional Development)
**Programa Especial para la Conservación y Desarrollo de la Selva Lacandona (Conservation and De-
velopment of the Lacandon Jungle)**

SOURCE: SEDESOL (1994), pp. 4–5.

TABLE 4.2   Principal Achievements of Solidarity, by Subprogram

Subprogram	Impact
Salud (Health)	Between 1989 and 1994, 10.5 million people were incorporated into institutionalized health services.
Infraestructura Educativa (Educational Infrastructure)	Between 1989 and 1994, 81,350 classrooms, laboratories, workshops, and annexes were built for more than 3.2 million students.
Escuela Digna (Adequate School)	Between 1990 and 1994, 119,706 buildings were improved, benefiting more than 19 million students.
Niños de Solidaridad (Children)	Between 1991 and 1994, scholarships were given to 1,169,611 primary students, 18.2 million meals were served to schoolchildren and more than 4.4 million medical visits were made to schools.
Servicio Social (Social Service)	Between 1989 and 1994, 910,611 scholarships were given to technical students and professionals.
Maestros Jubilados y Pensionados (Retired Teachers and Pensioners)	Between 1992 and 1994, compensation was given to 6,253 retired teachers.
Agua Potable y Alcantarillado (Drinking Water and Sewage)	Between 1989 and 1994, 4,000 systems of sewage benefiting 13.7 million people were built, enlarged, or improved, and 10,499 drinking water systems were built or improved, benefiting 16.3 million people.
Electrificación (Electrification)	Between 1989 and 1994, 5,230 low-income neighborhoods and 14,003 rural communities received electricity, benefiting over 20 million people.
Regularización de la Tenencia de la Tierra (Regularization of Land Tenure)	2.5 million land titles were legalized in 6 years, compared with 288,000 in the previous 15 years.
Vivienda en Solidaridad (Housing)	Between 1989 and 1994, 714,294 dwellings were built or improved.
Solidaridad Forestal (Forests)	In 1993, a Solidarity Forest Committee was founded in each of the states to plant around 170 million trees throughout the country by 1994.
Ecología Productiva (Productive Ecology)	Between 1992 and 1994, 530 projects were started in the Monarch Butterfly Biosphere Reserve in the States of México and Michoacán; special projects were initiated in the States of Campeche, Chiapas, Tabasco, Hidalgo, Morelos, Veracruz, and Puebla.
Fondos Regionales Indígenas (Regional Indian Funds)	Between 1990 and 1994, 142 funds were established. They have started 6,801 projects in 1,127 municipalities.
Fondos de Solidaridad para la Producción (Production)	Between 1990 and 1994, these productive projects benefited more than one million farmers who worked on 2.9 million hectares in 30 states.

(continues)

TABLE 4.2 (*continued*)

Subprogram	Impact
Empresas de Solidaridad (Solidarity Enterprises)	In 1993–1994, 19,905 Solidarity Enterprises were created and supported, 32.5% with risk capital, and 67.5% with financing and guaranteed funds.
Cajas Solidarias (Low-Interest Credit)	120 Solidarity funds were created to serve 2,115 local savings funds in 22 states.
Fondos Municipales de Solidaridad (Municipal Funds)	Between 1990 and 1994, 2,341 municipalities were funded (97% of the total). Over 113,000 projects were completed.
Infraestructura Carretera y de Caminos Rurales (Highways and Rural Roads)	Between 1989 and 1994, 218,561 kilometers of high-ways and rural roads were built: 23,963 kilometers were constructed; 15,601 kilometers were rebuilt; 178,997 kilometers were maintained.
Programas de Desarrollo Regional (Regional Development)	In 1989, regional development programs were started. In 1994, 16 programs were operating in 12 states and 395 municipalities, where 9.2 million persons reside.

SOURCE: SEDESOL (1994), pp. 37–39.

Although in itself the program was not really new to Mexico, given that in many ways it was a direct descendant of PIDER, its novelty rested in taking advantage of the bureaucratic mechanisms already in place to implement a program that ambitiously hoped to address the gaps in social service provision and promote more balanced regional development. For example, all funding decisions for Solidarity projects were incorporated into each state's CDS (Convenio de Desarrollo Social—Social Development Agreement, the successor to de la Madrid's CUD), thereby taking advantage of the COPLADE planning and development structure already set up in each state.[25] What did distinguish Solidarity from other regional development and poverty alleviation programs was a set of principles and guidelines that clearly favored decentralization and community involvement. Solidarity demanded, for example, community participation in the selection and implementation of projects through the local Solidarity Committees, shared responsibility for program implementation with state and municipal authorities, and shared costs among the three levels of government and beneficiaries.

Although the overall impact of Solidarity is difficult to measure because its programs were so wide-ranging, federal financing for it grew from US$500 million in 1989 to US$2.2 billion in 1993. The thirty-plus programs covered a broad range of investments, often designed to complement regular sector investments. For example, the Escuela Digna (Adequate Schools) program funded the renovation and construction of educational facilities and the Niños de Solidaridad (Solidarity Children) gave small scholarships to students; neither of these expenditures was included in the normal education budget. The overall results of the program are presented in Table 4.2;

at the end of the *sexenio*, the administration claimed that 523,000 projects had been completed throughout the country between 1989 and 1994 (SEDESOL 1994: 25).

The number of beneficiaries of, and projects completed under, the Solidarity umbrella is impressive, even though in many respects the political aspects of the program have overshadowed its accomplishments in terms of social welfare provision. But even if to a large extent Solidarity was engineered as a political consolidation mechanism and as a natural outcome of the economic development policies of the administration—as has been amply discussed in academic and other analyses (Cornelius, Craig, and Fox 1994; Dresser 1991)—what is important to underscore here is its intention to target specific regions and municipalities in a major effort of poverty alleviation.

As for decentralization per se, the most significant contribution of Solidarity is twofold: on the one hand, it provided a vehicle for greater citizen participation in government decision making through the Solidarity Committees and Municipal Solidarity Councils, especially for projects implemented at the local level; on the other, it promoted greater state and municipal control over public investment decisions as well as better input in the planning and implementation of public works and social programs in their own communities. As will be discussed in Chapters 5 and 6, Solidarity represented a genuine decentralization of both resources and decision making by allocating federal funds *directly* to project committees and their Municipal Councils, instead of going through the state governments. If the main decentralization shortcomings of the Municipal Reform consisted, precisely, in making allocations to local governments via their state governments, then Solidarity served as the vehicle for assisting municipalities in obtaining the autonomy they had been unable to achieve thus far.

Other Decentralization Efforts

A key, if largely unacknowledged, outcome of Salinas's political and financial "opening" and restructuring is decentralization. At least in geographical and economic terms, and particularly in the aftermath of NAFTA, all indicators are that the modern manufacturing *maquila* industries (assembly plants) located along the U.S.-Mexico border are taking the lead. If the *maquila*-type industries continue to expand from the border to other provincial areas of Mexico—what Sklair (1989) calls "the march to the interior"—then it will constitute an important vehicle for shifting the tendency away from centralization. The dramatic reorientation of the economy toward export manufacturing growth since Mexico's entry into GATT in 1986, and of course since the implementation of NAFTA, has meant that manufacturing industries are now the most dynamic and important contributors to GDP (superseding petroleum). Within the manufacturing sector, *maquilas* are at the leading edge, representing over 12 percent of total sales in 1992 (Lustig 1992; Wilson 1992), and this has reinforced those cities, mostly in the North and Center, that have included *maquila* plants as part of their urban development strategies.

In the education sector, Salinas proposed "the modernization of the state and of education," with the principal objectives of increasing the involvement of the states in the planning process, furthering teacher training, and restructuring the teachers' union. All of these objectives were fulfilled in the first three years of his administration. The reforms to Article 3 of the Constitution, the new Ley General de Educación (General Education Law) and, more important, the Acuerdo Nacional para la Modernización de la Educación Básica (National Agreement for the Modernization of Basic Education, ANMEB, signed in 1992 by the SEP, the SNTE, and the state governments), provided the basic framework for furthering the decentralization of the education sector that de la Madrid initiated. Salinas transferred to the state governments both responsibility *and* money for education and granted them full autonomy for spending these funds. Although significant achievements resulted from this transfer, in the end there were also negative outcomes, most notably an increase in the conflicts between the teachers and state government and a constant complaining by states and municipalities about the insufficiency of financial resources to carry out their newly assigned functions.

In the health sector, the decentralization program initiated under de la Madrid, which had transferred responsibility for the provision of health services to fourteen states (Aguascalientes, Baja California Sur, Colima, Guanajuato, Guerrero, Jalisco, México, Morelos, Nuevo León, Querétaro, Quintana Roo, Sonora, Tabasco, and Tlaxcala), did not advance much. Indeed, even though the decentralization of this sector was included in the National Development Plan 1989–1994 and in the Programa de Salud 1990–1994 (Health Program), no steps were taken to implement it because the states remained uneasy about assuming responsibility without assurances that adequate resources would also be transferred. If anything, with the creation of Solidarity and SEDESOL, the federal government centralized even more all resources for building, maintaining, and administering hospitals. The IMSS-Solidaridad program, for instance, provided health services without any involvement of either the state or municipal governments, thereby centralizing the sector further.

The Zedillo Administration

For President Zedillo, decentralization has become more than a standard rhetorical element in a campaign speech or a governmental program. It is the key element in his New Federalism project. With a pressure not really felt by any of his predecessors to take immediate action to remedy the abuses of overcentralization, Zedillo has been left with no alternative but to carry out a de facto redistribution of political and economic power.

New Federalism embraces several major areas: reform of the judiciary; reform of the revenue-sharing system; greater and more effective separation among the executive, legislative, and judicial branches; a reduction in the powers of the presidency itself (both constitutional and metaconstitutional); institutional strengthening of state and municipal governments; increased autonomy for the lower levels of government; separation of party (PRI) and government; further electoral reform and implementation of these reforms at the state and local levels; and the development of new forms and opportunities for both representative and participatory democracy in the process of government. Quite literally, it is a comprehensive, thorough Reforma del Estado (Reform of the State).

On the basis of my reading of official documents to date and several discussions with senior public officials charged with implementing New Federalism, it seems likely that there will be five broad areas of decentralization. First, some level of reform will raise the revenue-sharing allocations to the states, but this is likely to proceed only insofar as new and additional responsibilities are also transferred. During the Salinas administration, there were rising claims from several states to raise the proportion from 18.5 percent to over 30 percent, especially from the *panista* and other wealthier northern states (Rodríguez and Ward 1994a). While institutional resistance from Hacienda, the economic crisis, and the continually growing federal bureaucracy makes the level of this proposed change unrealistic, in addition to the 1.5 percent increase (to a total of 20 percent), some further across-the-board increase may be provided. Certainly, a redirection of resources is under way through the federal ministries to accompany the transfer of new sectoral responsibilities to the states. Specifically, there will be improvements and extensions to the existing decentralization of public education and health. In 1995, as mentioned earlier, only fourteen states were administering health services, while education was transferred to all the states. To date, the decentralization of these sectors in many states has proved unsatisfactory, has placed unreasonable demands on the capacity of the states, and, furthermore, has intensified conflict with the teachers' union. In addition, many areas in agriculture, communications, and transportation are being decentralized. The bottom line is that states will receive more resources only insofar as they respond positively to these newfound responsibilities.

Second, there will be expanded opportunities for states to raise income locally through taxation and other mechanisms. It is unlikely that this will occur through property taxes, as the right to collect this tax was transferred to the municipalities with the Municipal Reform of 1983. This means that these taxes will continue to be collected at the local level in most cases, except for those municipalities that are unable to do so for lack of administrative capacity. Nor is it likely to come from the value-added tax (IVA), since this tax has been centrally collected since 1990 and is not likely to be transferred to the states again. Therefore, the opportunities for raising state income will likely derive from developing other areas of taxation (e.g., taxes on automobiles, licenses, payroll, hotel occupancy, etc., as will be described in Chapters 5 and 6), and from the collection of fees for services.

Third, the lion's share of funds assigned for regional and social development through Ramo 0026 (formerly PRONASOL) will be to a far greater extent allocated to the states and thus controlled by state governments. Through 1998, 68 percent of the total resources in this budget line will be distributed directly to municipalities. Of this, approximately half is expected to be allocated by the states to the municipalities for social development projects, but in forms that are more transparent and equitable (see Table 4.3 for assignments and marginality indexes). The other half is to be incorporated into the yearly CDS for other integrated regional development projects, but also in forms that are more transparent and less discretionary. In both cases, however, the precise mechanisms for allocating these resources remain unclear, which may sustain the discretionary patterns that have caused inequitable development within the municipalities of a given state. Although in principle this change was designed to decentralize resources to the municipalities, which should have paramountcy in the allocation, in practice, in many states both state executive and SEDESOL officials appear to be successfully centralizing their control over both the allocation and the nature of approved projects (see Rodríguez and Ward et al. 1996).

Fourth, the decentralization measures in Zedillo's New Federalism also increase and strengthen the municipalities' administrative capacity. In the past, one of the principal arguments against decentralization was the poor training, corruption, and administrative inexperience of municipal officials. The problem has been exacerbated by a lack of training programs, low funding, and Mexico's three-year, no-re-election terms for local government officials, all of which produce a lack of continuity in policy design and implementation. Under New Federalism, the responsibility for improving institutional capacity at the municipal level will increasingly fall to state governments. In 1996, SEDESOL published its Programa Nacional de Desarrollo Urbano 1995–2000 (National Urban Development Program), which is quite bullish in the way in which it seeks to decentralize responsibility for planning to the local level, to train and upgrade the financial and administrative capacity to control land use, to engage in urban planning, and, above all, to be more successful in modernizing municipal ability to raise local revenues. Altogether, the program gives priority to federalism, decentralization, and equitable economic development.[26]

Fifth, New Federalism seeks to clarify the distribution of administrative functions across federal, state, and municipal levels. Although this seems rather imprecise, it follows the premises first incorporated in the Municipal Reform that were meant to eliminate (or at least to reduce) bureaucratic duplication and overlap.

Clearly, these proposed changes appear to target the weight and direction of decentralization much more toward the states rather than to municipalities. Indeed, in the emerging Pacto Federal (Federal Pact) between states and the federation, municipalities form part of the *régimen interior* (subgovernment) of each state. Although one assumes (and hopes) that the municipalities' autonomy will be respected, there is little doubt in my mind that the principal political beneficiaries of New Federalism will be the state governments.

Conclusion

We have seen in this chapter how centralization formed part of an imperative in the process of economic development and political consolidation in Mexico. In time,

TABLE 4.3 Distribution of Ramo 0026 Funds for the Fondo de Desarrollo Social Municipal, 1996

State	Marginality Index	Population	Ramo 0026 Allocation (1996 pesos)	Distribution (%)	Per Capita Allocation (1996 pesos)
Aguascalientes	−.88969	879,018	91,018,237	1.27	103.5
Baja California	−1.34464	2,051,102	81,392,738	1.14	39.7
Baja California Sur	−.96851	403,699	76,695,605	1.07	190.0
Campeche	.47741	620,651	158,045,411	2.21	254.6
Coahuila	−1.05344	2,280,623	107,185,352	1.50	47.0
Colima	−.75783	488,277	79,673,461	1.11	163.2
Chiapas	2.36046	4,185,704	569,455,898	7.96	136.0
Chihuahua	−.87224	2,754,802	161,791,559	2.26	58.7
Durango	.01175	1,463,300	199,203,741	2.79	136.1
Guanajuato	.21157	4,733,306	300,673,364	4.21	63.5
Guerrero	1.74666	3,078,484	377,799,312	5.28	122.7
Hidalgo	1.16952	2,134,124	302,156,686	4.23	141.6
Jalisco	−.76764	5,968,177	251,766,444	3.52	42.2
México	−.60422	11,517,233	366,621,863	5.13	31.8
Michoacán	.36274	4,043,089	318,365,861	4.45	78.7
Morelos	−.45714	1,378,617	126,579,676	1.77	91.8
Nayarit	−.13366	891,620	150,588,494	2.11	168.9
Nuevo León	−1.37660	3,524,723	110,429,045	1.54	31.3
Oaxaca	2.05526	3,315,403	526,257,440	7.36	158.7
Puebla	.83108	4,690,565	418,741,450	5.86	89.3
Querétaro	.16086	1,304,269	196,294,067	2.75	150.5
Quintana Roo	−.19119	796,347	134,435,868	1.88	168.8
San Luis Potosí	.74878	2,236,082	274,597,797	3.84	122.8
Sinaloa	−.14100	2,454,510	170,462,552	2.38	69.4
Sonora	−.85979	2,044,031	101,610,219	1.42	49.7
Tabasco	.51677	1,856,754	216,368,676	3.03	116.5
Tamaulipas	−.60855	2,475,827	148,874,673	2.08	60.1
Tlaxcala	−.03620	922,859	152,978,380	2.14	165.8
Veracruz	1.13030	6,806,201	525,105,922	7.34	81.1
Yucatán	.39959	1,587,080	209,305,228	2.93	131.9
Zacatecas	.56805	1,370,207	245,524,980	3.43	179.2
Total		84,256,684	7,149,999,999	100.00	
Average	.05477	2,717,958	230,645,161	3.23	111.1
Minimum	−1.37660	403,699	76,695,605	1.07	31.3
Maximum	2.36046	11,517,233	569,455,898	7.96	254.6
Stan. dev.	.96708	2,288,085	138,444,535	1.94	55.7
Greater than the average				38.7	
Less than the average				61.3	

SOURCES: Marginality index from CONAPO (1993). Population figures from CONAPO (1994). Table constructed from data in the *Diario Oficial* (Jan. 5, 1996).

however, this centralization reached the point that its negative consequences could no longer be ignored. In the last twenty-five years one presidential administration after another has attempted to tackle the problems of overconcentration, but with relatively little success. The policy of President de la Madrid, largely encompassed in the Municipal Reform of 1983, represents the most forceful effort to undo the damage wrought by the overcentralization of power and resources. To the extent that some decentralization *has* occurred, it has been a result of his initiative, further consolidated under some subprograms of President Salinas's National Solidarity Program. Under Zedillo, we hope to see a further consolidation of a de facto decentralization with his marked emphasis on New Federalism.

On leaving office, President de la Madrid stated that with decentralization one should not expect "spectacular results." He also affirmed that decentralization could not be the responsibility of the federal government alone; to succeed it requires the support of state and local governments and the consolidation of what was referred to, during his administration, as a "decentralization culture." The challenge, therefore, is to consolidate this "culture" while recognizing that, inevitably, any major reform will alter the status quo and impinge on vested interests. Although some of the decentralization efforts described here may have been well intentioned, major questions arise about their effective implementation. These questions center around two issues: one, whether these policies and programs have been designed to eliminate, reduce, or simply recast the dependence of the lower levels of government on the higher ones; and two, whether they require that local political heavyweights, state governors, and other high-ranking public officials give up some of their power in favor of lower levels of government. Thus far this latter point has not proved to be the case, as Chapter 5 demonstrates in the specific area of intergovernmental finances. To the extent that the decentralization efforts of the last twenty-five years have produced change, it has been in the emergence of a new brand of federalism, with larger powers concentrated at the *state* level.

5

Dependent Sovereignty:
Intergovernmental Finances
and the States

In this chapter my aim is to analyze intergovernmental fiscal relations in Mexico by focusing on recent trends in the revenue-sharing system, federal investment programs, and the National Solidarity Program. Although Mexico's intergovernmental fiscal system operates within the broader framework of federalism, we see a reflection of the special brand of federalism discussed in Chapter 2. As the descriptive and analytical data presented in this chapter demonstrate, the financial flows from the higher to the lower levels of government are designed to support a centralized system in which equity and effectiveness are far from being the predominant criteria for resource distribution.

Whereas the focus of this chapter is on the patterns of fiscal relations between the federal and the state governments, Chapter 6 will extend the discussion to incorporate the municipal level. The federal-state fiscal relations that will be discussed here are (1) the coordinated system of revenue collection and sharing; (2) the investment programs implemented by federal line agencies; (3) the National Solidarity Program, which between 1989 and 1995 involved a matching grant investment program that was coordinated between the federal and state governments and which in some cases included a municipal support component (e.g., Municipal Funds); and (4) the states' own revenue sources. The first section presents an overview of federal-state fiscal relations, and the second analyzes the structure of public finances at the state level, with special emphasis on the sources of revenue and the patterns of expenditure.

The Federal System of Revenue Sharing

The Mexican system of revenue sharing is in some ways similar to that of the United States until the 1980s. Through the office in charge of revenue sharing—the Coordinación General con Entidades Federativas of the Subsecretaría de Ingresos (Office of Federal-State Relations in the Underministry of Revenue) within the Secretaría de Hacienda y Crédito Público (Finance Ministry, SHCP)—the federal government mails checks each month to state and local governments for amounts calculated by an automatic transfer formula. Although the formal revenue-sharing system in the United States is no longer in effect—it was instituted by President Nixon in the early 1970s and distributed funds to states and local governments until it was eliminated during the Reagan administration—the American system of grants-in-aid has traditionally divided the assistance provided by the federal government to the other levels of government into categorical grants and block grants.[1] The Mexican government, too, has an equivalent for these types of grants offered through a variety of programs, not least among them Solidarity.

A formal system of revenue sharing was instituted in Mexico in 1943 and modified in 1953, but the revenues allocated to states and municipalities under this system were based on the collection of only a few federal taxes (labeled *impuestos especiales*, special taxes) and were never sufficient to cover state and municipal expenses. The system was modified again in 1980 and formalized into the Sistema Nacional de Coordinación Fiscal (National System of Fiscal Coordination, SNCF), which is the legal foundation for revenue sharing in Mexico. The SNCF was created as a mechanism to organize and discipline the fiscal system, especially to protect citizens from inequitable taxation procedures, given that there were instances of double and even triple taxation on a single source of income. Since 1980, states and municipalities have been entitled to receive a certain percentage of all revenue collected from federal taxes. The most important of these are the income tax (*impuesto sobre la renta*, representing around 43 percent of federal tax revenue), the value-added tax (*impuesto al valor agregado*, IVA, approximately 28 percent of federal tax revenue), and a special tax on production and selected services (*impuesto especial sobre producción y servicios*, 20 percent of federal taxes); the remainder comes from a variety of minor and variable sources. The system was modified yet again in 1990, establishing the guidelines that currently determine revenue sharing.[2]

With the purpose of developing, overseeing, and improving the SNCF, every year the Reunión Nacional de Funcionarios Fiscales, a national meeting of the states' finance secretaries and various officials from the Ministry of Finance, is held. There is also a Comisión Permanente de Funcionarios Fiscales (Permanent Commission of Fiscal Officials), formed by the finance secretaries from eight states chosen during the Reunión Nacional, which meets every three months to determine the issues that will be discussed at the yearly meeting and to ensure that these are executed. More important, this commission is in charge of guaranteeing that the distribution of funds among states follows the agreements made.

There are various working groups within the Permanent Commission, one of which develops new sources of taxation. For technical assistance to states and municipalities in fiscal matters, the SNCF created the Instituto para el Desarrollo Técnico de las Haciendas Públicas (Institute for Technical Development of Public Treasuries, INDETEC).[3]

The revenue-sharing system respects state sovereignty and operates through a voluntary agreement between state government and the Ministry of Finance. This agreement is optional for state governments and presents both advantages and disadvantages: the states that become part of the SNCF are entitled to a larger share of federal funds, but they are required to distribute *at least 22.1 percent* of these funds among their municipalities. Although the biggest disadvantage is that states lose their tax base, all have signed these agreements and are therefore incorporated into the national revenue-sharing system. Once states sign the agreement, the amount of revenue sharing that each state receives—called *participaciones*—is determined by a formula in the Ley de Coordinación Fiscal (Fiscal Coordination Law, LCF). The discussion that follows highlights the major changes in the regulations relating to *participaciones*. These changes are underscored because they allow us to assess the changes that are under way and their implications for the future of intergovernmental financial relations.

First, prior to 1990, this formula-determined revenue sharing was distributed among the states through three funds: (1) the Fondo General de Participaciones (General Revenue-Sharing Fund, FGP), made up of 13 percent of the total annual tax revenues of the federal government and distributed among the states according to each state's contribution to the collection of federal taxes;[4] (2) the Fondo Financiero Complementario (Complementary Fund, FFC), a compensating fund drawn from the same tax base as the FGP for the poorer states that contributed less to the FGP and therefore received smaller allocations from that fund; and (3) the Fondo de Fomento Municipal (Municipal Development Fund, FFM), made up of a fraction of the one percent additional tax on the export of oil and natural gas and assigned exclusively to municipalities. The 1990 reform amalgamated the first two funds into one, still called Fondo General de Participaciones (FGP).

Second, until the end of 1995, the system worked as follows. Tax revenues (as defined by the LCF) collected in the states went to Mexico City and formed the Recaudación Federal Participable (Federal Tax Collected for Revenue Sharing), of which 18.1 percent was distributed among the states as the FGP. Twenty percent of the FGP was to be distributed among the municipalities. The FFM was made up of 0.42 percent of the Recaudación Federal Participable and had to be passed on in its entirety to the municipalities. Thus, in total, the states received 18.5 percent of the federally collected revenue, 22.1 percent of which they had to distribute to their respective municipalities. *Participaciones* were paid to state governments monthly, with quarterly adjustments.

From 1990 to 1995, the FGP was distributed according to specific criteria. First, 45 percent was calculated based on the state's population. The second criterion allocated 45 percent according to the collection of certain taxes called *impuestos asignables*.[5] This latter 45 percent was not distributed according to the actual amount collected on any given year, but, rather, according to the previous year's coefficient multiplied by the ratio between *asignable* tax collection during the previous year and *asignable* tax collection two years past. Thus, a state with an increasing *asignable* tax base or increasingly diligent tax administration was rewarded by receiving increasing shares. Conversely, states whose tax base shrank relative to that of other states, or whose tax effort fell behind the average, faced decreasing revenue co-efficients. The remaining 10 percent was an "equalization share" given out in inverse proportion to the other two.

Prior to the 1990 reform, federal revenue sharing was distributed to the states based on their individual collection efforts, which inevitably meant that the poorer states received, on average, one third the amount per capita received by richer states. The implementation of the reform, following the new formula, resulted in a 64 per-cent real increase in federal transfers to the four poorest states (Chiapas, Guerrero, Hidalgo, and Oaxaca) from 1989 to 1992, while the remaining states received an average increase of 20 percent. Thus, the overall effect of the 1990 reform has been that the ratio of transfers to the three richest states (Nuevo León, Baja California, and the Federal District) compared with transfers to the six poorest states was re-duced from 3:1 in 1989 to 2:1 in 1992, and the expectancy was that it would con-tinue to decrease (see Table 5.1). This caused some friction between those richer northern states and Hacienda because they felt penalized for being better-off and more effective tax collectors and for contributing a larger portion to the federal cof-fers.

The increases to the poorer states are particularly noticeable when one takes into account federal *participaciones* per capita (see Table 5.2). For example, Oaxaca in-creased its federal *participaciones* from 89 (1992) pesos to 223 per person between 1990 and 1993. Note also the much higher per capita *participaciones* received by the oil-rich state of Tabasco, which has always benefited greatly from the special taxes (in this case, on hydrocarbons) built into the distribution formula.

The data in Table 5.3 show the distribution of *participaciones* as a percentage of total income for seven of the country's poorer states. As an overall percentage of to-tal income, the data show a consistently high dependence on federal revenue sharing among poorer states, often 80 percent or above. The exception of Guerrero may be explained by the fact that in 1992 it was going heavily into debt. The lowest level of dependence (except Guerrero) was that of Veracruz (67 percent); for Hidalgo, a full 90 percent of its total income in 1992 came from *participaciones*. The combined av-erage dependence of the seven states cited in Table 5.3, however, declined from 83 percent in 1987 to 70 percent in 1992; this follows an overall decline nationally as states have become more efficient in generating their own sources of revenue, a point to which I will return. Although the extent of dependence on federal income levels remains very high, it nonetheless declined from 90 percent in 1975 to 73.6 percent in 1992 (see also Table 5.4). The lion's share of the difference has increas-ingly been produced by the states' increased capacity to generate their own revenues (*ingresos propios*), from 8.6 percent to 21.9 percent (see Ortega Lomelín 1995).

In addition to the funds that states received in their own right through the FGP and the FFM, states were eligible to receive additional funds (called *incentivos fis-cales*) from Hacienda in the form of incentives and rewards for more effective collec-

TABLE 5.1   Federal *Participaciones,* by State, 1992 (millions of new pesos)

State	1990	% Change 1990–91	1991	% Change 1991–92	1992	% Change 1992–93	1993
Aguascalientes	179.5	48	266.3	14	304.6	0	306.2
Baja California	784.7	8	847.2	5	887.3	–5	845.5
Baja California Sur	139.6	34	187.4	–1	185.8	–1	183.8
Campeche	249.6	46	364.4	2	371.9	–2	366.1
Coahuila	560.7	13	633.2	7	676.2	–	674.3
Colima	118.4	63	193.3	10	213.5	–	212.3
Chiapas	993.7	11	1,101.0	9	1,196.8	–	1,186.6
Chihuahua	637.3	15	733.7	15	840.7	0	841.4
Distrito Federal	5,081.6	4	5,283	–3	5,129.2	–7	4,754.1
Durango	219.2	60	350.3	10	384.9	4	399.7
Guanajuato	631.9	21	766.5	21	925.9	6	978.9
Guerrero	325.0	52	494.3	14	561.1	10	618.5
Hidalgo	217.1	81	393.7	12	441.0	8	477.5
Jalisco	1,341.5	9	1,457.3	13	1,648.8	–1	1,625.8
México	2,283.9	7	2,441.8	9	2,664.9	4	2,766.3
Michoacán	395.1	46	578.6	24	717.2	10	785.4
Morelos	249.7	42	355.8	10	391.6	2	399.9
Nayarit	176.1	59	279.5	8	301.3	3	310.3
Nuevo León	1,268.2	2	1,294.6	4	1,349.7	–4	1,293.9
Oaxaca	267.9	77	475.2	22	579.6	16	673.5
Puebla	604.7	26	760.2	24	940.6	5	990.5
Querétaro	249.2	36	339.0	16	393.1	0	396.3
Quintana Roo	110.3	69	186.5	14	212.8	3	218.4
San Luis Potosí	276.2	54	425.2	11	470.9	7	503.2
Sinaloa	671.8	12	754.3	9	820.8	–2	802.5
Sonora	871.2	10	962.1	4	1,002.6	–4	959.8
Tabasco	1,603.1	0	1,610.4	–3	1,568.1	–18	1,293.1
Tamaulipas	632.8	15	728.7	9	790.8	0	793.7
Tlaxcala	115.7	107	239.8	11	266.6	6	281.8
Veracruz	1,439.7	12	1,614.2	11	1,785.3	0	1,798.4
Yucatán	250.6	45	362.9	11	401.8	3	415.4
Zacatecas	175.6	85	325.3	7	348.8	7	372.4

States' Marginality Index	1990	1991	1992	1993	% Change 1990–93
Low	7,014.8	7,959.7	8,719.9	8,763.5	25
Medium	1,073.8	1,460.1	1,601.6	1,613.2	50
High	4,050.5	5,122.7	5,583.1	5,510.5	36
Very high	3,848.2	4,838.6	5,504.5	5,744.9	49
Total	23,121.8	26,805.7	28,775.5	28,525.6	

SOURCE: SEDESOL/World Bank (1993).

TABLE 5.2 Federal *Participaciones* per Capita, by State, 1992 (millions of new pesos)

State	Participaciones 1990	Participaciones 1991	Participaciones 1992	Participaciones 1993
Aguascalientes	249.4	370.0	423.3	425.5
Baja California	472.5	510.0	534.3	509.1
Baja California Sur	439.5	589.7	584.8	578.4
Campeche	466.4	680.8	694.9	684.1
Coahuila	284.3	321.1	342.8	341.8
Colima	276.3	451.2	498.4	495.3
Chiapas	309.5	343.0	372.8	369.6
Chihuahua	260.9	300.5	344.3	344.5
Distrito Federal	617.0	641.0	622.8	577.3
Durango	162.4	259.6	285.3	296.2
Guanajuato	158.7	192.5	232.5	245.8
Guerrero	124.0	188.6	214.1	235.9
Hidalgo	114.9	208.5	233.6	252.9
Jalisco	252.9	274.8	311.0	306.6
México	232.7	248.8	271.5	281.8
Michoacán	111.4	163.1	202.1	221.3
Morelos	209.0	297.7	327.7	334.7
Nayarit	213.0	338.9	365.4	376.3
Nuevo León	409.2	417.8	435.6	417.6
Oaxaca	88.7	157.4	192.0	223.1
Puebla	146.5	184.3	228.0	240.1
Querétaro	237.0	322.5	374.0	377.0
Quintana Roo	223.5	378.0	431.6	442.8
San Luis Potosí	137.8	212.3	235.1	251.2
Sinaloa	304.8	342.2	372.4	364.1
Sonora	477.7	527.6	549.8	526.4
Tabasco	1,067.5	1,072.4	1,044.2	861.0
Tamaulipas	281.3	323.9	351.5	352.8
Tlaxcala	152.0	315.1	350.2	370.2
Veracruz	231.2	259.2	286.6	288.7
Yucatán	183.8	266.3	294.8	304.8
Zacatecas	137.6	254.9	273.3	291.8

States' Marginality Index	1990	1991	1992	1993	% Change 1990–93
Very Low	549.0	571.3	566.8	530.5	–3
Low	267.0	33.1	331.9	333.6	20
Medium	250.7	340.8	373.9	376.6	33
High	243.8	308.4	336.1	331.7	26
Very high	182.4	229.4	260.9	272.4	33
Total	142.3	164.9	177.1	175.5	19

SOURCE: SEDESOL/World Bank (1993).

TABLE 5.3 Distribution of *Participaciones* to Selected States as Percentage of Total Income, 1992

Income Source	Guerrero (%)	Hidalgo (%)	Michoacán (%)	Oaxaca (%)	Puebla (%)	Veracruz (%)	Zacatecas (%)	Total (%)
Participaciones	39.6	90.2	81.9	87.4	80.6	67.2	79.5	69.8
Own Revenue	60.4	9.8	18.1	12.6	19.4	32.8	20.5	30.2

SOURCE: World Bank (1993).

TABLE 5.4 Percentage of Total Income and Expenditures, by Different Government Levels

Year	Federal		State		Municipal	
	Income	Expenditure	Income	Expenditure	Income	Expenditure
1985	82.6	n/a	15.0	n/a	2.4	n/a
1988	n/a	90.3	n/a	7.8	n/a	1.9
1990	n/a	82.3	n/a	13.7	n/a	4.0
1991	81.1	77.6	15.5	17.2	3.4	5.2
1992	73.6	79.3	21.9	17.2	4.5	3.5

SOURCE: Horacio Sobarzo, "Federalismo fiscal en México" (mimeo), cited in Ortega Lomelín (1995). n/a means no data available.

tion performance. One of these incentives allows the state to conduct tax audits of businesses—the more audits performed, the more the state gets in incentives; another allows the state to collect tax fines and surcharges that might have not been collected by the federal government on behalf of Hacienda and keep a certain percentage. Evidently, the amount received by each state in terms of incentives varies greatly from state to state. Hacienda officials in Mexico City indicated to me that, while in monetary terms the amounts collected in the states were not significant, the fiscal presence of the states was enhanced in the public perception through these programs. These joint fiscal efforts are referred to as *fiscalización conjunta*.

Thus, prior to the 1995 modifications, there was a continuing heavy dependence on the federation for revenues, albeit accompanied by trends toward incentives to generate and retain direct income in the states. There was also widespread variation in the actual proportion of transfers versus direct incomes. This brings us to the third and current period of revenue-sharing arrangements associated directly with the initiatives toward a new fiscal federalism.

On December 15, 1995, the Fiscal Coordination Law was revised (see *Diario Oficial* December 15, 1995; see also Ordoño Pérez and Azpeitia 1996). In essence, the reform provided for three major changes. First, it increased *participaciones* from 18.5 percent to 20 percent of the *recaudación federal participable* (the total amount collected by the federation). Second, it provided new opportunities for the states to raise taxes and income in their own right, principally through a series of new measures such as taxes on new automobiles as well as adding their own taxes to existing federal taxes (e.g., hotel occupancy and, from 1997 on, car licenses). Third, it revised the allocation under the Municipal Development Fund, which remains at one percent, such that states and municipalities that opt to raise revenues through *derechos* (fees for licenses and services) in large part forfeit access to four fifths of the fund.[6]

Other Income Lines to States and Municipalities: Redressing the Imbalances

There are other budgetary transfer categories that are far more substantial than *participaciones* and are more open to discretionary management. These include federal government investments in the states, incorporated into the so-called Programa Normal of the federal budget (the country's yearly investment and expenditure budget).[7] Mexico's federal budget *(Presupuesto de Egresos de la Federación)* is divided into *ramos,* or budget lines.[8] In general, a *ramo* corresponds to a specific investment or expenditure program. In 1996 the most important of these to the states were Ramo 0025, for education; Ramo 0026, for social policy/poverty alleviation; and Ramo 0028, the *participaciones* to states and municipalities (see *Diario Oficial,* December 22, 1995).

Between 1988 and 1992, total federal investment increased from 41 billion (1992) pesos to 46.6 billion. In real per capita terms, this amounts to growth of approximately 3 percent annually (see Table 5.5).

TABLE 5.5   Total Federal Investment per Capita, by State (1992 pesos)

State	1988	1989	1990	1991	1992
Aguascalientes	504.6	400.5	431.5	261.4	484.9
Baja California	519.8	451.8	484.7	313.9	389.9
Baja California Sur	744.6	921.8	2,165.8	1,367.1	1,391.4
Campeche	5,119.1	2,559.7	3,557.7	2,830.3	3,482.0
Coahuila	416.4	550.4	649.1	867.5	529.9
Colima	756.3	717.8	628.7	778.1	847.9
Chiapas	136.1	180.0	200.8	262.3	309.5
Chihuahua	318.5	332.8	330.0	341.1	256.7
Distrito Federal	1,366.4	1,458.1	1,778.1	2,079.6	1,387.2
Durango	267.3	369.1	364.7	338.6	332.7
Guanajuato	167.0	135.5	150.7	122.6	161.5
Guerrero	276.1	242.3	438.6	417.4	505.6
Hidalgo	407.7	298.3	491.8	473.1	701.7
Jalisco	201.0	201.3	224.9	165.4	156.8
México	140.3	169.9	184.6	199.3	188.2
Michoacán	852.9	492.4	410.1	345.8	352.5
Morelos	266.3	328.6	326.4	294.2	315.7
Nayarit	337.3	368.6	593.8	1,217.9	1,558.7
Nuevo León	243.1	214.5	282.1	190.9	310.6
Oaxaca	558.6	300.4	477.2	299.7	484.8
Puebla	159.3	149.5	158.2	131.7	160.6
Querétaro	284.5	232.6	318.4	256.8	328.8
Quintana Roo	755.9	693.8	939.5	654.0	566.1
San Luis Potosí	272.3	433.0	549.8	194.6	360.3
Sinaloa	232.6	315.9	778.8	390.0	409.4
Sonora	778.1	336.5	416.3	310.3	371.9
Tabasco	529.4	592.7	541.9	1,173.2	1,382.6
Tamaulipas	466.5	83.2	331.2	473.7	381.5
Tlaxcala	264.1	216.7	289.2	268.7	253.5
Veracruz	630.5	708.9	703.1	444.4	716.6
Yucatán	240.1	534.9	579.0	497.8	483.5
Zacatecas	184.1	149.9	268.3	242.0	282.6
Total	18,396.8	15,141.4	20,045.0	18,203.4	19,197.0
Annual average	574.9	473.2	626.4	568.9	599.9

SOURCE: World Bank (1993) and author's calculations.

Federal investment varies widely from state to state. For example, during 1988–1992, Veracruz had an average annual federal per capita investment of 641 pesos compared with 218 pesos for Chiapas. Although the federal investment budget is one of several ways to redress imbalances in the less-advantaged states, this discrepancy between what are in effect two of the poorest Mexican states demonstrates two things. First, federal investment responds to the economic development needs favoring those states perceived to have more dynamic economies and that require additional economic infrastructure, such as Veracruz. And, second, it demonstrates how much discretion there is in federal-to-state investment programs.

One way of portraying the marginality level of individual states in Mexico is by adopting the CONAPO poverty index, which differentiates between five groups of states, ranging from "very high" marginality to "very low" (see Table 5.6).[9] The table shows that, with the notable exception of oil-producing Tabasco, there is a close relationship between GDP per capita and marginality index for each state (see Figure 5.1). This is not unexpected. What *is* unexpected, however, is the way in which federal investment and federal *participaciones* are distributed among these states. As we have seen, federal investment tends to vary by state and by each state's marginality index, but it is inconsistent and tends to be skewed in favor of the wealthiest states. As we see in Table 5.7, average annual per capita federal investment in the poorest states remained less than half that of the wealthiest states.

Solidarity funding might have alleviated this inconsistency. It must be remembered, however, that even in 1992, Solidarity represented only 15 percent of federal investment. While the data in Tables 5.8 and 5.9 indicate substantial increases in Solidarity funding in real per capita terms between 1990 and 1992 (with the exception of the very low marginality group after the Federal District was exempted from Solidarity funding in 1990), there is little suggestion of progressivity in the allocation of these resources for the four categories—low marginality to very high marginality. This is surprising in light of the fact that PRONASOL was always seen as a poverty alleviation program targeted at the poorest states. The lack of targeting at the state level may have resulted from the absence of a systematic allocation method, and it also suggests that policy makers had some discretion in allocating PRONASOL resources (see, for example, Fox and Aranda 1994; Fox and Moguel 1995; Molinar and Weldon 1994). For instance, I have already commented on the anomalously high per capita federal investment received by the state of Veracruz compared with Chiapas, but this anomaly is redressed, somewhat, by the fact that after 1989 Veracruz received very little Solidarity support. This highlights discretion or lack of systematic application of resources to poorer states, or both.

Finally, one would expect federal *participaciones* to narrow the differential between rich and poor states. Certainly, one sees that the states with a very high marginality index and those with a medium marginality (albeit the latter embraces only 5 percent of Mexico's population) have benefited from changes in the formula at the expense of the richest states. The real growth rates from 1989 to 1992 tell the story well: while the very low marginality states' income from *participaciones* decreased at an annual average rate of 1.1 percent, that of the very high marginality states increased at 14.3 percent—well above the average of 7.3 percent for all states combined. In percentage terms, the very high marginality states increased their share of the revenue-sharing pot by almost 50 percent, whereas those of the low marginality group rose by only 25 percent and the very low marginality group remained broadly stable (see Tables 5.1 and 5.2).

TABLE 5.6   Category of Marginality, GDP per Capita, and Marginality Index
(1993 pesos)

Category of Marginality	GDP per Capita	Marginality Index
Very low		
Distrito Federal	11,156	−1.68
Nuevo León	6,571	−1.37
Baja California	4,412	−1.34
Weighted average	9,200	
Low		
Coahuila	3,846	−1.06
Baja California Sur	3,279	−0.97
Aguascalientes	2,820	−0.89
Chihuahua	3,496	−0.87
Sonora	3,743	−0.86
Jalisco	3,768	−0.77
Colima	3,291	−0.76
Tamaulipas	3,330	−0.61
México	3,213	−0.6
Morelos	2,506	−0.46
Weighted average	3,960	
Medium		
Quintana Roo	3,167	−0.19
Sinaloa	3,246	−0.14
Nayarit	2,711	−0.13
Tlaxcala	2,919	−0.04
Weighted average	3,076	
High		
Durango	3,267	0.02
Querétaro	3,363	0.16
Guanajuato	2,606	0.21
Michoacán	2,222	0.36
Yucatán	2,660	0.39
Campeche	2,663	0.47
Zacatecas	2,068	0.57
San Luis Potosí	2,609	0.75
Tabasco	6,929	n/a
Weighted average	2,982	
Very high		
Puebla	2,559	0.83
Veracruz	2,785	1.13
Hidalgo	2,171	1.17
Guerrero	1,810	1.75
Oaxaca	1,585	2.05
Chiapas	1,902	2.36
Weighted average	2,258	

SOURCE: SEDESOL/World Bank (1993). n/a means no data available.

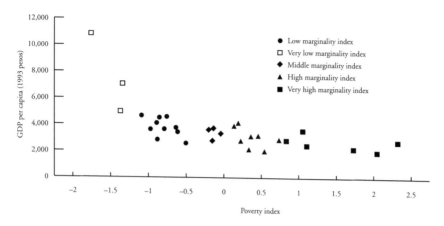

FIGURE 5.1   Distribution of state per capita GDP in 1993 pesos, by CONAPO
marginality index

TABLE 5.7   Federal Investment per Capita, by States' Category of Marginality
(1992 pesos)

States' Category of Marginality	Total Federal Investment			Solidarity Investment			Solidarity as % of Total Federal Investment		
	1990	1991	1992	1990	1991	1992	1990	1991	1992
Very low	1,258	1,403	1,003	22	16	25	2	1	3
Low	314	317	283	38	41	62	12	13	22
Medium	675	558	621	70	73	117	11	13	19
High	472	427	504	56	64	103	12	15	21
Very high	436	334	485	49	51	102	11	15	21
Average	631	608	579	47	49	82	7	8	14

SOURCE: SEDESOL/World Bank (1993) and author's calculations.

These comparisons can, however, be misleading. By comparing ratios of the richest to the poorest groups, the effects on middle-income states may be masked. One
way to examine changing equity is to look at Lorenz curves and their corresponding
Gini coefficients. Although these techniques are typically used to measure income
distribution rather than intergovernmental fiscal relations, I looked at the overall
distribution of *participaciones* by population for each state.[10] Although these data are
not reproduced here, the analysis indicates quite clearly that the distributional effects of the new formula are becoming more equitable over time. The Gini coefficients fall from 0.31 in 1989 to 0.27 in 1990 to 0.23 in 1991 and finally to 0.20 in
1992. In conclusion, therefore, as a result of investment programs and *participaciones*, we have seen a modest shift toward redistribution of revenues to the poorest
and most marginalized states; however, per capita figures still favor the wealthier
states.

TABLE 5.8 Solidarity Expenditures, by State, 1989–1994 (millions of new 1992 pesos)

State	Federal Expenditures	State Expenditures	Total Expenditures	% of Federal Expenditures
Chiapas	2,232.6	941.2	3,173.8	6.5
Oaxaca	2,204.4	763.4	2,967.8	6.4
Guerrero	1,806.9	440.7	2,247.6	5.2
Michoacán	1,757.5	968.0	2,725.5	5.1
México	1,635.7	1,574.6	3,210.3	4.7
Yucatán	1,546.5	390.0	1,936.5	4.5
Veracruz	1,347.4	860.7	2,208.1	3.9
Sonora	1,257.5	865.2	2,122.7	3.6
Coahuila	1,164.2	436.1	1,600.3	3.4
Hidalgo	1,127.1	527.9	1,655.0	3.3
Chihuahua	1,040.5	724.9	1,765.4	3.0
Nuevo León	1,034.0	726.9	1,760.9	3.0
Puebla	1,009.1	853.5	1,862.6	2.9
Jalisco	1,002.2	970.1	1,972.3	2.9
Guanajuato	869.7	708.7	1,578.4	2.5
Tabasco	801.1	476.9	1,278.0	2.3
Durango	769.8	235.3	1,005.1	2.2
Sinaloa	769.3	520.1	1,289.4	2.2
San Luis Potosí	759.5	280.2	1,039.7	2.2
Zacatecas	752.5	290.9	1,043.4	2.2
Tamaulipas	746.2	601.6	1,347.8	2.2
Campeche	688.4	287.3	975.7	2.0
Baja California	637.7	570.9	1,208.6	1.8
Morelos	605.5	270.5	876.0	1.8
Tlaxcala	599.6	287.4	887.0	1.7
Quintana Roo	535.2	163.4	698.6	1.5
Querétaro	506.8	375.4	882.2	1.5
Nayarit	506.1	205.4	711.5	1.5
Aguascalientes	505.2	552.8	1,058.0	1.5
Colima	408.6	182.4	591.0	1.2
Baja California Sur	363.8	91.5	455.3	1.1
Subtotal	30,990.6	17,143.9	48,134.5	89.6
Central funding[a]	3,304.3	81.9	3,386.2	9.6
Pronass[b]	176.1		176.1	0.5
Distrito Federal	116.9	4,816.2	4,933.1	0.3
Total	34,587.9	22,042.0	56,629.9	100.0

NOTES: The figures for 1994 are close estimates.

[a]Includes resources allocated to certain federal agencies to support their investment programs.

[b]National Program for Social Service.

SOURCE: SEDESOL (1994) p. 26, and author's calculations.

TABLE 5.9   Solidarity Investment per Capita, by State (1992 pesos)

State	1988	1989	1990	1991	1992
Aguascalientes	42.2	51.1	91.7	86.2	101.1
Baja California	22.7	44.5	70.9	43.3	86.7
Baja California Sur	64.5	86.3	121.9	124.3	222.2
Campeche	62.7	94.6	166.2	159.5	279.5
Coahuila	13.7	34.5	58.7	78.6	111.9
Colima	98.9	206.8	134.1	109.9	169.1
Chiapas	10.6	33.0	81.0	101.4	152.6
Chihuahua	12.1	33.8	49.4	75.4	98.4
Distrito Federal	594.9	567.0	1.1	1.3	0.0
Durango	18.4	27.2	106.9	89.7	119.6
Guanajuato	5.0	12.2	25.0	19.0	40.5
Guerrero	9.2	26.2	57.8	63.7	154.5
Hidalgo	18.7	26.3	61.4	67.5	140.5
Jalisco	14.8	12.6	22.0	20.5	29.4
México	6.6	9.1	18.8	20.6	34.6
Michoacán	8.8	22.3	42.3	48.6	122.5
Morelos	14.9	29.2	69.9	70.5	89.0
Nayarit	29.8	67.6	72.2	67.8	107.3
Nuevo León	15.1	51.4	49.6	40.3	56.8
Oaxaca	28.5	40.6	95.0	84.5	145.4
Puebla	7.5	8.5	27.2	25.7	62.1
Querétaro	34.8	35.6	53.1	60.0	70.5
Quintana Roo	60.8	81.1	127.6	129.1	248.8
San Luis Potosí	6.1	17.0	39.5	41.7	54.9
Sinaloa	16.3	24.8	41.3	51.6	82.2
Sonora	44.5	48.8	71.2	53.0	107.1
Tabasco	2.9	11.3	21.8	22.9	49.4
Tamaulipas	13.1	24.3	32.1	42.5	70.2
Tlaxcala	33.7	70.5	13.3	102.7	141.5
Veracruz	3.7	7.3	15.4	13.8	46.5
Yucatán	20.3	38.1	112.4	206.1	245.5
Zacatecas	27.1	46.1	102.8	115.4	168.1
Total	1,357.7	1,889.7	1,450.3	1,176.2	3,608.4

SOURCE: SEDESOL/World Bank (1993) and author's calculations.

The National Solidarity Program

Between 1989 and 1995, federal investment was divided into two categories: Solidarity and Programa Normal. Solidarity's budget line, Ramo 0026,[11] was integrated into each state's Convenio de Desarrollo Social (Social Development Agreement, the former Development Agreement, or CUD, discussed in Chapter 4).[12] Prior to 1989, Solidarity's budget line was called Desarrollo Regional (Regional Development); after 1989, Ramo 0026 became Solidarity, and all other federal investment became the Programa Normal. Thus, hereafter, between 1989 and 1995 Solidarity will be considered synonymous with Ramo 0026.

In theory, from 1989 to 1995 the program required 25 percent to 50 percent matching state funds. Total Solidarity expenditure by state for the period 1989 to 1994 is shown in Table 5.8, while the per capita Solidarity investments from 1988 to 1992 are shown in Table 5.9. One must also note that, since 1990, the Federal District has been removed from Ramo 0026, although it continues to take the largest share of total federal investment.

It is critically important to underscore that, contrary to popular belief, Solidarity did not revolutionize federal investment in Mexico. Although the program grew from US$600 million in 1989 to US$2.2 billion in 1993, this represented no more than 15 percent of total federal investment (the other 85 percent being the Programa Normal). Table 5.7 presents data that demonstrate the proportion of Solidarity funding relative to total federal investment for the five marginality categories and shows that, even for the very high marginality states in 1992, Solidarity represented only 21 percent of investment per capita. With the exception of the very low marginality states, the percentage of Solidarity investment in all of the other categories was broadly similar (Table 5.7). As already noted, this lack of progressivity in the allocation of Solidarity resources is surprising, given that the program was deliberately created as a poverty alleviation program targeted at the poorest states.

In terms of actual programs on the ground, Solidarity did, however, have a very strong effect on state and municipal investment. One of its most significant—and underappreciated—features was its stimulation of intergovernmental cooperation. Almost all Solidarity programs were funded by both federal and state government (usually 50 percent federal/50 percent state, or 75 percent federal/25 percent state), thus giving state government an important say in the allocation of these resources (although once again, these proportions and levels of state involvement vary markedly). In 1992, as shown in Table 5.10, in eight of the poorest states, the Solidarity contribution made up an average of 34 percent of federal investment; this included two extreme cases: Zacatecas, where 59 percent of federal investment came through Solidarity, and Veracruz, which received only 6 percent. Clearly, criteria other than need or poverty dictated the various routes through which federal investment was channeled.

At the municipal level, the Solidarity program that often had the largest impact was Municipal Funds. This program was initiated in 1990 with two principal objectives: first, to transfer resources and strengthen municipal governments throughout the country so that works of wider social benefit could be executed; and second, to strengthen community participation and involvement in decision making (SEDESOL 1993, *Guía Técnica*).[13] The maximum for any single project was set at US$50,000, but the average project investment was usually less than US$14,000. From 1990 to 1992, Municipal Funds represented between 8 and 9 percent of the Solidarity Program, and the number of states embracing the program rose from thirteen to twenty-seven.

TABLE 5.10   Federal Solidarity Funds as a Percentage of Federal Investment in Eight of the Poorest States

State	1988	1989	1990	1991	1992
Chiapas	8	18	40	39	49
Guerrero	3	11	13	15	31
Hidalgo	5	9	12	14	20
Michoacán	1	5	10	14	35
Oaxaca	5	14	20	28	30
Puebla	5	6	17	20	39
Veracruz	1	1	2	3	6
Zacatecas	15	31	38	48	59
Average	5	12	19	23	34

SOURCE: SEDESOL/World Bank (1993).

As was generally the case with Solidarity programs, Municipal Funds involved a federal-state matching grant of 75/25 percent for the poorest states, including the eight listed in Table 5.10, and 50/50 for the wealthier states. In addition, communities were expected to match the funds received for a specific investment by contributing a minimum of 20 percent of the total cost themselves. Given this emphasis on community participation and the relatively small absolute amounts involved, this program was targeted almost exclusively to rural areas. In general, rural areas require less complex infrastructure, have active community organizations, especially through the *ejidos*, and little local government presence, which provides greater opportunity for community participation. In many rural municipalities, almost all of the income received through *participaciones* is spent on administration, with little capacity to raise internal income through taxation (unlike their larger city counterparts, discussed in Chapter 6). Therefore, even these small amounts represent a major—if not the only—opportunity for some level of investment to be undertaken on behalf of the community.

Given the argument that in terms of efficiency and impact these resources were best spent if targeted at rural municipalities, it is possible now to analyze the extent to which this happened. While certainly the rural municipalities received almost twice the statewide per capita average, when we examine the distribution of Municipal Funds *between* municipalities and also between different states, we observe that there is considerable room for improvement in targeting. While some municipalities received over ten times per capita what others did in the same state, those benefiting were not, necessarily, those whose infrastructure needs were greatest. Often there was a poor relationship between need and fulfillment, and in several states for which I analyzed the data (plots not reproduced here), municipalities most in need were not necessarily receiving the most funds per capita.

The high visibility of Solidarity brought about not only wide-ranging praise, but criticism as well, especially from the academic community, which focused most of its analyses on the political impacts of the program (e.g., Cornelius, Craig, and Fox 1994; Dresser 1991). According to some interpretations, Solidarity was little more than a political tool designed to strengthen popular support for the PRI. In effect, some analysts argue, the program's funding did little to address the issue of poverty (Lustig 1994), and spending was not determined by the poverty index of a given municipality (Molinar and Weldon 1994). Generally speaking, the main criticisms of Solidarity are that it allowed state and local leaders to select project investments based on electoral considerations rather than need; that it had very little community involvement in some projects, particularly the bigger and more expensive ones; that it undermined grass-roots organizations that refused to affiliate themselves with the PRI; and finally, that once these projects were implemented, there was inadequate follow-up in regard to operation and maintenance of the works completed.

While all these criticisms are indeed valid and well documented, what is most interesting is how funding decisions regarding Solidarity projects were reached. For instance, while for the Municipal Funds projects all decisions were reached through public discussion and ample community involvement, most of the larger projects (e.g., Empresas de Solidaridad—Solidarity Enterprises) were decided at the federal level with no input whatsoever from the localities where these projects were to be located. Thus, it appears that democratic and participatory mechanisms of decision making were instituted only for those programs that were the least expensive. Indeed, I had the opportunity to witness negotiations in a community among the representatives of several Solidarity Committees over which Solidarity projects were going to have priority, given the limited resources available. The proposed projects were a basketball court, a water system, repairing a school, building a rural road, and paving a street; there was funding available only for two of these. After hours of bargaining and negotiation, the rural road and the basketball court were the winners. For the larger, more expensive programs, as far as I could see, no discussion ever occurred.

Thus, because of the discretionary nature of the Solidarity Program, decision making regarding investments in states and municipalities was not always transparent and on occasion gave rise to allegations that partisan political considerations affected the allocation of resources. For example, during the 1992 gubernatorial election in Michoacán, strong allegations were made that Solidarity funds were channeled to a variety of projects in PRD strongholds in order to garner support for PRI candidates (see Chávez 1992). In other places governed by the opposition, there was also evidence of flooding the locality with Solidarity projects around election time. Conversely, the argument has also been made that localities governed by the opposition were punished by not directing any Solidarity projects to them. Molinar and Weldon, for example, found that in some cases "the government usually allocated more PRONASOL funding to those states which were loyal to the PRI, while it punished states that had voted for the opposition" (1994: 133–134).

As I have already noted, however, not all Solidarity programs were susceptible to manipulation. The Municipal Funds program, in particular, seems to have overcome some of the inequities built into the distribution of resources by following clear criteria (poverty index, population, etc.) in the distribution of funds to the municipality. Nonetheless, while programs such as Municipal Funds and, more significantly, the revenue-sharing system, may have guaranteed that states and municipalities would not be starved of resources, discretionary mechanisms for the transfer of additional resources undeniably remained intact. By way of a preliminary conclusion, for rural municipalities, Municipal Funds and similar programs were very important in terms of both efficiency and impact. Many rural municipalities reaped considerable benefits from increases in Municipal Funds, Escuela Digna, and other programs that increased their investment resources while providing a mechanism for community participation. In order to ensure that Municipal Funds was targeted at the poorest municipalities, the adoption of a general formula or rule for the distribution of these funds would have been useful. This would have reduced the apparent arbitrariness in the distribution of funds and ameliorated criticisms that targeting was politically motivated. This is one reason why PRONASOL has now been "downgraded" and the resources of Ramo 0026 transferred to the states and put more squarely under the aegis of the governors and state legislatures.

As a result of the reforms instituted by Zedillo in December 1995, the lion's share of funds assigned for regional and social development through Ramo 0026 (formerly PRONASOL, now called Superación de la Pobreza) will be to a far greater extent allocated to the states and thus controlled by state government. As of 1996, the resources of Ramo 0026 will be distributed among three funds: Fondo de Desarrollo Social Municipal (Municipal Social Development Fund); Fondo de Prioridades Estatales (State Priorities Fund); and Fondo para la Promoción del Empleo y la Educación (Fund for the Promotion of Employment and Education). Of these, the largest share is for the Municipal Social Development Fund, which takes 65 percent of the total allocation; second is the Fund for the Promotion of Employment and Education, which takes 30 percent; and finally, the discretionary State Priorities Fund, with the remaining 5 percent (*Diario Oficial* December 22, 1995). By 1998, the last two are to be phased out entirely (education resources will be channeled through Ramo 0025), and therefore all resources will go into the Municipal Social Development Fund.

As of 1996, the resources of the Municipal Social Development Fund will be distributed among the states according to a formula based on poverty indicators in states and municipalities (*Diario Oficial*, January 5, 1996). Following this formula, the four states taking the largest share of the fund would be Chiapas, Oaxaca, Veracruz, and Puebla (in that order). SEDESOL remains in charge of designing social policy at the national level and retains control of the budgetary resources of Ramo 0026. Thus, the mechanisms for the distribution of resources from the federal government to the states appear to be more transparent and equitable, given that they favor the poorer states; however, the precise mechanisms of decision making for the allocation of these resources from the states to the municipalities remain unclear, which may sustain the patterns of state and federal discretionary power that have existed in the past and that have caused inequitable development both among states and among the municipalities of a given state.

State Government Finances

As I observed earlier in this chapter, federally financed investments in the states are nearly twice the amount states receive from revenue sharing and, more significant, their allocation is not formula-driven. As Table 5.6 shows, on a per capita basis the disparity in federal investment received by the states is very large, with a handful of states and the Federal District receiving three times the average level of investment per capita as the rest of the states combined. Moreover, while state incomes more than doubled between 1980 and 1982 as a percentage of total government income, they remained about one fifth of the total national fiscal revenues and therefore heavily dependent on federally dispensed funds (see Table 5.4).

State-level financial systems also operate within the framework determined by the Fiscal Coordination Law (LCF). There are, however, some variations in the way states manage their finances, given that within the bounds imposed by the LCF, each state's legislature determines that state's tax and revenue policies. The LCF states very clearly that, of the total amount of federal *participaciones* transferred to the states, at least 20 percent must be distributed by the states to the municipalities. Thus far only two states have led the charge in increasing the percentage allocated to municipalities by changing their respective state fiscal coordination laws: Coahuila, to 35 percent, and Hidalgo, to 25 percent.[14]

State resources are distributed among the state's municipalities according to a variety of criteria, but in essence the distribution tends to be formula-driven. In principle, each state arithmetically determines the formula for the distribution of funds to its municipalities based on certain "standard" indicators: population, poverty, amounts collected in taxes, and so on.[15] Hidalgo, for instance, distributes its funds according to the following criteria: 45 percent proportional to population; 45 percent proportional to each municipality's marginality index; 5 percent proportional to the state's own tax collection; and the remaining 5 percent proportional to the number of localities in each municipality (Decree no. 161, *Periódico Oficial* December 30, 1989: 2). Thus, while in some cases the distribution coefficients that determine how much each municipality will get are arrived at as a result of systematic analysis and an effort to be equitable, in others, the amount that municipalities receive is simply published by executive decree in the *Periódico Oficial* without stating any explicit criteria. In such cases, the potential for arbitrariness is much higher. In Veracruz and Chiapas, for example, the coefficients were published in the states' *Diario Oficial* without stating how they were arrived at.[16] Where formulas do exist, they are calculated jointly by the Secretaría de Finanzas and the Contaduría Mayor de Hacienda (Finance Committee) of the state legislature and then approved by the entire state legislature, with little or no overt interference from the federal level.

Each state legislature's Finance Committee reviews the annual budgets of the municipalities and then presents them for approval to the entire legislature (Article 115 of the federal Constitution stipulates that every municipality must present its annual budget to the state legislature for approval). The *participaciones* that a municipality will receive are thus entirely determined at the state government level by both the Secretaría de Finanzas and the legislature. Because the Fiscal Coordination Law gives only rough guidelines about how states should allocate revenue sharing to municipalities, state legislatures are almost completely free to choose their own criteria—or lack thereof. For example, Article 6 of the LCF stipulates that the state government must allocate the federal funds assigned to municipalities within five days after the state receives them; otherwise, the state must pay the municipalities interest on the funds. Article 6 also establishes that these allocations must be made in cash (rather than in goods or works), without any restrictions on how they will be spent and without any deductions. Although Article 6 and other provisions of the LCF determine and ensure that a set appropriation will be made to the municipalities, the law is fundamentally flawed since it offers no guidance about the criteria that should govern how much each municipality receives. Indeed, in 1995 *only twelve states* had a formal Fiscal Coordination Law (governing transfers from states to municipalities); under New Federalism, however, several other state legislatures were proposing similar arrangements by early 1996. Thus, state legislatures can subjectively decide how much each municipality will receive, with the almost inevitable consequence that some municipalities will receive larger shares according to criteria that in some cases may be politically determined.

Funding levels may be analyzed in two ways: first, in terms of the total amount allocated to all municipalities in any year; and second, in terms of the levels of bias in allocations among municipalities according to various criteria, for example, rural/urban, per capita income, level of need and marginality. As a result of my fieldwork as a member of the World Bank's missions to strengthen municipalities in Mexico, I can analyze in greater depth the fiscal relationship between state and municipality in the eight poorest Mexican states. I believe these states offer insight into the general pattern of intergovernmental relations in Mexico. Looking first at the amounts actually allocated by states to municipalities, we see in Table 5.11 that there is considerable variation between states, notwithstanding the LCF's insistence that at least 20 percent of federal *participaciones* be passed on to the municipalities. In the seven states for which data are available (unfortunately, Chiapas is not included), only Hidalgo has consistently sought to give out significantly more than 20 percent (except in 1989). Most other states give out less, some significantly less, for example, Oaxaca, Puebla, and Veracruz. Guerrero stands out for its very low level of transfers, as would, I suspect, Chiapas were data available.

Second, looking at the extent to which there is bias in the allocations to specific municipalities, I have analyzed the data available for the eight states included in Table 5.11 in three ways: first, per capita allocations to large and small municipali-

TABLE 5.11   Percentage of State Budget Transferred to Municipalities, in Eight of the Poorest States, 1987–1993

State	1987	1988	1989	1990	1991	1992	1993
A. Chiapas	n/a	n/a	n/a	n/a	n/a	n/a	n/a
B. Guerrero	15.2	18.2	17.0	12.1	9.5	7.2	6.6
C. Hidalgo	22.2	20.6	14.2	22.6	22.5	26.1	25.8
D. Michoacán	20.0	18.8	18.6	18.9	19.0	18.2	17.5
E. Oaxaca	18.1	14.8	15.4	11.5	16.9	16.8	14.7
F. Puebla	18.7	16.4	15.1	17.7	17.9	14.8	18.0
G. Veracruz	18.5	17.1	18.5	15.7	16.1	15.8	17.3
H. Zacatecas	22.1	24.9	20.2	18.0	19.0	20.0	16.7
Average for states C–H	19.9	18.8	17.0	17.4	18.6	18.6	18.3

SOURCE: SEDESOL/World Bank (1993); n/a means no data available.

ties, respectively; second, Gini coefficient calculations for the distribution for each year for each state; and third, correlation coefficient calculations between *participaciones* per capita on the one hand, and size, percentage rural, and the CONAPO marginality index on the other.

Revenue-sharing and population graphs (not reproduced here) suggest that Chiapas, Veracruz, and, particularly, Guerrero have biases favoring large municipalities, and that Hidalgo, Michoacán, and Zacatecas have a bias in favor of small municipalities. Oaxaca appears to favor neither small nor large.[17] These implicit biases may be examined by plotting revenue-sharing distributions for equity and for urban/rural orientation. One should be looking for moderate to high levels of equity associated with partiality of orientation according to whether that state is predominantly urban or rural. In Figure 5.2 the x-axis comprises the Gini coefficient (a measure of the distribution's per capita equity), while the y-axis represents the correlation between *participaciones* per capita and the size of population (a measure of whether small rural or large urban municipalities are receiving a higher share).

In essence, therefore, my analysis seeks to identify the relationship between level of equity and per capita revenue sharing for urban and rural municipalities. Four clusters emerge. The first consists of the states of Hidalgo, Zacatecas, and Michoacán to the left of the chart, indicating a clear policy of favoring small municipalities (and thus with only a moderately equitable distribution in per capita terms). The second comprises Oaxaca and Veracruz, which show very unequal distributions and which favor neither small nor large municipalities but appear to be randomly distributed as far as size is concerned. Chiapas also appears to fall in this group, but the inequity in its distribution is much less pronounced. The third group consists of Puebla, whose distribution appears to reflect the number of inhabitants and nothing else. The final cluster contains Guerrero, which is the mirror image of the first group—intermediate equity and strong urban bias. From a normative point of view, one can say that, although there is nothing inherently desirable in a strict per capita distribution, distributions such as those in Oaxaca and Veracruz are sufficiently un-

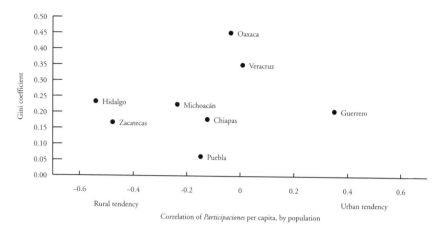

FIGURE 5.2   Revenue-sharing distribution, by per capita equity and rural/urban bias
SOURCE: World Bank (1993).

equal as to be highly questionable. On the other hand, Guerrero's policy of favoring the larger and therefore richer municipalities also does not appear to be very satisfactory, given that it is a highly rural state with large numbers of rural municipalities. One would have expected it to be closer to the first cluster, with Hidalgo and Zacatecas.

Thus, the importance of the criteria for distribution—and the biases therein (as, e.g., in Guerrero)—becomes evident when analyzing the impact of the criteria. Moreover, one of the major problems with the lack of transparency surrounding the distribution criteria of the state-local system of revenue sharing is that, by and large, municipalities do not know how much they are legally entitled to receive in *participaciones*. The municipal presidents I interviewed in the poorest states, including those of some important cities such as San Cristóbal de las Casas, knew only that they could count on their *participaciones* arriving on a given date, but not how much they were getting, and certainly not how the amount was determined. Indeed, some of them were totally unaware that a formula existed; others looked puzzled when a question about the coefficient that determines the amount they receive was posed to them.

All of this underscores the desirability of making the process more transparent. If municipal officials knew the formula and how it is applied, they would be fully aware of how much their municipality is entitled to receive. In addition, there would no longer be room for political (or other) considerations in the decisions of how much a municipality would get.

If there is ambiguity about the criteria for transfers of *participaciones*, the problem is compounded when it comes to federal investment projects. Traditionally, these have been highly discretionary and depend on deals struck between the governor and the federation. Only in the past two years have one or two states (e.g., Guana-juato) sought to standardize this line of funding for municipal investment projects, again following a series of explicit criteria similar to those for the *participaciones*. Thus, while transparency in the allocation of all federal funds is clearly necessary, it is especially pertinent for the more discretionary lines of funding, for example, Ramo 0026 funds, given the potential for partisanship discussed earlier.

State Revenues

In addition to federal allocations, which represent the most significant source of in-come, all states raise their own revenue through a variety of sources, but particularly through taxes and *derechos* (the fees charged for public services). Among these, the most important are property taxes and water levies. In addition to the revenues raised through taxes and *derechos*, states also collect fees for a variety of services (e.g., license plates, *registro civil, espectáculos públicos*), which make up the bulk of the *pro-ductos* (patrimonial goods) and *aprovechamientos* (benefit fees). To the degree that states are better able to raise their own revenues, their dependence on federal alloca-tions (at least in principle) would decrease. Between 1990 and 1992, the states re-ceived on average twice as much revenue in *participaciones* as they raised themselves (Ortega Lomelín 1995: 60).

In 1992, *derechos* and taxes combined represented only 5.6 percent of total state income for the six states (C–H) in Table 5.11; this was almost double the amount of previous years. Within the context established by the Mexican Constitution, federal fiscal legislation, and each state's constitution, each state legislature determines the specific taxes that will be collected in the state. The more typical state taxes are on the use and ownership of a car (*tenencia*) and on property transfers (*traslación de do-minio*). Recently, some states have begun to collect payroll taxes (*impuesto sobre nóminas*), but are surprisingly loath to make an issue of enforcement.[18] In addition to these state taxes, some states also collect the shared tax on hydrocarbons (*hidro-carburos*) and the customs tax (*impuesto sobre comercio exterior*). The latter can be collected only in those states that are on the border or the coast. Although these are federal taxes, the states that collect them get a certain percentage. Thus, Chiapas, for example, appears on paper to have a very healthy financial picture: it has oil, ports, and customs, plus it received a significant proportion of Solidarity funds; nonethe-less, it is one of the poorer states.

Clearly, given that not all states can collect these taxes, there is some inequity built into them. Allowing states to collect a wider range of local taxes to increase their revenue seems inevitable and, as I have observed, is on the New Federalism agenda. To the extent that the states aggressively pursue these tax and fee opportuni-ties, however, they have a lesser claim upon the 0.83 percent allocation of the Mu-nicipal Social Development Fund (*Diario Oficial*, December 15, 1995).

Of all the taxes collected locally, the most important, by far, is the property tax (*impuesto predial*), which became a *municipal* tax after the Municipal Reform of

1983. Although we will return in Chapter 6 to the importance of the property tax as a significant income generator in large municipalities, here it is worthwhile noting that since the late 1980s there has been a noticeable effort by the states and municipalities to improve collection of this tax. Since 1989, the absolute amount in nominal new pesos of property taxes collected nationally has increased 469 percent. Yearly increases in the property tax in 1990 and 1991 were 39 percent and 35.5 percent, respectively (Ortega Lomelín 1995: 62). Despite this increase, however, Mexico still has a very low level of property tax collection by any international standard (see Chapter 6). In fact, in 1992 all the states in Mexico collected only US$798 million from this tax.

Collection of water charges also remains low in Mexico,[19] at only US$946 million in 1992. From the states' perspective, even though the growth rate of collection of water charges was more moderate than the growth rate of property taxes, it still reached a significant level—229 percent in nominal new pesos between 1989 and 1992. In the 1989–1992 period, especially high increases were achieved in the Federal District (566 percent), the state of Mexico (383 percent), and Hidalgo (382 percent).[20]

State Expenditures

As Table 5.4 demonstrates, state expenditures as a proportion of total expenditure remains relatively low, at around 17 percent. The major item among recurrent state expenditures is administration (salaries and general operation and maintenance). As Table 5.12 indicates, recurrent expenditures in 1993 averaged 36 percent across the seven states, but this average obscures the states where it was much higher (Oaxaca, Puebla, and Veracruz). Education has become a major expenditure item in the states as a result of the decentralization of education in the 1980s, and particularly after the 1992 Acuerdo Nacional para la Modernización de la Educación Básica (National Agreement for the Modernization of Basic Education, ANMEB). The ANMEB transferred to the states responsibility for expenditures on primary and secondary education. In Baja California, for example, basic education absorbed 67 percent of what the state got in *participaciones* (*Revista INDETEC*, no. 83 [July–August 1993]: 98).

In addition, several of these states invested a considerable proportion of their resources (around 17 percent), with Michoacán and Hidalgo leading the way with almost a third of their expenditure in investment. In assessing expenditure patterns in the eight states listed on Table 5.11 for the 1987–1993 period, it is interesting to note that, with the notable exception of Guerrero, which has increased its public debt considerably since 1989 (running at approximately one third of total expenditures in 1990 and 1991 and remaining high through 1993), none of the other states show a deficit or debt in their budgets. Evidently, this does not mean that they spend only what they have, but, rather, leads us to believe that the public debt they incur is channeled through other expenditure items.[21]

TABLE 5.12   State Expenditures for Seven of the Poorest States, 1993

Expenditure	Guerrero		Hidalgo		Michoacán		Oaxaca	
	Millions of new pesos	*%*	*Millions of new pesos*	*%*	*Millions of new pesos*	*%*	*Millions of new pesos*	*%*
Total expenditures	2,761.8	100.0	630.6	100.0	1,271.7	100.0	284.3	100.0
Recurrent expenditures	435.7	15.8	198.7	31.5	500.8	39.4	191.8	67.5
Total transfers	1,587.6	57.5	233.2	36.9	346.3	27.3	69.5	24.5
Transfers to municipalities	181.6	6.6	162.4	25.7	222.5	17.5	41.9	14.7
Total state investment	238.0	8.6	198.6	31.5	416.3	32.7	19.7	6.9
Solidarity	108.9	3.9	144.5	22.9	0.0	0.0	0.0	0.0
Programa Normal	107.4	3.9	54.2	8.6	0.0	0.0	0.0	0.0

Expenditure	Puebla		Veracruz		Zacatecas		Total	
	Millions of new pesos	*%*	*Millions of new pesos*	*%*	*Millions of new pesos*	*%*	*Millions of new pesos*	*%*
Total expenditures	1,170.0	100.0	2,759.2	100.0	514.5	100.0	9,392.1	100.0
Recurrent expenditures	587.0	50.2	1,309.1	47.5	136.9	26.6	3,359.9	35.7
Total transfers	317.0	27.1	886.5	32.1	239.7	46.6	3,679.8	39.2
Transfers to municipalities	211.0	18.0	476.8	17.3	85.8	16.7	1,382.1	14.7
Total state investment	217.0	18.5	365.7	13.3	98.2	19.1	1,553.6	16.5
Solidarity	32.0	2.7	147.8	5.4	78.2	15.2	511.5	5.5
Programa Normal	28.0	2.4	217.9	7.9	20.0	3.9	427.5	4.5

SOURCE: World Bank (1993).

As the data in Table 5.12 show, in 1993 a significant proportion of state investment expenditures was channeled through Solidarity, particularly in the form of matching percentages; in some states the matching figures were 25 percent state/75 percent federal, while in others it was 50 percent state/50 percent federal, depending on state finances and political relations with the center. As indicated earlier, expenditure patterns have changed since the creation of Solidarity in 1989. In total, the distribution of state expenditures appears to have been (in general terms) 60 percent to the Programa Normal and 40 percent to Solidarity. In some states, however, the proportion to Solidarity was larger than to the Programa Normal; in Hidalgo, for example, Solidarity's percentage was bigger than the Programa Normal's after

1990, and the proposed expenditure for 1993 was three times that of the Programa Normal. The same pattern is evident in the case of Zacatecas in 1992. As a whole, the state contribution to Solidarity in the eight poorest states grew 64 percent a year, while the contribution to the Programa Normal showed an average growth of 21 percent a year.

Conclusion

Mexico has evolved a complex system of fiscal policy in which the lion's share remains firmly controlled by the federal government, notwithstanding the changes and attempts at decentralization that have been undertaken. Whether in terms of taxation, *participaciones* to states, or federal investment programs, ultimate control over the amount and direction of cash flows continues to rest with the federal government. Moreover, thus far the federal government has been reluctant to make an across-the-board increase in the share that it returns to the states for recurrent and investment expenditures. This has been accentuated through the recentralization of the IVA.

Notwithstanding the federal government's reluctance to "let go," the revenue-sharing system does appear to have become more equitable in recent years. The evidence for this lies in the absolute real and relative increase in the transfer of resources to states and in the systematic application of criteria and formulas that deliberately redistribute resources in favor of the poorer states, albeit only to a limited extent.

Federal investment funding, however, remains a very significant proportion of total state income. The allocations of federal investment lines to states are variable and arbitrary and appear to favor the better-off and more productive states. PRONA-SOL, of course, at least partially offset this imbalance. Although it came to represent less than one fifth of total federal investment, it did become an important mechanism for decentralization by targeting directly the poorest areas, by bypassing state and municipal government, and by emphasizing marginal rural areas that now counted on investment resources that previously had rarely trickled down. Even this process, however, was criticized for the funders' discretionary power and arbitrariness, and one suspects that governors and municipal presidents will be more satisfied now that Ramo 0026 will be under their control.

The system of state-to-municipality revenue sharing remains the most problematic. Fewer than half of the states have developed objective and transparent criteria for the allocation of *participaciones* to the municipalities according to the LCF guidelines; very few states have developed similar criteria to govern the allocation of investment expenditures to municipalities. It appears that many states did not transfer the mandatory 20 percent of *participaciones* to municipalities, and there is considerable variability both in the actual proportion allocated in any one year and between specific municipalities themselves. By and large, allocations often benefit the better-off and urban municipalities.

Although, technically, states are improving their administrative capacity to raise income and to distribute resources in a fair and equitable manner, they remain heavily dependent on the federal government. Federal investment income is much higher than *participaciones*, and most states currently have a low capacity to generate income through local taxation. All states spend a high percentage of their income on recurrent costs, but most also seek to undertake a significant level of investment, and almost all hesitate to take on major debt. As long as the capacity to *raise* funds is restricted, states will continue to depend heavily on the center's purse strings. Unlike the urban municipalities studied in Chapter 6, to date states have not found much autonomy—at least not in the financial sphere. They remain dependent sovereign states.

6

Municipio Libre: Ten Years of Decentralization in Practice

Since 1917, the principle of municipal autonomy has existed in Mexico only on paper. When the Constitutional Convention met in Querétaro that year, the issue of how to structure and strengthen municipalities was hotly debated and led to a series of constitutional provisions that sang the praises of the *municipio libre* (free municipality) as the bedrock of the country's federal system. But in practice, the municipality's constitutional autonomy never grew beyond this well-intentioned rhetoric.

In an effort to redress the lack of enforcement of the Constitution, the most important constitutional provisions dealing with the municipality have been revised many times, but, by far, the most important amendment to the Constitution is the one initiated by Miguel de la Madrid in 1983. The reform of Article 115 proposed to devolve to municipalities the autonomy they had not enjoyed, in spite of constitutional provisions. The reform, as discussed in Chapter 4, was to strengthen municipal governments (and hence federalism) by granting municipalities greater independence from the higher levels of government.

Early evidence suggested that the political and financial autonomy promised by the reform did not materialize during de la Madrid's administration. Moreover, the little autonomy that municipalities were able to achieve brought with it responsibilities that municipal governments often could not handle; this inevitably meant that the central government retained supervisory powers and continued to play a critical financial role. In short, the reform of Article 115 was designed to grant a measure of autonomy to local governments by transferring *some* power and resources, but with the underlying proviso that the center would retain ultimate control.

More than ten years have passed since President de la Madrid's reform, and we are now in a position to evaluate it. Most of the analysts who have assessed it (and decentralization in general) tend to be rather pessimistic because they see the municipality's continued dependence on the higher levels of government. My contention, however, is that *some* decentralization has occurred. There is still a considerable way to go to achieve *full* autonomy and for the municipality to become genuinely free (financially and politically), but as this chapter will show, significant advances have indeed been made. If nothing else, whatever discretion that existed at the local level was officially acknowledged and formalized with the Municipal Reform of 1983. A critical point argued in Chapter 5, however, is that this discretion in decision-making procedures has become much more evident at the *state* level, even if intended for municipalities. Both overall fiscal policy and the Municipal Reform, albeit perhaps unintentionally, have allowed the states to develop and maintain significant control methods over their municipalities, particularly through the distribution of financial resources.

Following on the description of how funds are distributed among the three levels of government presented in Chapter 5, this chapter presents an overview of the principal functions performed by a typical municipal government in Mexico, emphasizing financial administration because it is the arena that lends itself better to assessing the actual practice of decentralization. The data analyzed here further show that the Municipal Reform has favored state governments instead of municipalities. This has forced municipalities to be creative and assertive, however, in finding ways to meet their obligations to the community by generating revenue locally. Thus, a new type of municipal government has been created in Mexico, one, indeed, that is much closer to the constitutional precept of *municipio libre*.

Functions of Municipal Government

As described in detail in Chapter 2, *municipios* are politico-administrative units roughly equivalent in size and governmental function to counties in the United States. The municipality is governed by an *ayuntamiento*, or council, headed by a municipal president who is elected every three years, but who cannot be reelected to consecutive terms. In addition to the municipal president, the *ayuntamiento* comprises other elected officials who are elected on the president's coattails—one or two *síndicos* and several *regidores*, whose presence and number are determined by state constitutions and electoral codes—and several other appointed officials. When the top-level members of the *ayuntamiento* meet in full session, they constitute the *cabildo*, which is the highest decision-making body of a municipality. The *cabildo* approves all plans, programs, projects, and budgets within the municipality. In addition to being responsible for guiding the development of their respective municipalities, among the most important functions performed by municipal governments are (1) planning and executing development projects; (2) delivering public services; (3) providing a forum for citizen representation and participation; and (4) administering municipal finances.

Planning

An important function of a municipal government is to participate in the formulation of federal and state development plans, as well as to formulate, implement, and control its own plans and programs.[1] In an effort to involve all levels of government and the community at large in the planning of development programs, President de la Madrid created the Sistema Nacional de Planeación Democrática (National System for Democratic Planning, SNPD) in 1983 by amending Article 26 of the Constitution. The SNPD established the state's obligation to promote social and governmental participation and cooperation in all matters concerning municipal and regional development. Before de la Madrid, this participation, more often than not, tended to be more nominal than real, particularly for the lower tiers of government. The SNPD was also instituted to keep the citizenry informed about the governing mechanisms followed in pursuit of specific development objectives. Although the SNPD's legal precepts are well thought out and to date have remained unchanged, the overall intergovernmental planning process in Mexico, generally speaking, remains burdened by bureaucratic inefficiency and leaves much to be desired.

In the last fifteen years most municipal and regional development plans have been contained in the Development Agreements—CUDs—and in the Social Development Agreements—CDSs—signed by the president and the governor of each state (discussed in Chapter 4). In principle, each governor includes in the yearly plan the various local projects proposed by the state's municipal presidents; thus, the agreements provide the basic framework for a variety of programs targeted at promoting regional development. More significant, the primary importance of both the CUD and the CDS consists in their being formal agreements designed for the transfer of federal resources to the states. From a municipal perspective, the CUDs and the CDSs have been critically important because through them the state and federal governments have promised to strengthen the municipalities. For instance, specific provisions deal with the process of strengthening municipal governments by directly transferring to them resources that in the past both the state and the federal governments retained. Under these provisions, federal allocations are to go directly to the municipalities without passing through the states, thereby allowing municipal governments to decide which projects to fund. But with some notable exceptions (e.g., Solidarity's Municipal Funds), by and large, this has not happened, as the states quickly contrived new mechanisms through which to control the allocations destined for each municipality. As we saw in Chapter 5, the access to federal investment resources is conditioned by factors that more often than not are beyond the municipality's control.

The principal mechanism through which the higher levels of government control the flow of resources to the lower ones is the so-called *proyectos especiales* (special projects). These one-time projects, targeted to a particular state or municipality, are heavily subsidized by the higher levels of government (especially the federal). Roads, hospitals, and large-scale housing projects constitute examples of projects normally falling in this category, and altogether seem almost tailor-made for PRONASOL. Under President Salinas the planning and construction of large-scale urban development projects was enhanced substantially through Solidarity, although, clearly, some states and municipalities were favored.

Indeed, as discussed earlier, one of the major criticisms of Solidarity concerned its centralized decision-making process, which led to such favoritism. For example,

Solidarity funding allowed for the construction of El Cuchillo dam on the outskirts of Monterrey. It was built to eliminate the need for residential water rationing and reflected well on the governor. Within Monterrey, it allowed the municipal administration to prioritize and showcase the provision of water and drainage to neighborhoods that in some cases had lacked these services for more than thirty years. Nuevo León's then-governor, Sócrates Rizzo, and Monterrey's then-municipal president, Benjamín Clariond, were both close friends and collaborators of President Salinas (although not of each other); indeed, the president himself officially dedicated the dam in January 1994. In this instance at least, Solidarity funding was crucial for both projects—and for both men's careers (Rodríguez and Ward 1996).

Planning is centralized in other ways as well. From all accounts and from my observations, it is clear that most planning decisions are actually made in the state COPLADEs, created under the de la Madrid presidency and which have remained more or less intact since 1983.[2] The COPLADE is where all levels of government and different social groups meet to negotiate their interests and priorities and to find ways of integrating them into specific policies and plans. As Luis Aguilar (1994) suggests, the COPLADEs have become the primary location of the actual practice of intergovernmental relations. All states have their own COPLADE, and, indeed, several municipalities have replicated the structure at the local level. Nonetheless, as demonstrated in Chapter 5, there are a variety of obstacles (the most critical of which are the funders' discretionality in the allocation of resources and the inability of states to generate income locally) that state and local governments must clear to have access to federal funding and thereby to be able to carry out the programs included in their development plans. Thus, to implement any aspect of their development plans, the lower tiers of government are left with no alternative but to remain subordinated to the central government. Since 1995, there has been a resurgence in the development of the Comité de Planeación de Desarrollo Municipal (Municipal Development Planning Committee—COPLADEMUN), which increasingly are likely to represent the organ of state-municipal development planning agreements. Thus far, COPLADEMUNs have developed in a limited number of municipalities, principally larger cities; in some cases (e.g., in Guanajuato), reportedly, COPLADEMUNs are replacing the statewide COPLADE as the organization in charge of regional development.

Altogether, the planning function of municipal government has tended to be mostly nominal. Given the centralization that characterizes the planning process in Mexico, there is very little room for municipal initiatives in the plans formulated at the higher levels of government. Nonetheless, the plans from which municipalities are usually excluded tend to be the more wide-ranging and grandiose in scope. For small-scale projects, municipalities enjoy an almost free hand, the principal restriction being the availability of resources. But with only a handful of exceptions, the construction and maintenance of the type of public works included in most development plans continues to depend on state and federal agencies. Clearly, since municipal governments seldom have either the resources to embark on substantive works or the necessary equipment and infrastructure to maintain them, they must seek credits and secure investments from various agencies of federal and state government, as well as from the private sector, if they wish to promote and sustain local development.

More recently still, many large *panista* cities have created a quasi-autonomous planning institute in the municipality. These *institutos de planeación* are modeled broadly on a similar entity in Curitiba, Brazil, a model that was developed by charismatic and many-time municipal president Jaime Lerner. Under the PAN, these planning institutes have all the regular functions of a planning department—elaboration of a master plan, ordinance passing power, land use development approval power, and so on. The principal difference appears to lie in their semiautonomous status, given that their close interaction with the private sector helps bridge the gap between the public and the private sectors. Also, the very name "institute" carries with it an academic and independent image.

The planning process at the municipal level thus seems to be acquiring a new style yet retaining much of the old way of doing things. In San Pedro Garza García, for example, when Mauricio Fernández took office (1990), he immediately began work on an urban development plan designed by professionals and university professors from around the world and that is expected to guide the municipality's development until the year 2010. All this is indeed a novelty. Nonetheless, he vowed to follow the plan with two specific objectives that ring familiar: to better regulate urban development and slow down growth; and to shift government attention to small projects that serve the majority of San Pedro's citizens, rather than, as he stated in interview, "large projects that become monuments to the government" (Rodríguez and Ward 1996).

Public Services

Until the mid-1980s, when the Municipal Reform was enacted, considerable ambiguity existed (even in the Constitution) regarding which specific services fell under the responsibility of municipal government. This ambiguity, coupled with the inability of some municipalities actually to provide public services, led the state and federal governments to take primary responsibility for their provision. More often than not, local needs were not met. The Municipal Reform of 1983 clearly delineated municipal government's responsibility for the provision of services, partly in an attempt to respond more effectively to local needs and conditions.

The public services now under municipal control are classified as (a) basic: water, drainage, streets and sidewalks, street lighting, roads; (b) basic complementary: street cleaning, markets and supply centers, elementary education, graveyards, slaughterhouses; (c) security: public safety, traffic, fire department, emergency medical attention; (d) community protection: health, disaster prevention, pollution protection, social communication; and (e) social well-being: parks and gardens, protection of the historical, artistic, and cultural patrimony. As this list cannot be comprehensive, federal and state governments assist local governments to provide all necessary services.

The responsibility for the provision of services to municipal governments was also transferred to grant municipalities more control over their own resources and, consequently, more autonomy. Since under the Reform municipalities get to keep the fees collected for the provision of services, the general assumption was that these fees would constitute an important source of revenue. Significantly, also, local governments became entitled to decide how to spend these funds.

While on paper these intentions appear laudable, the reality of municipal administration and intergovernmental relations has thwarted their implementation. The scarcity of resources, on the one hand, and the dependence on patron-client ties to the governor for special projects, on the other, have exacerbated several of the major problems built into this transfer. Since most municipalities lack the equipment and trained personnel required to deliver services independently of other levels of government (particularly since they had always relied on them to do so), the shift in responsibilities almost invariably has led either to less effective delivery of services or to renewed forms of dependence on the higher levels of government through arrangements of "administrative cooperation." Therefore, municipal performance in providing urban services has tended to be measured in terms of lightweight activities that require no lump sum investment and that fall unequivocally within the aegis of the municipal president. Typical here would be local policing, public lighting, street repairs, market and slaughterhouse supervision, regulation of cantinas and street vendors, and so on.

There are several major problems built into this transfer of responsibility from state to municipality. First of all, the rates charged for public services most often are insufficient to cover the costs of providing them. For example, the fees collected for the provision of water seldom cover the maintenance costs of the water supply system, thereby turning it into a major expense rather than a source of income.[3] Second, many municipalities lack adequate human, technical, financial, and administrative resources to handle the delivery of services, as well as the infrastructure and equipment required for the maintenance of public works. Third, if local governments decide which services to fund and which not, there is the obvious risk of favoring those services that are more useful to certain constituencies than to others, which sometimes leaves essential services ignored. And finally, there is the critical issue of a lack of political will to institute an effective system of charging fees for providing services. In many localities these services have traditionally been subsidized by the higher levels of government, and people are simply not accustomed to paying for the services they receive. At least until non-PRI municipal presidents were elected, very few municipal presidents were prepared to buck the traditional orthodoxy of power relations and tackle the issue by taking the first steps to change the people's mentality to a culture where public services must be paid for. The reason is obvious: it was felt that the political cost for the PRI would be too high.

Nonetheless, there are some remarkable success stories where municipalities have indeed been able to overcome these structural obstacles and dramatically raise the level of services provided by the *ayuntamiento*. Invariably, the first examples of these successes came from PAN governments in large cities such as Ciudad Juárez and Chihuahua (1983–1986), León (since 1989), and subsequently from the PRI itself in cities such as Aguascalientes, Monterrey, and Naucalpan. As we shall observe, a key component of these municipalities' capacity to provide services has been their ability to raise more money. But in addition, their successes have been born of the infusion of new ideas and personnel from different career tracks coming into government (Rodríguez and Ward 1992, 1994). For example, in Ciudad Juárez and Chihuahua, municipal presidents Barrio and Álvarez (1983–1986), respectively, set about professionalizing, remodeling, and re-equipping the police force in order to raise morale and improve service. Ernesto Ruffo, as municipal president of Ensenada (1986–1989), set out to clean the streets, restrict street vendors to certain locations, and improve sewage removal and treatment facilities. While these are individual examples of service improvements achieved in each of these cities, they were not, of course, the only new activities undertaken by these municipal presidents. Rather, they are indicative of the types of action undertaken across the board.

Not all administrative improvements set in train by the opposition were well received, however. In Morelia, PRD municipal president Samuel Maldonado made the not-unreasonable decision to turn off some public street lighting after 10:00 PM in order to save the municipal treasury money; however, this provoked such an outcry that he was forced to back down immediately. This PRD experience also illustrates the intense opposition the party evoked from the PRI and the Salinas government. In Morelia, not only the street lighting issue became a *cause célèbre* around which the opposition PRI could mobilize: almost every action undertaken provoked similarly hostile reaction and mobilization (Beltrán del Río 1993; Rodríguez and Ward 1994c).

Since around 1989, many PRI-governed cities have also begun to demonstrate greater civic responsibility and effectiveness in responding to citizens' service needs. This has largely been for pragmatic reasons, since governors and party alike have begun to accept that within Mexico's new electoral environment their candidates will be elected only if their PRI predecessor governments have been effective and credible. On occasion, these actions bring them into direct conflict with party corporatist organizations such as the CTM and the former CNOP. For example, PRI municipal president Benjamín Clariond in Monterrey moved PRI-affiliated street vendors out of the Macro Plaza in downtown Monterrey, sparking heated conflict with workers' unions. Other actions involved relatively low-cost investment in improvements to street paving, measures to relieve traffic congestion, improved storm sewers, and the remodeling and improvement of public buildings. Between 1992 and 1993, five thousand street signs and ninety-three traffic lights were installed in Monterrey, and 250 kilometers of road were freshly marked (Rodríguez and Ward 1996). In order to tap into Solidarity funding, Clariond prioritized the provision of water and drainage to neighborhoods that, in many cases, had lacked these services for over two decades. Solidarity investment income almost doubled at a stroke the investment income going into public works in the city; it also underscored the importance of cultivating good intergovernmental relations if major infusions of additional income were to be secured.

There are other alternatives for improving the level and effectiveness of service provision. Few municipalities have resorted to debt contracting in order to finance major infrastructure or urban development improvements. In one case, Ciudad Guzmán, where the municipality borrowed a large sum to finance the development and improvement of the aqueduct, the effect on city finances was extremely onerous. Also, as we have seen, there are constitutional restrictions on incurring debt at the state and local levels.

A more widely tried alternative is privatization. Increasingly, city governments have begun to explore the possibility of transferring public service provision to the private sector or contracting out some level of activities. Experiments include, for example, partial contracting out of police services and the transfer of garbage collection to private contractors in Naucalpan in 1992–1993. In Aguascalientes, the water system was privatized in 1993. The limited degree to which urban public service provision is considered profitable (*rentable*) in Mexico, however, makes widespread privatization an unlikely option for the near future. Moreover, privatization to date has been far from a resounding success. In Naucalpan the concession was revoked after only a few months due to inadequate service and citizen complaints, which led to a major lawsuit with international dimensions because part of the contracting consortium involved U.S. interests (Conde 1996). In Aguascalientes, where the municipal government had long worked closely with private contractors to provide water, once the concession was handed over, the price for the service rose higher than anticipated. The political cost proved to be high also: in the 1995 elections the PAN took the capital city, which had always been a PRI stronghold. In part, this was triggered by the rising cost of water (García del Castillo and Díaz Flores 1995).

Citizen Representation and Participation

Although the centralized nature of the Mexican political system allows little room for direct citizen participation in policy making and planning, various mechanisms have evolved at the local level that enable the public to have access to their local government. In Mexico, as elsewhere, it is most useful to conceive of two forms of participation: representative democracy, and participatory democracy.[4]

Representative Democracy in the Mexican Municipality. Mexico remains weak in terms of the extent to which people are represented by local elected officials. Although the *cabildo* acts as a form of representational council, it is far from being genuinely representative. *Regidores* and *síndicos* are elected on the municipal president's coattails as part of a slate, as described in Chapter 2. Given that they do not run for the position on their own, they have no real mandate or a constituency to represent. In short, therefore, the one constitutionally mandated forum for democratic representation within the *ayuntamiento,* the *cabildo,* has limited value and effectiveness. Even though *cabildo* sessions are in theory open, in practice they seldom are, and even then few people attend.

This failure of the *cabildo* to represent citizen views effectively in municipal government has been compensated by a host of other participatory mechanisms, ranging from corporatist organizations, clientelism, routinization, Solidarity committees, and, most recently, the creation and active involvement of consultative councils, citizen councils, and numerous other nonexecutive ad hoc bodies. Each of these will be analyzed in detail later.

Participatory Democracy in the Mexican Municipality. Traditionally, political participation in Mexico at all levels, but particularly in the municipality, has occurred along two broad lines: first, in regime-supporting activities that, until recently, were largely ritualistic; and second, in petitioning public officials for the allocation of goods and services.

Regime-supporting activities included voting and participating in government-sponsored campaign rallies or demonstrations. Until recently, voting tended to be overwhelmingly ritualistic because citizens knew that the votes they cast simply ratified the selection of the candidates chosen by top (PRI) party officials. Nonetheless, as the PRI has lost elections, recognized important victories of the opposition, and appears to be undergoing substantial change internally, ritualistic voting seems to have diminished greatly, leading to more genuine political participation in terms of voting behavior. As discussed earlier, a new civic culture that demands respect for the electoral process has emerged in Mexico since the late 1980s, rendering elections more genuinely competitive.

Nonelectoral forms of participation appear to have changed less, as citizens are still obliged to collaborate in activities that will have some material payoff for them, their families, and their neighborhood. In the past these activities consisted, basically, of petitioning an agency or official for something specific, such as a school or piped water. There were also experiments with state-sponsored *faenas* (groups that volunteered for one day), such as Governor Jiménez Cantú's Ejército de Trabajo (Work Army) scheme in the state of Mexico.

Today, as the sectoral composition of the party dissolves, these activities are orchestrated primarily through the Movimiento Territorial (Territorial Movement— MT), which has become, as was described to me, "el brazo político del partido" (the political arm of the party). The MT (which replaced the CNOP and the UNE) has taken over the function of promoting group organization for requesting goods and services from the government.[5] The MT's success at organizing local groups to collaborate with municipal authorities in carrying out a number of public works has been built on the notion that participation instills in the individual a sense of responsibility and cooperation in the community's development while helping break the apathy caused by government paternalism.

"Routinization" as a mode of community-local authority interaction in large part arose as a reaction to clientelism and corporatism, particularly where public officials needed to circumvent local leaders (caciques) (Eckstein 1988; Ward 1989). Such leaders and other local bosses often were unrepresentative of local communities and opposed the programs that public officials were seeking to implement. As the political climate changed and municipal presidents and executive officers were less likely to be required by the PRI to cultivate and tolerate such leaders, so public officials sought to individualize links between the *ayuntamiento* and community residents. This meant, for example, contracting directly with households over land regularization, water and electricity installation, street paving, and so on. Campaigns and procedures were developed to bring citizens into the routines of regular government. In order to ensure that this did not "grow" the bureaucracy and increase inefficiency as individuals were passed from department to department, residents' interactions with local government would be through a consolidated, "single window" (*ventanilla única*) administrative system. Brokers (leaders) were redundant.

Prior to the MT and Solidarity, the most popular forms of organization during the de la Madrid administration (some of which still operate) were the Consejo de Colaboración y Consulta Municipal (Council for Municipal Cooperation), which worked closely with municipal authorities to organize and execute a number of works demanded by the community; the Asociación de Colonos (Tenants' Association) and the Junta de Vecinos (Neighborhood Board), both of which sought to solve the problems of a specific area of the community; and the Comité por Obra Determinada (Committee for a Specific Work), a committee established to carry out a particular work in the community. Another form of participation that has become increasingly popular since de la Madrid first used it so successfully in his presidential campaign is the *consulta popular*, in which both the community and the authorities work out the plans and programs that will be incorporated into the presidential candidate's policy agenda. To a large extent, the Salinas administration gave a more official character to all these forms of participation, given that most community public works carried out under the auspices of Solidarity were initiated by citizen petitions and group organization (the Comités de Solidaridad, Solidarity Committees).

As mentioned earlier, the failure of the *cabildo* to represent the citizenry effectively in municipal affairs has spawned alternative mechanisms to increase public participation. In León, for example, the *panista* municipal administration of Medina Plascencia (1989–1991) created a Dirección de Integración Ciudadana y Educación (Citizen Integration and Education Board), which sought to integrate and serve as liaison with citizen groups, residents' associations, and so on, as a means of bypassing traditional PRI corporatist municipality-community links. In addition, León's *panista* administration created some eighteen ad hoc councils that covered a wide range of municipal activities, from public services to planning (Instituto Municipal de Planeación Urbana, Municipal Urban Planning Institute—IMPLADE) to the integration of rural communities to a *patronato* (advisory board) for the zoo (Cabrero 1995). This structure remained under Medina Plascencia's successor, although the new PAN municipal president sought to "take the municipality to the people" by ordering his section directors to make regular neighborhood tours and to hold an "open house" once a week to receive petitions and hear citizen views.

Similarly, in San Pedro Garza García, municipal president Rogelio Sada created Consejos Consultivos Ciudadanos (Citizen Consultation Councils) to advise each principal municipal office (e.g., public works) on policy matters. In addition, locally elected Juntas de Vecinos (Neighborhood Boards) were designed to bring citizen concerns directly to the city administration.

The importance of participation in allowing a community to make its needs known to the authorities and for offering help in having its demands met is nothing new in Mexico or elsewhere. The importance of such self-help initiatives throughout the world has been proved time and again. In some cases, however, they tend to be underestimated because, individually, they appear relatively modest and not to have major consequences except for those benefited directly. In aggregate, however, the impact of these projects can be substantial. Community participation has entered the mainstream of urban and rural development projects in developing countries in the last decade (Moser 1989; Skinner and Rodell 1983). In short, community participation offers opportunities to reduce the costs of development projects, thereby spreading resources more widely; it encourages beneficiaries to use and maintain the project if they have participated in its creation; the project itself is more likely to reflect what people need, rather than what outsiders think they need; and, perhaps most important of all, it foments democratic participation and a belief in a "bootstrap" approach to social change.

But it is also criticized as an abrogation of government responsibility (i.e., as leaving people to do things themselves) and for being an end in itself rather than a means to more successful and appropriate forms of organization and social change (Gilbert and Ward 1985; Moser 1989). Nonetheless, the benefits to the community often outweigh these criticisms; evidently, the philosophy behind self-help initiatives suited President Salinas's Solidarity program particularly well.

From the municipal government's perspective, self-help initiatives also make the population aware of the importance of sharing with the authorities its problems and concerns. Motivating the community to engage in works that benefit everyone could generate a number of services that the government cannot provide and hence deflect somewhat the pressure on government. Solidarity was remarkably successful in motivating community participation and in delivering services that otherwise might not have been provided, which served the Salinas government rather well. Moreover, as Gilbert and Ward (1985) and many others have argued, a motivated community can become a particularly useful political asset for mobilizing local political support. Specifically, in conjunction with the PRI's efforts, Solidarity helped reinstate to party ranks many who were dissatisfied with government performance and had moved to the opposition. In this respect, then, Solidarity helped reestablish political support for both the PRI and the government, a fact that has become the source of extensive academic debate.[6] Zedillo's Superación de la Pobreza (Overcoming Poverty) also makes extensive use of the erstwhile Solidarity Committees, which are now constituted into Municipal Committees more closely under the aegis of the municipal president and the local SEDESOL representative.

Municipal Finances

Given the well-known fact that Mexican municipalities lack sufficient resources to cover their expenditures, municipal governments of all political parties are continually forced to seek assistance and financial support from the federal and state governments in order to meet their obligations. Necessarily, this pattern of dependence reduces the autonomy that all municipalities, regardless of their party affiliation, should have as a result of the reforms to Article 115.

The legal dispositions governing municipal finances and fiscal policy are found in legislation at different levels: at the federal level, Article 115 of the Constitution, the Ley de Ingresos (Income Law), and the Fiscal Coordination Law; at the state level, the state constitutions, their Leyes de Ingresos, and their Fiscal Coordination Laws; each municipality's fiscal code; and the collaborative agreements between the municipality and its state government. Within the municipality proper, the most important legal dispositions are the municipal fiscal codes and financial regulations, as well as each municipality's yearly fiscal laws (Ley de Hacienda and Ley de Ingresos).

Every year, in October and November, each municipality's *ayuntamiento* presents to the state legislature its Ley de Ingresos and its Ley de Hacienda for approval. The Ley de Ingresos specifies the municipality's sources of income by taxes and tariffs (i.e., what is to be included in the various entries—*impuestos, derechos, productos, aprovechamientos*) and estimates the amounts expected to be collected from these sources. The Ley de Hacienda determines how the *impuestos, derechos, productos,* and *aprovechamientos* are to be collected. Many municipalities resent the fact that the state legislature provides them with a template for these laws, which, in effect, gives them the opportunity to fill in the blanks but not to provide any real input. Indeed, some municipalities have resisted this state imposition and written their own laws (with sometimes rather unfortunate results). Other municipalities have refused to present these laws for approval, even though the state legislature may impose administrative and financial sanctions (e.g., delaying payment of *participaciones*) for failing to submit them.

The most important provision dealing with municipal finances is Section IV of Article 115 of the federal Constitution. This provision is also the heart of the Municipal Reform of 1983, since, at least in theory, it grants municipal governments the freedom to decide how to spend their resources. According to Section IV, local governments are entitled to collect revenues from three main sources: (1) fees for the

TABLE 6.1   Municipal Revenue Categories

Standard Revenues		Supplementary Revenues	
Impuestos (taxes)	Property, income, sales, etc.	*Subsidios* (state and federal government subsidies)	Health, education, salaries, public services
Derechos (fees)	Water, drainage, street lighting, garbage collection, slaughterhouses, etc.	*Contribuciones ciudadanas* (citizen contributions to public works and services)	Fees assessed to the beneficiaries of a specific work (e.g., for paving in front of one's house)
Productos (patrimonial goods)	Sale or lease of real estate or liquid assets, ownerless goods, sale of garbage	*Deuda* (loans, credits, other financing)	From federal and state government, commercial banks, or development banks
Aprovechamientos (benefit fees)	Fines, surcharges, donations, grants, and other bequests	*Transferencias* (transfers)	State and federal revenues allocated for specific programs or works (e.g., CUDs, CDSs)
Participaciones (federal allocations)	Revenue sharing through two funds: FGP and FFM		

delivery of public services, (2) property taxes, and (3) federal allocations. State legislatures may include other sources of revenue, but that is determined by each state government. Municipal autonomy, however, is still very limited, particularly as the Contaduría Mayor de Hacienda (Finance Committee) of each state legislature continues to review the annual budgets that all municipalities are required to submit and then presents them for voting approval to the entire legislature.

Municipal Revenues

Municipal governments in Mexico collect two types of revenue: *ingresos ordinarios*, or standard revenues, and *ingresos extraordinarios*, or supplementary revenues (see Table 6.1 for the various revenue categories). In its entirety, municipal revenue is derived from revenue-sharing (*participaciones*), taxes (*impuestos*), user fees charged for public services (*derechos*), income from government assets (*productos*), and other income from public services or assets classified neither as *derechos* nor as *productos* (*aprovechamientos*). *Impuestos, derechos, productos,* and *aprovechamientos* make up the municipality's own revenues. These revenues, plus the *participaciones*, make up the standard revenues, or the income over which the municipality has, within the limitations of the law, full control.

Supplementary revenues include the monies *ayuntamientos* receive from federal and state government in the form of subsidies and other contributions for the execution of public works, covering operational deficits, and emergency situations. This implies, naturally, that the municipality is subject to the priorities of state and federal governments. These revenues are collected irregularly by the municipality and therefore do not represent a constant source of income. With the advent of Solidarity, however, supplementary revenues gained importance.

Figure 6.1 shows the steady and substantial increase in municipal income since 1975. The first sharp increase occurred in 1979, as the economy was reinflated by López Portillo on the crest of the petroleum boom. After the crisis of 1982 one observes a second sharp rise in 1984, associated with the implementation of the Municipal Reform; as we shall see later, the increase in federal revenue sharing was specifically in *participaciones*, although the economic shocks experienced in 1985–1986 reduced levels of municipal income somewhat in 1986 and 1987. The third major increase coincides with the changing political landscape after 1988, so that from 1989 on we observe a consistent increase in municipal income.

Table 6.2 presents the relative proportions of income coming from indirect sources in the form of *participaciones*, the direct income generated locally through the four categories (*impuestos, derechos, productos, aprovechamientos*), and other income, which since the early 1980s has been negligible. Looking first at *participaciones*, one observes a dramatic increase in their importance beginning in 1982. Although they were already rising steeply during the last years of the López Portillo administration (1980, 1981), they positively took off with de la Madrid's Municipal Reform in 1983–1984 and held steady until they began to decline in 1989, once direct incomes increasingly formed a larger share.

This overall national trend is even more accentuated when one looks at large city municipality budgets. The concomitant to this is the growth in direct income that until the Municipal Reform had always dominated (often supplemented by "other income"—see Table 6.2), and that has grown nationally from 32 percent in 1988 to over 40 percent in 1991. Once again these national data smooth the sharper upward trend observed in large city budgets. Much of this increase in direct income stems from the *impuestos* category, which as Figure 6.2 shows, began to rise dramatically in 1989.

As we now know, among the standard revenues at the municipal level the most important are the *participaciones*, *impuestos*, and *derechos*, and of these only the last two are self-generated. As the analysis in Chapter 5 demonstrates, *participaciones*, in particular, are the primary source of municipal income. On average, a typical rural municipality depends for more than 80 percent of its income on the revenue-sharing funds it receives from the higher levels of government, while urban municipalities traditionally have been able to supplement their *participaciones* with locally generated direct income. Thus, the same pattern of dependence that we observed between the state and the federal level is replicated between the municipality and the state. In order to break out of the dependency circle, municipalities must neces-

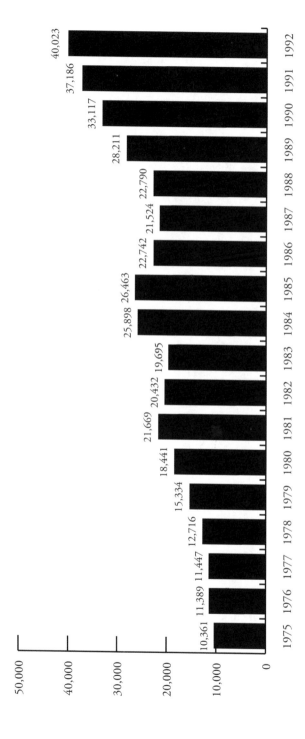

FIGURE 6.1   National municipal income, 1975–1992 (constant pesos)
SOURCE: INEGI.

TABLE 6.2   Municipal Income and Expenditures, 1975–1991 (%), National Aggregate

Income Source	1975	1976	1977	1978	1979	1980	1981	1982
Direct Income	54	55	51	51	52	45	44	43
Impuestos	17	17	16	15	15	12	10	8
Derechos	10	10	10	10	10	11	9	8
Productos	12	13	12	11	10	8	7	7
Aprovechamientos	14	15	13	15	17	14	17	19
Indirect income								
Participaciones	13	12	14	15	17	26	29	46
Other income	30	29	32	28	26	26	24	8
Supplementary income	3	5	3	5	4	2	3	3
Expenditures								
Gasto corriente	59	61	63	61	59	59	57	61
Gasto de inversión	25	24	23	22	23	23	29	28
Gasto de deuda	6	6	6	8	7	7	5	3
Transferencias	4	3	3	4	7	4	4	4
Other expenditures	5	6	5	5	4	8	6	5

Income Source	1983	1984	1985	1986	1987	1988	1989	1990	1991
Direct income	31	31	34	33	33	32	37	38	40
Impuestos	6	11	12	11	11	11	13	17	18
Derechos	7	5	6	6	6	7	7	8	8
Productos	6	6	5	5	5	4	5	5	5
Aprovechamientos	12	9	11	10	11	10	11	8	9
Indirect income									
Participaciones	64	59	57	59	57	58	51	48	47
Other income	2	6	4	2	4	6	6	8	8
Supplementary income	3	4	4	5	6	4	6	6	5
Expenditures									
Gasto corriente	57	51	55	60	57	56	57	56	56
Gaso de inversión	30	34	33	28	25	25	25	27	26
Gasto de deuda	4	4	4	4	4	4	4	4	4
Transferencias	3	3	5	4	5	6	6	6	7
Other expenditures	5	8	4	4	10	8	8	7	7

SOURCE: INEGI (1975–1983, 1979–1988, 1989–1991).

sarily find mechanisms for generating their own sources of revenue if they are to be truly autonomous. If they are unable to do so, their resources will comprise the *participaciones* and any windfall state and federal investment income that they can leverage.

Once again, it was the newly elected opposition governments of the 1980s that broke the logjam of dependency and first took advantage of the reforms instituted by President de la Madrid (Rodríguez and Ward 1992). Specifically, incoming

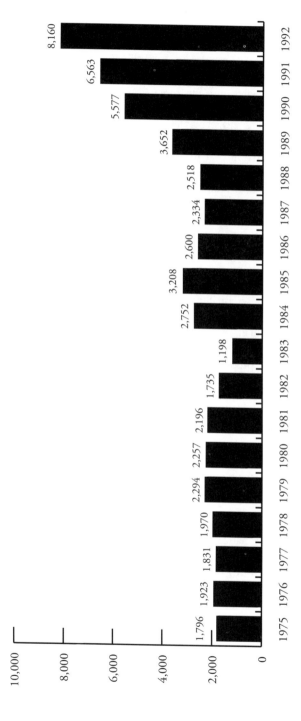

FIGURE 6.2 National municipal income derived from taxes (*Impuestos*), 1975–1992 (constant pesos)
SOURCE: INEGI.

panista city administrations such as those of Francisco Barrio in Ciudad Juárez and Luis H. Álvarez in Chihuahua (1983) feared that they would probably be penalized in the arena of *participaciones*, and certainly insofar as they could expect to receive discretionary investment income. Earlier work on these two cities (subsequently corroborated) demonstrates that in fact non-PRI governments were not in any way penalized because of the safeguards incorporated into the Fiscal Coordination Law, but they did suffer in a variety of ways from reduced investment in special projects (Rodríguez and Ward 1992: 72).[7] This element of intergovernmental relations is important, since it highlights the ways in which governors and the federal government are able to exercise discretion over the allocation of funds to municipalities. Luis Álvarez commented that, although he had gotten along well with then-governor Oscar Ornelas, and that the governor always reassured him that he would of course transfer the funds, he was never precise about when that would occur; as Álvarez put it when I interviewed him, "Siempre me decía que sí, pero no cuando" (He always told me yes, but not when). *Tortuguismo* (slowing down, from *tortuga*, "turtle") thus serves as a most useful mechanism of gubernatorial control.

For these reasons, most opposition municipal presidents, upon taking office, seek ways of cushioning the expected shortfall of investment income. Once again the Barrio and Álvarez responses are illustrative of what has become the pattern. By increasing the levels of local taxes and the efficiency with which they were collected, during a single triennium the traditional dependence on *participaciones* relative to own income (70/30 approximately) was turned around. When Barrio and Álvarez left office (in 1986), the proportion of indirect income had been reduced from 70 percent to 38 percent, and this trend continued in successive PRI administrations. Some "new PRI" administrations, such as that of Benjamín Clariond in Monterrey, also set in train similar changes. Between 1990 and 1993, direct income rose from 41 percent to almost 60 percent, with a concomitant decrease in *participaciones* (from 58 percent to 36 percent). Much of the increase was obtained by raising taxes, particularly the property tax and the *adquisición de inmuebles*.[8] Similarly, Clariond's *panista* contemporary in neighboring San Pedro increased internal revenues such that when he left office, 74 percent of municipal income was generated directly (Ward 1996).

Not all PAN administrations were able to reverse the *ingresos propios/participaciones* proportions so dramatically. For example, in Ciudad Guzmán, major debt was contracted by a *priísta* administration in 1988–1989 and again in 1991, but repayment was deferred until 1992—coincidentally, the year in which Alberto Cárdenas (the current PAN governor of Jalisco) was elected municipal president. Thus, under his administration debt payments rose quickly and represented one quarter of total municipal expenditure. Since 1989, user fees have dramatically increased from around 15 percent to twice as much (Hernández Claro 1995).

A similar pattern began to emerge in most large municipalities in 1989, which can be explained only partly by the arrival of non-PRI administrations (Table 6.3). The election of a PAN administration in León in 1989 saw a 10 percent rise in direct income over *participaciones*, most of it due to increased *impuestos* and *derechos*. Tijuana, also *panista*, reduced its dependence on *participaciones* by 23 percentage points in 1989, and although there was some rise initially in the *impuestos* category, most of the additional public income appears to have come from contracted loans; in the last triennium the *impuestos* line was less aggressively pursued in order to avoid the political fallout that might have ensued prior to the 1995 elections (Guillén López 1995). In Aguascalientes, too, we observe a major decline in the *participaciones* share beginning in 1989, with a sharp rise (21 percent) in direct incomes between 1989 and 1991.[9] This increase was entirely due to a rise in *derechos,* which were almost nonexistent between 1983 and 1989 and which rose to around 30 percent of total municipal income between 1991 and 1993. The decline beginning in 1994 reflects privatization of the water service.

The important point to recognize is that, notwithstanding those cases in which municipalities are penalized by withdrawal of or reduction in investment income, the total income available to them has *increased.* Far from having to "do more with less," as was originally anticipated by the likes of Barrio and Álvarez, cities have begun to "do more with more" (Ward 1995). Later we will observe how they have also been able to achieve better value for money through more streamlined and efficient expenditure patterns.

Since the Municipal Reform of 1983, the most important tax for the municipalities is the property tax (*impuesto predial*), which formerly was collected by the state government and now, with the reforms to Article 115, belongs exclusively to the municipality.[10] Prior to the Municipal Reform, the states not only collected the taxes, but also decided, according to their own legislation, how much of the amounts collected at the municipal level would be redistributed to the municipalities they came from; often, municipal governments got nothing. As is the case with the provision of public services, however, one of the largest problems in implementing the revised property tax provision of Article 115 is that most municipalities do not have the administrative infrastructure required for collecting the tax (including an updated cadastre) and therefore have had to sign collaborative agreements with their state governments to collect the taxes for them. As a result, some states still have responsibility for collecting municipal property taxes and keep a certain percentage of the revenue collected. Although it might be an exaggeration, an informed observer commented to me that in his estimation municipalities get to keep, on average, approximately one third of what the state raises in property taxes. One noteworthy example is the state government of Chiapas, which continues to collect the property tax in all of the state's municipalities. State officials categorically indicated to me that all the revenue collected is then transferred back to the municipalities, and that the state keeps only "una pequeña fracción" (a tiny fraction); no one would say exactly how much this "fraction" amounts to.

The increased importance of taxes nationally is apparent in Table 6.2 and Figure 6.2. This rise is almost entirely the result of municipal governments' taking control of their cadastre, updating it, and raising tax levels. In León, for example, the collec-

TABLE 6.3   Relative Levels of Public Income and Expenditure in Four Large Cities, 1979–1994 (%)

Income/Expenditure Item	1979	1981	1983	1985	1987	1988	1989	1990	1991	1992	1993	1994
Tijuana (Baja California)												
Public income												
Direct	95	54	36	46	43	44	44	45	45	46	40	37
Impuestos	20	7	6	19	20	23	27	22	27	26	22	19
Derechos	24	12	10	7	5	5	4	6	6	7	7	6
Productos	4	2	2	2	3	3	3	3	2	1	1	1
Aprovechamientos	47	34	17	18	16	13	10	15	10	12	11	10
Indirect												
Participaciones	5	46	64	54	57	56	33	36	35	39	32	31
Public expenditure												
Gasto corriente	59	67	83	74	79	72	50	65	71	77	78	55
Gasto de inversión	25	24	11	16	12	20	30	16	10	13	13	4
León (Guanajuato)												
Public income												
Direct	100	56	34	47	53	46	56	60	56	60	56	48
Impuestos	19	22	2	27	24	18	22	27	29	31	28	21
Derechos	13	17	9	6	5	14	18	22	11	11	12	9
Productos	n/a	10	5	22	13	12	11	10	6	10	7	4
Aprovechamientos	58	13	1	1	12	4	6	5	6	11	11	14
Indirect												
Participaciones	n/a	44	66	53	47	54	43	37	43	39	38	42
Public expenditure												
Gasto corriente	56	71	86	45	45	50	65	51	57	75	70	71
Gasto de inversión	38	27	12	55	55	44	27	34	30	25	30	29

(continues)

TABLE 6.3 (continued)

Income/Expenditure Item	1979	1981	1983	1985	1987	1988	1989	1990	1991	1992	1993	1994
Aguascalientes (Aguascalientes)												
Public income												
Direct	81	72	63	44	42	40	40	47	61	63	63	56
Impuestos	8	3	1	16	15	17	12	13	13	18	19	23
Derechos	13	21	7	4	7	4	0	20	30	29	30	19
Productos	n/a	42	38	18	20	16	14	17	3	4	6	4
Aprovechamientos	19	10	37	3	4	5	10	11	14	11	9	10
Indirect												
Participaciones	20	28	37	56	58	60	31	32	35	36	37	44
Public expenditure												
Gasto corriente	62	67	40	64	57	60	49	43	47	54	53	61
Gasto de inversión	38	31	59	34	41	40	48	56	47	42	38	28
Naucalpan (México)												
Public income												
Direct	41	36	29	60	52	59	51	48	58	58	44	49
Impuestos	8	8	4	41	34	27	23	25	28	35	33	35
Derechos	3	24	18	13	18	21	18	19	24	17	7	9
Productos	n/a	16	0	1	0	4	2	1	1	2	2	2
Aprovechamientos	15	5	6	6	6	9	9	3	5	4	2	3
Indirect												
Participaciones	59	64	71	40	38	41	27	25	27	28	32	38
Public expenditure												
Gasto corriente	89	55	83	76	88	79	73	70	77	75	72	74
Gasto de inversión	10	40	10	22	6	15	12	25	5	12	8	14

NOTE: Expenditures do not add up to 100, since not all items are included (e.g., debt payments, *transferencias*).
SOURCE: Compiled from data in Cabrero (1996).

tion of taxes as a proportion of public income rose 11 percent from 1988 to 1991, an increase brought about by updating the cadastre and extending the property tax base itself. Interestingly, Tijuana, where the PAN has won a narrow majority continuously since 1989, the government has been very circumspect about raising property taxes and, indeed, revenues from this source have declined since 1992 under the second PAN administration—a ploy that has obviously been successful, since they won again in 1995. Balancing the political gains and possible losses associated with raising revenue through the property tax route has been a major issue for almost all municipal presidents and for the political parties as well.[11]

Together with property taxes, the fees charged for the delivery of public services (*derechos*) constitute the major source of self-generated income in a typical municipality. One of the most significant drains on municipal resources, however, is unreimbursed expenditures for public services, especially for water supply and public lighting. In the most urbanized and largest municipalities, the public sector has created semiautonomous water companies, and fees are generally sufficiently high to cover normal operating and maintenance costs. In some rural municipalities, the municipality delegates water supply to a local water commission, which, having no access to other revenues, must charge to recoup operating costs. In many municipalities, however, the water supply system is managed by the municipality itself, and since costs are frequently not covered by the minimal charges imposed, other revenues are diverted to subsidize the system. Because the poorest of the municipal population often receive no water, this in effect becomes a subsidy by the poor of the more well-to-do. The information available on the collection of water charges unfortunately does not include an analysis of costs, which makes it impossible to judge the apparently significant increase in collections. Nevertheless, as we saw in Chapter 5, water charges remain relatively low in Mexico, totaling only US$946 million in 1992.

That fact notwithstanding, urban municipalities in particular have become more aggressive and insistent about recovering the recurrent costs and installation costs of water and other services through the *derechos* category (see Figure 6.3). Although nationally the proportion of income derived from *derechos* appears to have increased by under two percentage points since 1987, in absolute terms this increase is considerable, if we take into account the sharp rise in overall income. In Table 6.3 the significance of this increase is more apparent in cities such as León and Ciudad Guzmán (the latter is not shown on Table 6.3; see Hernández Claro 1995). In the latter, as we have seen, *derechos* represented the major source of a sharp increase in locally generated revenues, far exceeding that of *impuestos*.

Municipal Expenditures

Municipal expenditures are classified into five large groups: *gasto corriente, gasto de inversión, gasto de deuda, transferencias,* and *otros gastos.* Of these, *gasto corriente,* or recurrent expenditures—which are mostly for administration and for operating mu-

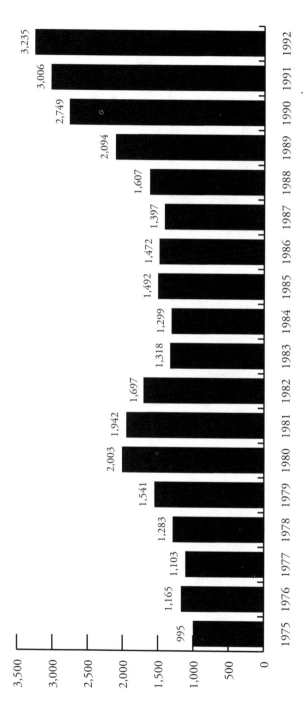

FIGURE 6.3 National municipal income derived from user fees *(Derechos)*, 1975–1992 (constant pesos)
SOURCE: INEGI.

nicipal services—and *gasto de inversión,* or capital expenditures—destined for the construction of public works and services and the purchase of equipment—take the lion's share.

Table 6.2 indicates that, traditionally, recurrent expenditures occupies just over one half of total municipal expenditures, with one quarter going for investment and the remainder for all other costs combined. These national averages, however, obscure very important differences between large cities and predominantly rural municipalities. The latter, in particular, spend 90 to 95 of their entire budget on administration, not because they are inefficient but because their *participaciones* are so meager and because their capacity to raise local taxes is nil. Large cities, however, have much wider opportunities and potential for raising income directly, as we have seen, but here, too, recurrent expenditures are high, often on the order of 70 percent (see Table 6.3). This high level of administrative costs may reflect inefficiencies, although research suggests that city administrations in Mexico have become more streamlined and efficient. Governance of large cities is a highly complex process and will, necessarily, carry high administrative costs. All municipalities, therefore, have a high level of dependence on federal and state support for their investment programs.

Thus, most of the expenditures for a typical municipality go for administrative costs and, interestingly, for electricity used for public lighting. While there is some recovery of cost for public lighting through the property tax, the fees component collected is very low; nonetheless, the municipality must pay the Comisión Federal de Electricidad (Federal Electricity Commission—CFE—the federal government's giant electricity conglomerate) for this service. Given the existing scarcity of resources, and the secondary importance of having public lighting, many local governments adamantly resist having public lighting installed in their municipality and, certainly, are reluctant to bring electricity to low-income neighborhoods, where they have little chance of recovering any of the costs.

For all municipalities, but in particular for the rural, poorer ones, Solidarity made an enormous difference, as it represented the only available funding for investment of any type. In many of these rural municipalities, indeed, the Solidarity appropriation for a handful of projects far exceeded the entire yearly municipal budget. As discussed in Chapter 5, at the national level approximately one third of the general Solidarity funds were directed mostly to rural municipalities and managed by them through the various Solidarity programs (Fondos Municipales, Fondos para la Producción, Escuela Digna, and Niños de Solidaridad). That such a large percentage of funds was targeted to the municipality certainly supports Solidarity's claims to have promoted decentralization.

Conclusion

This chapter has demonstrated that municipalities, particularly the larger ones, are on the march. The Municipal Reform and the greater plurality of parties in government have caused dramatic changes in governance at the municipal level in the last ten years. Overall, there has been a sharp increase in real financial resources at the local level, much of it a result of rising direct income; there is also less reliance on the indirect income from the higher levels of government through revenue sharing. Peso for peso, too, cities and large municipalities are getting better value for money by improving public administrative practices through initiatives such as streamlining departments, computerizing management systems, contracting directly with individual households, reducing subsidies, and so on. In addition, they are increasingly seeking to become more transparent, sometimes publishing their financial statements in local newspapers even on a weekly basis. This fiscal transparency has become imperative as they have sought to raise taxes and fees and as people have come to expect better services in return. Above all, municipal presidents have tried to take responsibility for the activities mandated to them by the state and municipal codes and in the Constitution, and less and less have gone cap in hand to the governor.

This newfound partial autonomy derives in large part from the municipalities' decreased dependence on federal revenue-sharing schemes. But it also reflects greater political autonomy between municipal president and governor, unlike the traditional pattern described so well by Fagen and Tuohy in 1972. This rupturing of orthodoxy in intergovernmental relations came about once the PAN, in particular, broke the logjam and entered public office in the 1980s. No longer did municipal presidents have to follow the party line nor were they subject to the directives and whims of the governor. They, and most municipal presidents today, regardless of their political party, are much more pragmatic, recognizing as they do that they have to get the job done if their party is to be reelected. Some governors, too, are actively supporting decentralization as a means of improving the level of public responsiveness and reducing their own need to get involved with the day-to-day running of their municipalities (see Rodríguez and Ward 1994b).

In these respects, therefore, the ideal of the *municipio libre* is beginning to emerge as a reality. These achievements and changes have touched only a relatively small number of municipalities, however, specifically those with significant urban populations. For the remainder, particularly those that did not benefit from Solidarity funding, the ideal has yet to be fulfilled.

7

Retaining Power by Giving It Away: From Reforma Municipal to Solidaridad to Nuevo Federalismo

As I stated at the beginning of this book, *descentralización* has persisted as a key element in the Mexican political discourse of the last fifteen years. Significantly, it has also held a prominent place in the discourse of policy makers, academics, and international organizations, even though when it first began to be seriously promoted in the early 1980s it was received with great skepticism. Given Mexico's enormous centralist tradition and the host of unsuccessful policies for economic and administrative deconcentration, there appeared to be very little hope that anything substantial would be achieved. While it was generally recognized that decentralization was indeed imperative, very few seriously believed that it had a real chance of succeeding and of changing the way things had been done for decades.

In Mexico, as elsewhere, most decentralization programs tended to emphasize administrative, spatial, and economic deconcentration, all of which had been pursued to some extent under Echeverría and López Portillo. The difference in the 1980s was that decentralization began to focus on the Constitution and the federal character of the Mexican system and to emphasize, specifically, the role played by the municipality in the arrangement of intergovernmental relations.

To Centralize by Decentralizing

One of the principal contentions of this book is that the last three presidential administrations—of Miguel de la Madrid, Carlos Salinas de Gortari, and Ernesto Zedillo—have in some guise or other pursued decentralization as a means of holding on to power, although not only for themselves as individuals. Rather, they have wanted to hold on to power to ensure the continuity of their political party, the powers accumulated by the federal executive, and many of the institutions and privileges that sustained the PRI's control of government for more than sixty years.

By 1982, and particularly after the political reforms initiated in 1977, some of these traditions and institutions had become obsolete and the demands for change had become so pressing that, in effect, successive presidents had little choice but to seek ways to redistribute some power and authority. This is especially true of Ernesto Zedillo's administration, which has explicitly made clear that the president is no longer willing to use the metaconstitutional powers associated with the office. In Zedillo's words, "It is my conviction that the president of the republic should not have or exercise any powers other than those explicitly conferred on him by the Constitution and the law . . . the executive branch is not authoritarian and does not benefit from exercising powers not granted by the law" (Presidencia de la República 1996: 22–23).

The various types and modes of decentralization discussed in Chapter 1, ranging from measures to deconcentrate and delegate activities at one end of the spectrum to granting full autonomy to the subordinate unit through devolution at the other end, have been adopted in Mexico by different presidents during the past twenty years. Throughout all of these successive administrations, however, devolution has clearly been the least-desirable option. Nonetheless, the excessive levels of centralism and presidential control had become counterproductive by the late 1970s, generating growing resentment in the periphery toward the center and intensifying political alienation. In part, political reform and opening were designed to counteract that growing resentment and to give the federal government, led by the PRI, greater legitimacy. The need to "let go" in order to hold on to the reins of power also helps explain the trend toward decentralization.

In discussing the various types and modes of decentralization of the last three administrations, we might characterize the de la Madrid government as having advocated devolution, although in practice his initiatives resulted primarily in deconcentration rather than in full devolution. Salinas carried de la Madrid's underlying intent to devolve greater power to the municipalities a step farther through his Solidarity Program, in effect granting local communities an autonomy previously unknown. It is paradoxical, however, that in order to do so he had to strengthen further the control of the center and, more specifically, of the presidency itself. On balance, both presidents made substantial progress toward administrative deconcentration, but stopped short of conceding an effective delegation of powers. Only when pressed by the incipient opposition were they compelled to make any concessions, but even these were discretionary between parties and regions. The willingness to decentralize political power still did not exist.

Thus, whereas Presidents de la Madrid and Salinas could use decentralization because it was politically expedient and because it served as a means to regain some of the regime's lost legitimacy, Zedillo cannot afford the luxury of choosing whether to use it or not. If de la Madrid and Salinas were in a position to centralize by decentralizing, Zedillo's reality is to *survive* by decentralizing. Moreover, for Zedillo decentralization has extended to include not only the lower tiers of government but, more significant, the other branches as well. In addition to strengthening state government, he has reformed the judiciary and encouraged the legislative branch to take a more active role in government. Thus, the paradox of decentralizing in order to hold on to centralized power has taken on different hues and stems from different origins under the three presidents.

For Miguel de la Madrid, part of the paradox is that, while his presidency is often considered gray and unimaginative, he was the one who broke the ground for instituting long-term change in intergovernmental relations, strengthening local government, and bringing autonomy to municipalities. Moreover, he also took the lead in opening the political space for the opposition. The reasons that prompted decentralization during his term were both economic and political. The 1982 economic tailspin into which his predecessor had thrown the country so alienated the private sector elites, particularly in the North, that de la Madrid's first task as president was to restore their confidence and the Mexican public's faith in government. Thus, he began to reprivatize the banks, renegotiate debt repayments, and implement a stabilization package. Politically, too, he started building bridges to restore some of the luster to the government's tarnished legitimacy by recognizing important victories of parties other than his own and by developing a national process of *consultas populares* (popular consultations). The Municipal Reform, requiring as it did little new investment, became the principal means whereby he was able to reach out to the people at the local level and give them greater opportunities for participation in government. It was also the means whereby the federal government began to shift some of the responsibilities for governing back to the states and municipalities. This was the first major attempt at weaning municipalities from their traditional dependence on state and federal government.

As we have seen, these changes laid the groundwork for what were to become profound changes in municipal governance (particularly of cities), although the impetus for change came from the opposition, not the PRI. This break in the PRI's monopoly of local government, combined with the increasing difficulty of sustaining the party's support base and delivering the vote, generated a great deal of resentment and concern within the party leadership. In fact, by 1985 the PRI had successfully trimmed de la Madrid's wings. In return for CTM support for a continuation of the austerity package, particularly after the second series of oil price shocks, the president found himself unable to insist on respect for electoral results and the electoral process in general. Thus, the elections in San Luis Potosí in 1985, and in Chihuahua the following year, resulted in what many analysts consider some of the most flagrant examples of electoral fraud in recent history.

The extent to which de la Madrid was ultimately successful in sustaining centralized control allowed him to get his own way and impose Salinas as his successor. This he did notwithstanding the usual expectancy that one *sexenio*'s imbalances would be redressed in the next, following the traditional swing of the pendulum in Mexican politics. It was also against the wishes of many in the party and in the so-called *corriente democrática* (democratic current); the latter actually broke away from the party when they saw the writing on the wall as a de la Madrid lookalike was chosen to be the next president. In the end, and notwithstanding his adherence to austerity programs throughout, de la Madrid concluded his administration with an invigorated federal executive.

The Salinas paradox is that, while he decentralized extensively, he ended up being one of the most centralizing presidents in modern Mexico. As I have argued in this book, Solidarity was one of the most effective decentralizing forces ever introduced in Mexico, bringing as it did small-scale but significant investment resources to a large number of the most impoverished municipalities and communities. More important, it allowed them to decide among themselves what projects would receive the allotted funding. Salinas also laid the groundwork for a more competitive electoral process and for greater pluralism in government by "recognizing" opposition victories at the state level and in numerous municipalities.

Once again, the reasons for decentralization were both economic and political. Solidarity was designed specifically as a buffer to the neoliberal economic restructuring process on which Salinas had staked Mexico's future, but which was likely to cause further hardship in the poorest communities. Moreover, the so-called lost decade of austerity, declining real wages, and the need to renew the social pact in order to bring down inflation demanded a massive infusion of new social welfare resources effectively targeted at the populations most in need. Politically, too, Salinas needed to restore the legitimacy of the presidency and to win the popular support that had been notable for its absence at the polls during his election in 1988. This he did in a variety of ways: by destroying caciques in some of the more powerful unions; by reforming the electoral process with the COFIPE in 1989 (further amended in 1993 and 1994); by creating the IFE and entirely revamping the electoral register; and by beginning to recast the bases of party organization and mobilization.

Very quickly, and certainly by midterm, Salinas had restored the electoral fortunes of the party and raised his personal popularity to an unprecedentedly high level. Much of this success hinged on his Solidarity Program, which, although until then relatively decentralized, beginning in 1992 was brought more formally under the control of a newly empowered federal ministry, SEDESOL.

Paradoxically, in order to achieve these levels of decentralization of social welfare and to open up the electoral process nationwide, Salinas had to strengthen the centralized powers of the presidency itself. For example, his lack of confidence that state governors would implement and target Solidarity effectively meant that he had to work around and above them; this he did at least until 1992, by which time the battle had been won. In fiscal terms, too, he contracted all states into an agreement to recentralize the IVA and further tightened federal control over revenue sharing. In order to force through his economic and political programs, he was obliged to wield an iron hand and ruthlessly manipulate state governors in and out of power, using in each of these cases his metaconstitutional powers. Whether he was a confirmed decentralizer or not is moot: political pragmatism required that reform be instituted only by presidential fiat from on high.

After Salinas's strengthening of the presidency, what was required was a strong president who would be prepared—and capable—of letting go, someone who would open up the horizontal political space between the three branches as well as decentralize vertically by trusting state governors, increasing the amount and transparency of revenue sharing, and empowering local government—in short, a strong president who could begin to share and divest himself of some of his centralized powers without a loss of authority. Salinas's first choice for successor, Luis Donaldo Colosio, was therefore a good one, since Colosio had proven leadership ability and a strong basis of support and authority within the party. As PRI president from 1989 to 1991, he had set about recasting the party's organizational base, recognizing as he did the need to shift toward a more territorial organizational structure and away from the traditional sectors. More important, he realized that within Mexico's new electoral environment the PRI needed candidates with a local following and credibility who were capable of winning the vote and then doing a good job. No longer could the party's central hierarchy expect to foist its candidates on local constituencies. For legitimacy reasons, too, the boundaries between party and government required clarification. The imperatives of decentralization were clear. In his words, "es la hora de superar la soberbia del centralismo, de apoyar decididamente al municipio; es la hora del nuevo federalismo; es la hora de dotar de mayor poder político y financiero a nuestros estados" (Now is the time to overcome the arrogance of centralism, to fully support the municipality; now is the time for new federalism; now is the time to grant larger political and financial powers to our states) (Morales and Palma 1995: 179).

Colosio's assassination and Zedillo's replacement as candidate meant that these imperatives, now labeled Nuevo Federalismo (New Federalism), would be confronted by someone whose political authority was considerably less well established and who, judging by his past performance, would not exercise strong leadership. Whether it is at all possible in Mexico to *simultaneously* be a strong leader and a weak president is doubtful. It is a question of semantics, however, since Colosio's assassination meant that it was no longer a question of someone strong's being prepared to loosen the reins of power; from the very beginning of his administration, Zedillo's grip was loose anyway. As events have unfolded, it has become obvious that both horizontal and vertical decentralization are occurring, but it is also apparent that this process is coming about because of both the president's willingness to step back *and* the ability of other political actors to articulate their demands effectively.

The challenge for Zedillo, therefore, is to modernize the country and the party in ways that will enable the PRI to hold on to overall power. He, too, began his administration by confronting a legitimacy crisis, in his case born of his being the second-choice candidate, of not having the strong backing of his party, of being heavily dependent on Salinas's popularity at the time, and of not having a team to speak of. Also, when he took over, Mexico was in the throes of political turmoil, with political assassinations allegedly prompted by factions within the party, a judicial system heavily compromised by drug barons, contested election results in two key states, and so on. Instead of closing ranks, Zedillo's response was to distance himself from the party. In the event, as discussed earlier, it was the seriousness of the economic crisis that intensified his need to decentralize by sharing power with the other branches, on the one hand, and with other levels of government, on the other. The PRI's future, it appears, depends heavily on finding ways to institute and promote modernized and "good" government; this is to be achieved, Zedillo hopes, by decentralization.

The Zedillo paradox, therefore, is his apparent willingness to give away power at a time when, because of economic and political crises, the country most requires strong, consolidated leadership. Ultimately, as I will argue, retaining a decisive amount of power will be achieved by giving a share of it away—at least in the first instance.

Vertical and Horizontal Decentralization

While the distribution of powers in a federal system is often referred to as "dual federalism," in the Mexican case I prefer to talk about "vertical and horizontal" structures because it reminds us that what is at stake is the distribution and sharing of powers among three branches as well as among three levels of government. Although in theory this distribution may not be new in Mexico, in practice, all branches and all levels of government have been overshadowed by an overpowering federal executive. As the need to reconsider the distribution of power became more pressing, decentralization was added to the agenda. Discourses on decentralization, however, have overwhelmingly focused on levels, that is, the vertical, and not on branches, that is, the horizontal. The New Federalism agenda, for the first time since the presidency of Benito Juárez, has turned government's attention to the other branches as well. Moreover, the changes occurring in the last few years, and those more likely to continue, demand the implementation and practice of a genuine federated system. What are the dimensions of these changes?

In terms of vertical decentralization, the major changes involve genuine autonomy, which will allow the municipalities and states to undertake and fulfill their mandates. This will require clarification of the duties and obligations of each level as well as a strong financial base to support implementation. Paramount here will be a new pattern of intergovernmental relations, particularly insofar as fiscal issues are concerned. As we saw in Chapters 5 and 6, the revenue-sharing structure currently in place makes inevitable the dependence of each tier on the one above. Both federal-to-state and state-to-municipality methods of revenue sharing need to be substantially revised in order to raise the absolute amount shared and, more important, to remove discretionality by ensuring that clear, transparent criteria are used for calculating the distribution of funds.

But this new arrangement of intergovernmental relations does not depend on the federal government alone. Governors, too, must be willing to become active partners in the sharing of power and to "let go"; as Salinas himself stated, "descentralizar no es crear pequeñas repúblicas" (decentralization doesn't mean creating mini-republics). In Baja California, Governor Ruffo, perhaps because he had been on the receiving end as municipal president of Ensenada, undertook to actively pass on to the municipal level as many functions and responsibilities as feasible. He recognized that there was no good reason for dealing at the state level with many of the day-to-day needs and problems of the municipalities. Having done what he could to make the municipalities financially independent and to ensure the transparency of their basis of funding, he did not seek to interfere in the affairs of his state's municipalities.

The realm of horizontal decentralization is a less familiar one, since there is no tradition of real separation of powers in Mexico; the Mexican system comprises a *sharing* of powers rather than a *separation* of powers. It is unlike the U.S. system, where the structure of checks and balances accompanies the sharing of powers and prevents one branch from controlling another. Moreover, in a vertical sense, states and localities also have far greater independence in the United States. In Mexico, the federal executive has remained firmly in control of the legislative and the judiciary. In spite of the many advances achieved in the legislative branch—increased plurality; having important commissions headed by opposition representatives; heated and articulate debate; and the forging of cross-party alliances in order to have constitutional changes approved and to achieve legitimacy for major pieces of legislation—the executive still dominates. While no longer the rubber-stamping body of the past, under de la Madrid and Salinas the legislative branch was unable to break away and become an independent counterweight to the presidency.

Similarly, the judiciary, until very recently, was entirely captive and dominated by the executive. Not until Zedillo's reforms, instituted at the end of 1994 and intensified during the first two years of his administration, had there been any systematic attempt to revamp this branch. Even here, however, the inspiration has come not from horizontal decentralization and a wish to redistribute and balance powers, but, rather, from a very pressing need to attend to the uncontrolled levels of corruption and the unresolved political assassinations, and to confront the penetration of drug rings into the system. Paradoxically, the latter was the one area where presidential powers seemed incapable of bringing about effective change. Zedillo has taken steps not only to reform the judiciary, but also to cleanse the judicial system and to uphold the rule of law: "My position remains steadfast: on the one hand, respect and support for the independence of the judicial branch; and, on the other, ensuring that the Federal Public Prosecutor's Office, under the Office of the Attorney General of the Republic, acts in strict compliance with the law" (Presidencia de la República 1996: 20). Such is the novelty of these notions in Mexico that the president was obliged to chide the nation: "It is essential for all of us, absolutely everyone, to get used to obeying the law" (Presidencia de la República 1996: 21).

At the local level, state legislatures have traditionally been weak and unable to balance the powers of the local executive. Even where the two levels have been highly conflictual and divisive, the executive has dominated, looking more to the president of the republic for approval than to the locally elected and sovereign chamber of government. As state legislatures are increasingly integrated along pluralist lines, and as representatives themselves become more independent of the governor and national party orthodoxy, so they are likely to play an increasingly important role as an effective counterweight in state affairs, although thus far this is one area of New Federalism that appears to be moving more slowly—certainly much more so than is the case with Congress. In the municipalities, the rough equivalent of the legislative branch is the *cabildo*, but this body has similarly been subordinate and ineffective, limiting its role to little more than rubber-stamping the initiatives of the municipal president. In most municipalities, this tier is so weak and undervalued that it has not mattered terribly much whether the *cabildo* is not a strong counterweight to the municipal president. Indeed, *cabildo* members are even elected on the municipal president's coattails. In large municipalities, however, the absence of a legislative council has become a serious issue, with regard to both legitimizing policy design and implementation and representing the citizenry's interests.

Another important issue here is to create opportunities whereby independent civic groups and individuals at the local level may achieve representation in municipal governance without having to run for office under the label of a registered political party. For the first time, the possibility of running for office as an independent is an item for discussion on the political agenda, although it has been successfully resisted by all three major parties and was not incorporated into the August 1996 electoral reforms.

In the future, however, the dimensions of vertical and horizontal decentralization will have validity only if they occur in an electoral environment that allows and stimulates free, periodic, and open elections. That is the ultimate checks and balances in democratic theory and practice. Without it, all attempts at redistributing power have limited value.

Two Steps Forward, One Step Back

Notwithstanding the important advances in Mexico's decentralization, some significant setbacks have occurred along the way. Indeed, each of the last three presidential administrations has, in essence, taken two steps forward, one step back.

President de la Madrid's decentralization initiatives, particularly the Municipal Reform, may be regarded as the most important contribution to the advancement of decentralization in modern Mexico. Single-handedly, he set in train measures that would strengthen the capacity of municipalities to take on major governance responsibilities. At least for some municipalities, as documented in Chapter 6, the Reform laid the groundwork for the birth of a new type of municipal government in Mexico—one that is less dependent on the higher levels and that is well on its way to fulfilling the *municipio libre* ideals enshrined in the Constitution.

Where the Reform fell short, however, was in failing to intensify implementation during the second half of the *sexenio* for reasons of political expediency. It also fell short insofar as the innovations in many cases were "hijacked" by state governors. Few *priísta* municipal presidents, for example, felt able to take on the newly mandated powers and opportunities, such as raising local taxes, providing basic services, and taking control of the police. To do so would have breached the political loyalty they owed to the governor and to party higher-ups and that continued to be demanded of them. Indeed, given that de la Madrid failed to push more forcefully for the widespread implementation of his reforms and instead allowed the states to take over, suggests that this may very well have been what he anticipated and wanted all along.

Nevertheless, as president during most of the so-called lost decade, de la Madrid's accomplishments in the area of municipal devolution are often also "lost." His *sexenio*, to a large extent, has come to be associated with a host of memorably negative events, including the collapse of oil prices in the world market and the devastating earthquakes in Mexico City in 1985. Nonetheless, while his reforms may be somewhat modest when compared with those of others (not least the highly visible and lustrous Solidarity), his principal merit is to have started down the path for long-term change. Moreover, as president, perhaps his major accomplishment is best encapsulated in a statement he made when asked during a 1992 interview what he considered to be his most significant achievement as president; he reflectively responded, "poder andar entre la gente" (to be able to walk among the people). This ability to walk among the Mexican people, as we know, was a luxury that neither his predecessor nor his successor could afford.

Under Salinas, the principal steps forward in decentralization have already been amply enumerated: Solidarity, targeted at the poorest communities and municipalities; new local leadership structures and civic involvement in the governing process; major and widespread opposition victories, which have also generated new styles and experiences of governance; party reform; and a more equal (if still unfair) electoral environment. Above all, Salinas sought to give back to the states responsibility for problem solving and attending to citizen demands. On one occasion, midway through his *sexenio,* he called on then-*regente* Manuel Camacho to make a major public statement on his behalf explicitly criticizing those governors who were not resolving problems locally and were allowing them to be shipped to Mexico City to stage demonstrations and *plantones* (sit-ins) in the Zócalo. When approached with petitions for public works or services during visits to the states, Salinas would call the governor to his side and ask that the petition be redirected to him, thereby putting the governor on the spot by insisting on a firm commitment and, more specifically, a time frame for project initiation and completion. Salinas also sought to decentralize responsibility to local community groups, often bypassing municipal and state power hierarchies, to the point that there was increasing criticism that Solidarity committees and their like were operating as "parallel governments," given that they, not the municipalities, were the recipients of federal resources. This concern was expressed more overtly once Salinas left office and while the initial blueprint of New Federalism was being drawn. Both municipal presidents and governors were determined to bring this parallel structure back into the formal structure of government.

Ultimately, one cannot be sure just how committed Salinas was to decentralization per se. I have argued in this book that insofar as he was concerned, decentralization was the handmaiden of political and economic liberalization. His big step back was the intensification of centralization in the presidency itself, manifest in his excessive political control and use of metaconstitutional powers, particularly insofar as intervention in the states was concerned (e.g., the removal of governors described earlier). Notwithstanding Solidarity, his administration further concentrated fiscal policies, both in the collection of revenue and in the establishment of parameters governing revenue sharing. It could also be argued that he further concentrated economic power in the private sector through his privatization schemes, which benefited and further enriched a small number of Mexican business empires. There seems little doubt, in retrospect, that in the last months of his *sexenio*, power and ego clouded his judgment and prevented him from taking the necessary steps to achieve a managed devaluation of the peso and arrange for a smooth handover of power to his successor. Also, the alleged involvement of members of his own family in the Ruiz Massieu assassination, as well as their personal enrichment associated with the privatizations and other government-related transactions, has blighted his presidency.

Although only two years have elapsed since Zedillo took office, there have been several major steps forward in implementing the New Federalism agenda. This notwithstanding, the economic crisis has demanded priority and has left many agencies severely underresourced. As I discussed in detail in Chapter 4, Zedillo's New Federalism embraces both the vertical and the horizontal dimensions of decentralization and covers five principal areas of action: first, reforms designed to raise revenue-sharing allocations to the states; second, an expansion of the states' capacity to raise income locally through taxation and other mechanisms; third, the lion's share of funds assigned for regional and social development through Ramo 0026 are now allocated to the states and thus controlled by state governments; fourth, an increase and strengthening of the administrative capacity of municipalities; and fifth, clarification of the distribution of administrative functions among the federal, state, and municipal levels. In addition, substantial progress has been made in the further decentralization of major sectoral areas, namely, education and health. Education has now been decentralized to all of the states and in many cases is now being passed on to the municipal level. Late in 1996, Zedillo had signed agreements with all the states for the completion of the decentralization of health care.

If all of these are implemented, then the course of decentralization will be greatly advanced. We are now beginning to discern, however, the potential reverses. No fewer than four of the measures just outlined are designed to strengthen *state* government rather than the municipality specifically. Ramo 0026 funds to municipalities are increasingly being earmarked by state and federal officials for projects of their choosing, even though these projects are benefiting municipalities first and foremost. Moreover, initial negotiations in the emerging *pacto federal* (federal pact) between states and the federation appear to have clearly placed municipalities in a subordinate position as part of the *régimen interior* (internal government) of each state. As under de la Madrid, the primary beneficiaries of these reforms may very well end up being, once again, the governors, although in this case there is very little pretense that it is otherwise.

What Next?

Notwithstanding the decentralization experiences spanning more than a decade, the numerous programs of the last five presidential administrations described in this book, and the increase of research and academic study on the municipality, there remains a paucity of knowledge on which to base and develop normative theory. In particular, there is an almost total dearth of analysis at the state level, especially important if, as predicted earlier, it is precisely that level that will be affected most by New Federalism. There is an urgent need for new and systematic research initiatives to examine the practices of state governance, intergovernmental relations, intragovernmental relations, transparency of revenue-sharing practices, decision-making procedures, and so on. Each of these areas is crucially important, yet we know precious little about them.

Another area of research that has been so far largely neglected concerns the small and mostly rural municipalities—still the majority of the 2,412 municipalities in Mexico. These municipalities remain grossly underfunded and dependent on higher levels. Because their population is spread across many small and medium-sized communities around the *cabecera municipal* (municipal seat of government) and their possibilities for generating their own revenues are limited or nonexistent, any effort to meet their specific needs requires systematic study and sensitive incorporation into a genuinely federalist agenda. To date, it has been almost exclusively the larger urban municipalities that have been the focus of attention and modernization. In these latter cases, there has been a dramatic improvement in administrative capacity and performance, particularly since 1989; for them at least, the Municipal Reform has amply fulfilled its objectives.

The fifth goal on the New Federalism agenda is clarification of the responsibilities of all levels (federal, state, and municipal). Here, too, there is a need for further research and imagination in identifying who is responsible for what, and how higher levels may support lower ones without infringing on their sovereignty. In particular, greater objectivity and understanding are required by higher-level officials about the institutional capacity of the lower levels to govern themselves. Sophisticated techniques of cost-benefit analysis, budgeting, and general management are not required; what is needed is a strengthening of the assistance linkages that the higher levels can offer in areas such as fiscal reform; providing training expertise that will allow employees to build capacity locally; creating incentives to promote a career civil service; and instituting simple and transparent accounting procedures. One immediate way to achieve this would be to allow reelection of municipal presidents. Currently, they are barely beginning to understand the requirements of the job when their three years in office are up. The no-reelection clause not only makes difficult any policy continuity but, more important, also prevents the building of institutional capacity. It also reduces the incentive to do a good job.

Similarly, from the horizontal perspective, changing the law to allow for reelection of state and federal deputies would have much to recommend it. Since 1934, deputies have not been allowed to be reelected for consecutive terms—an initiative deliberately designed to *prevent* independent development of a constituency that might distract from party loyalty. Now it is precisely more concern and activity for their constituency that is demanded of representatives, but without the possibility of reelection, there remains little incentive.

As is the case with Congress, state legislatures need to be empowered and to grow into their responsibilities for co-governance. To date, their role has been one of occasionally challenging the executive and approving municipal budgets. All too often they have become embroiled in political conflicts with municipalities, particularly those governed by a different political party. Indeed, in many states the nature of intergovernmental relations remains antagonistic rather than cooperative.

What does all this add up to? In essence, Mexico might benefit most from seeking to develop a cooperative federalism based on mutually supportive intergovernmental relations between levels and effective co-governance between branches, rather than an autonomous federalism that emphasizes sovereignty and individuality. Although not federalism in the truest sense, in practice it could prove to be a good, solid, working federalism. In short, it would be another version of federalism *a la mexicana*, but one in which the various levels of government help each other out rather than attempting to undermine and outdo the others. Horizontally, too, the respective branches of government would bear responsibility for providing a greater counterbalance to executive powers. Federal cooperation in this context of clarification of responsibilities would be a "nesting" of activities, where each level would have a clear understanding of what it ought to be doing—and would take responsibility for it. Such a system of federal cooperation, instead of fostering conflict, would serve as a framework for conflict resolution, recognizing that all conflicts must be dealt with individually according to particular circumstances and cannot be resolved by following a single blueprint elaborated in Mexico City.

Ultimately, successful decentralization in Mexico requires that the concepts of devolution, empowerment, and accountability become reality. The New Federalism agenda promises to go some way toward that reality, but whether the full meaning embedded in those terms will be realized is uncertain. Thus far, for the first time in the transition from Reforma Municipal to Solidaridad to Nuevo Federalismo, we appear to be on the threshold of a genuine process of decentralization.

Notes

Chapter 1

1. Although technically the Municipal Reform began in 1984, it is commonly referred to as "the Reform of '83" because it was approved by Congress on February 3, 1983. Even though in other places I have referred to it as the Reform of 1984, in this book I will refer to it as the Reform of 1983.

2. For a detailed discussion of the Reform, see Martínez Assad and Ziccardi (1989), Rodríguez (1992), and Chapter 4 in this volume.

3. See, for example, Cornelius, Craig, and Fox (1994) for different interpretations of the program's outcomes.

4. See Wolman (1990: 30) for a discussion of the public choice justification for decentralization.

5. In Mexico, the Aztecs built the foundation for a strong centralist state. By 1519, Tenochtitlán, the area now occupied by Mexico City, had an estimated population of 300,000, organized in small states and governed by lords and high priests. Society was rigidly stratified according to class; there was a nobility, a peasantry, and a rather authoritarian state. The center held firm political and administrative control and dominated all economic activity. The state also had absolute control over the distribution and exploitation of land, water usage, and the labor force, which enabled it to control all the means of production. Overall, Tenochtitlán was a sophisticated urban center that efficiently provided its inhabitants with potable water, street cleaning, police protection, and building maintenance.

6. One of the most ambitious and controversial contemporary decentralization programs is France's, initiated under Mitterrand.

7. All translations are mine unless otherwise noted.

8. It should be noted, however, that most of the literature on decentralization focuses on administrative decentralization.

9. Although various typologies for decentralization have been developed in the literature, the most widely used is based on the work of Rondinelli and his collaborators. See especially 1981, 1989, 1990; Cheema and Rondinelli (1983); Rondinelli and Nellis (1986). See also Ashford (1976), Bennett (1990), Conyers (1983), Maddick (1963), Silverman (1992).

10. The debate is nothing new and, in fact, neither is the concept itself. Even a cursory examination of the literature will provide abundant examples of the implementation of decentralization in ancient times. If anything, the scholarly discussion on the topic gained increased attention beginning in the eighteenth century. Starting in the late 1950s, as Conyers (1983) documents, decentralization became "the latest fashion."

11. The literature on privatization has grown dramatically in the last few years. One particularly useful source is Savas (1987). See also Ramamurti (1996) and Roth (1987).

12. Although Rondinelli refers to these modes as *degrees* of decentralization, they can also be applied when referring to other *types* of decentralization. For this reason, I have chosen to refer to them in the broader sense. Moreover, no matter how clear the theoretical distinctions may appear to be, all types of decentralization are interrelated. For instance, almost any student of development would argue that it would not be very useful to have political decentralization if it did not translate into some improvement in the population's standard of living through economic decentralization. Similarly, the overall purpose of administrative decentralization should be to produce more balanced regional development; if a region's development is to be complete, some sort of cultural decentralization should also evolve. See Silverman (1992) for further discussion of two additional forms of decentralization: bottom-up and top-down agencies.

13. Curiously, just as there is no accurate translation for devolution, neither is there an appropriate Spanish word for two other terms that are critical for effective local government: empowerment and accountability. *Empoderamiento* and *rendir cuentas,* like *devolver,* do not really convey the meaning—and relevance—of these terms.

Chapter 2

1. Centralism existed to the extent that the individual provinces of the new country were accountable to the central government in Spain, but operated within a federal system in the sense that the provinces were independent of one another; i.e., no one province had control over any other.

2. For a thorough discussion of centralism in Latin America, see Véliz (1980).

3. The 1821 discourse is especially illustrative for today's debates about the desirability of creating a new federalism in Mexico restoring the paramountcy of the regions over the center, and for the issues of separation of powers discussed in the remainder of this chapter: "En lo que refiere al escenario político, se encontraba un gobierno con pretensiones nacionales y que vivía con particular efervescencia, la beligerancia de los intereses locales y regionales, que buscaban impulsar un proyecto político que les permitiera mantener un control sobre su territorio con la menor ingerencia del centro, y que se justificaba dado 'que en un país tan vasto, con clima y condiciones diferentes, era imposible hacer frente a las necesidades provinciales con leyes uniformes', además se 'sostenía que únicamente los funcionarios locales podían entender los problemas regionales'"(With respect to the political scenario, there was a government with national pretensions that lived with particular effervescence the belligerence of local and regional interests, which sought to promote a political project that allowed them to maintain control over their own territory without the slightest interference from the center, justifying it under the premise that "in a country so vast, with different weather and conditions, it was impossible to confront the provincial needs with uniform laws," in addition to the fact that "only local officials could understand regional problems")(Gortari 1996: 212).

4. It is important to note that separation of powers and checks and balances are separate ideas, both theoretically and practically. The Constitutions of both Mexico and the United States, however, call for three separate branches of government (executive, legislative, and judicial) to share power. This is distinct from European parliamentary systems, in which the executive and legislative branches are fused and where the three branches often perform differentiated functions (see Huntington 1968). A system of fused powers (i.e., functions) requires checks and balances to protect against the tyranny of one branch. Moreover, Mexico and the United States are federalist systems, constitutionally based on popular sovereignty.

Political accountability is, therefore, more difficult and requires an active system of checks and balances. While the idea of checks-and-balances is often viewed as a distinctively American innovation, the constitutional structures of Mexico and the United States are sufficiently similar to merit discussion of the need for checks and balances in the Mexican political context.

5. This is one alternative; another is for the aggrieved group to withdraw local party support for the nominee and for the disaffected candidate to run as an independent (sometimes successfully).

6. In 1989, Ernesto Ruffo Appel became the first member of the opposition PAN to win a gubernatorial election. In 1992, Chihuahua became the second state to be governed by the PAN as a result of an electoral contest. The state of Guanajuato was also governed by the PAN, but that was on an interim basis and a result of a different type of political negotiation. In the 1995 elections, Jalisco, Guanajuato, and Baja California were won by the PAN.

7. The figure of the president so permeates the entire system with his policy preferences that the whole government seems to be speaking through one voice. The decision making of the political elite is extremely sensitive to the president's initiatives because following his wishes promotes career advancement.

8. The *camarilla* system is one of the most difficult and inaccessible concepts of the Mexican system, particularly for foreigners. Even for Mexicans, it is something that is learned gradually through personal experiences. Basically, a *camarilla* is a patron-client relationship in which the patron, who has high political status, provides benefits and the opportunity for upward mobility to his or her clients in exchange for loyalty and political support. The supreme patron is the president; when a new president assumes power he brings into high office his most loyal followers, i.e., the members of his *camarilla*, who in turn bring their own followers, and so on all the way down the system. Most of the political conflict within the system is related to the struggle between rival *camarillas*, especially those at the top, which form around presidential prospects in the last years of a *sexenio*. These vertical chains of politicians are assembled over a long period and an elaborate process of alliance building and are bound together by personal loyalties rather than ideologies. For an extensive (and classic) discussion of the *camarilla* system, see Smith (1979).

9. Traditionally, personal contacts have been much preferable to the use of demonstrations or violence. See Stevens (1974: 94) on this point. For an analysis of nonviolent strategies used by urban migrants in Mexico City, see Cornelius (1975). See also Bennett (1995), Eckstein (1988), Montaño (1976), Varley (1989, 1993).

10. Many would contend that this is still the practice even with the governors of the opposition. Allegedly, the first three *panista* governors (Ruffo, Barrio, and Medina Plascencia), in different ways and for different reasons, arrived at their governorships with Salinas's blessing.

11. For example, *panistas* Francisco Barrio in Ciudad Juárez in 1983 and Rogelio Sada in San Pedro in 1991. We have also found evidence of "new PRI" municipal presidents doing the same (Rodríguez and Ward, 1992; Ward 1996).

12. The role played by these local political bosses has been critical for the electoral success of the PRI—in the past, at least—given their ability to effectively provide PRI candidates with the support of the urban workers and peasants they control in exchange for personal favors. This system of patronage mediated through governance cemented the PRI's grip on power for decades.

13. For the opposition municipal presidents, the position of municipal president quite often represents not only an important victory for their party and themselves but often, also,

the end of the road as far as their political career is concerned. For *priístas,* on the other hand, being municipal president often serves as a stepping-stone to higher political office.

14. Some states have no *síndicos* whatsoever. In the state of Chihuahua, for instance, the two most important commissions (Gobernación [Governance] and Hacienda [Finance]), whose functions would usually be carried out by *síndicos,* are replaced by two additional *regidores.*

15. These various methods of election to office represent a serious flaw and undermine any separation of powers between the executive and the collegial body of the *cabildo.* If, in the future, there is to be an effective separation of party and government at the *ayuntamiento* level, then independence of the *cabildo* should not be left to chance, but should be legislated for by having members elected in their own right (i.e., not as one of an "all or nothing" slate tied to the candidate for municipal president). Additionally, all or some *regidores* might be chosen to stand as representatives for different geographic entities within the municipality. This would resemble the election of city council members by district in the United States.

16. "El municipio es concebido como la escuela básica de la democracia en México, por ser la institución política que tiene más contacto con el pueblo. Democracia se entiende como la participación del pueblo en las decisiones que le afecte; es un sistema de vida fundado en el constante mejoramiento económico, social y cultural del pueblo" (The municipality is considered the basic school for democracy in Mexico, given that it is the political institution that has more direct contact with the people. Democracy is understood as the people's participation in decisions that affect them; it is a life system founded on the constant economic, social, and cultural improvement of the people) (Ochoa Campos 1986: 136).

17. The argument has been made, indeed, that in the past the masses were sometimes mobilized by the regime itself in an effort to make the revolutionary goal of "social justice" more believable. This mobilization occurred especially when resources were available to be distributed, but was firmly discouraged when resources became insufficient or when the demands placed on the system endangered its stability (or, for that matter, the power or position of a politician). Formerly, the PRI served as one of the primary instruments for mobilization and control. For further discussion of the party's role in this regard, see Anderson and Cockroft (1966), Brandenburg (1964), Hansen (1974), Padgett (1966).

18. For an extensive discussion of *sexenio* turnover and of the *camarilla* system, see Smith (1979). *Sexenio* turnover is so great because at the beginning of each administration all high-level officials are replaced, and all replacements bring with them their own subordinates (members of their own teams, or *camarillas*). Broadly speaking, the six years in office are employed as follows. The first two years are dedicated to the formation and coordination of teams and to breaking ties with predecessors, as well as to securing finances for implementing favorite programs. This implementation takes places during the third, fourth, and fifth years. The fifth year is also devoted to forming close alliances with those who are likely to figure in the coming administration. The sixth year, once the new presidential candidate is unveiled, is for strengthening the ties formed during the previous year, especially if the official in question had the vision to associate with the right *camarilla.* During this last year, few new projects are initiated.

Chapter 3

1. For various interpretations of the authoritarian nature of Mexico's political system, see Centeno (1994), Cornelius, Gentleman, and Smith (1989), Garrido (1993), Grindle (1977),

Harvey (1989), Molinar Horcasitas (1991), Purcell (1975), Purcell and Purcell (1980), Reyna and Weinert (1977), Roett (1993), R. Scott (1959), Smith (1979), Teichman (1988).

2. The Mexican "economic miracle" refers to the period beginning in 1940, when the country sustained an annual economic growth rate of 6 percent or more, coupled with low inflation and political stability. The miracle ended abruptly in the 1970s (Hansen 1974). Yet, Mexico has managed to maintain its position as one of the fifteen largest economies in the world.

3. Indeed, as corrupt government officials have become increasingly tied to Mexican and other Latin American drug rings, and as the *narcos* have more openly interfered in political affairs, this more open corruption has led many analysts to foresee the making of a new Colombia in Mexico.

4. For an academic analysis of the government's response to the earthquakes, see the special issue of the *Revista Mexicana de Ciencias Políticas y Sociales*, no. 123 (1986).

5. For a thorough review of economic policy from the early 1980s on, see Jones, Jiménez, and Ward (1993). In their analysis of land market investment opportunities and returns, they track economic and stock exchange performance throughout the de la Madrid and Salinas administrations, focusing on the upturn in the economy and the dynamics of the real estate market and land values.

6. Of course, there have also been occasions to suspect the use of fraud to prevent opposition candidates from winning office. Specifically, many Mexicans believe that the opposition candidate won the presidential election in 1929, 1940, and 1988 (Camp 1993:62). Similarly, others have argued that at various times in the recent past, opposition candidates were denied the governorships of the states of San Luis Potosí, Chihuahua, and Baja California Norte (see Aziz 1987; Bezdek 1995; Guillén López 1993). There are many more examples when it comes to municipal victories that have not been recognized.

7. Cárdenas, a former governor of Michoacán, is the son of President Lázaro Cárdenas (1934–1940), who was enormously popular. Indeed, it has been argued that one of the major reasons why Cárdenas did so well in 1988 was name recognition, particularly in the rural areas, where his father was a most beloved figure. Clouthier was a well-known businessman from the state of Sinaloa who provided the PAN with real charismatic leadership. Eventually the Frente disappeared and provided the foundation for the creation of a new political party, the Partido de la Revolución Democrática (Party of the Democratic Revolution, PRD).

8. The last two organizations overlap somewhat; each incorporates a host of NGOs whose concern is to develop and protect citizens' rights, protect the vote, encourage awareness of political and electoral rights, etc.

9. The most important achievement of the reforms of the 1960s was the establishment of the system of proportional representation. The 1963 reforms allowed for the representation of parties obtaining a minimum of 2.5 percent of the national vote. Five congressional seats were to be assigned for the first 2.5 percent of the national vote obtained, and an additional seat for every additional half percent of the vote obtained. However, a twenty-seat cap was placed on the opposition's representation, which demonstrates the limited reach of the reform. In fact, seats were also given to the PARM and the PPS (both parties closely associated with the PRI), even though neither one of them obtained the required 2.5 percent of the national vote. This in effect inflated the congressional representation of these parties vis-à-vis their electoral proportions and, more significantly, gave the PRI an unquestioned majority (Favela 1992; Klessner 1991; Molinar 1986). The constrained nature of the reform was especially relevant for the PAN; although it continued to increase its vote at the national level, the

twenty-seat cap on any non-PRI party kept the PAN's proportional representation within the Chamber of Deputies to below 10 percent (Mabry 1974). The 1972 reforms lowered the total vote threshold from 2.5 percent to 1.5 percent, and the twenty-seat cap for opposition parties was raised to twenty-five.

10. In Mexico, as in the United States, federal legislative power is divided into two houses: in Mexico the lower house is the Chamber of Deputies; the upper house is the Senate. Elections are held at staggered intervals for all three levels of government: federal, state, and municipal. State and federal representatives (*diputados*) serve three years, senators for six.

11. The principle of *representación mayoritaria* (majority representation) formed the basis for the election of representatives to the so-called *uninominal* elected offices, such as the president, governors, senators, three hundred federal deputies, and a number of state deputies, determined by each state's constitution. In some municipalities the same principle applies to the election of the municipal president, *síndicos*, and *regidores*. The principle of *representación proporcional* (proportional representation) was designed to enable more members of the opposition to hold public office. This made possible the election of representatives to positions referred to as *plurinominal*, comprising one hundred federal deputies, a number of state deputies (again determined by each state's constitution), and a proportion of *regidores* in each *ayuntamiento*. In 1988, there were 1,314 *regidores* from opposition parties in local government (SPP 1988). That number has increased dramatically in subsequent elections as the PAN and the PRD now govern over one third of Mexico's population.

12. Opposition parties now had 100 of the then 400 seats. These *plurinominal* seats were to be distributed on the basis of proportional representation to the qualifying minority parties. The remaining 75 percent of the congressional seats would be determined on the basis of the official electoral returns from the single-member districts, the *uninominal* seats. A second outcome of the 1977 reforms was to facilitate the formation of new (but small) parties at the regional or national level, thus potentially fragmenting the political opposition further.

13. The series of reforms for increasing the opposition's representation described here clearly illustrate that the PRI has not been willing to make changes that would lead to its losing overall control of the electoral process. The PRI had a majority on both the Electoral Commission and the Electoral Tribunal and, at that time, the commission chair, the secretary of Gobernación, had both vote and, if necessary, tie-breaking vote.

14. For an in-depth analysis of the 1994 election from various perspectives, see Ward et al. 1994.

15. The PRI wanted a proviso that the opposition had to receive "a respectable proportion of the vote" and suggested a threshold of 25 percent, eventually to be reduced to 0 percent (i.e., no threshold). Tactically, this is very clever, since it reduces the likelihood of PAN-PRD coalition candidates. Each party will want to compete for the fourth senatorial spot. Even where the PRI loses the direct elections in a state, it could always expect to come in second, and thus it is almost certain to enjoy a large majority in the Senate.

16. Since 1992, no party has been permitted to obtain more than 63 percent of the seats in Congress. Therefore, any party wishing to propose constitutional changes will have to build an agreement with another party.

17. This is obviously aimed at the PRI, whose party symbol uses the colors and alignment in identical configuration to those of the national flag and to government programs like Solidarity, which also incorporate them into their logo. For more on this conflation of PRI-government nationalism, see Rodríguez and Ward (1994b). It seems likely that in the long run this will also be conceded by the PRI, but only after it has been able to educate and wean

its traditional followership into recognizing a new set of colors. Obviously, this change was not one it felt able to undertake within twelve months.

18. The extension of proportional representation to the state and municipal levels came as part of the 1977 and 1986 reforms described earlier. Formulas, however, vary from state to state. Each legislature determines the distribution of party representation in state and municipal government. These statewide formulas generally set minimum percentages of the popular vote that must be obtained, and may exclude parties that win single-district elections. In some cases, all parties are included in the distribution of proportional (*plurinominal*) seats.

19. Although, naturally, all these negotiations are secret, the general interpretation is that the PRI and the PAN have reached a modus operandi whereby the PRI is willing to let electoral results stand in some places in exchange for social tranquillity in other elections and in other places. Only in this way can one explain cases that seem rather bizarre. In the 1993 election in Baja California Sur, for example, the PAN won a majority in the congressional elections and took several of the leading cities, yet lost the governorship. The losing gubernatorial candidate, outraged, declared openly that his defeat had been traded by the PAN party leadership against victories elsewhere; thus, he affirmed, the PAN was allowed to keep the congressional seats and the municipal governments in exchange for the PRI's keeping the governorship.

20. A third state, Guanajuato, was also governed by a *panista*, but he was an interim governor placed in office by President Salinas. Carlos Medina Plascencia was not even a candidate in the 1991 gubernatorial elections in that state; he came into the position only because the PRI candidate's electoral conduct had been discredited and President Salinas wished to make a conciliatory gesture to the PAN. Even among *panistas* his governorship was seen as lacking in legitimacy. Elsewhere, doubts over the conduct of elections or postelection civil disturbance obliged President Salinas to remove or withdraw successful candidates, even though, in theory, under state constitutions, only the state legislature can remove a governor and designate an interim governor. In this way, the PAN was given its third governorship, of Guanajuato. In other notable cases, such as Tabasco, San Luis Potosí, and Michoacán, interim PRI governors were installed.

21. The *dedazo,* or "fingering," is the process by which the outgoing president selects his successor by "pointing" at him

Chapter 4

1. See SEDESOL (1992) for a complete description of this program.

2. Netzahualcóyotl comprises several low-income (self-help) neighborhoods that formed in the eastern part of Mexico City during the 1960s. Netzahualcóyotl currently has a total population of 1.3 million. In the 1996 election, the PRD candidate for municipal president won, making Netzahualcóyotl the largest city held by that party. Partly because of the continued investment in social infrastructure in Chalco, the PRI retained control there in the 1996 election.

3. The programs explicitly intended to support regional development and economic decentralization were divided into three general categories: those oriented to rural areas, those aimed at urban areas, and those that included both rural and urban areas. Rural programs, in addition to PIDER, included a National Plan for New Ejido Centers; urban programs included two important presidential decrees about industrial decentralization issued on November 23, 1971, and July 20, 1972, in addition to the Lázaro Cárdenas and twin-plant pro-

grams; the urban-rural programs included the Program for the Economic Development of the Border, and the Coordinating Commissions for the Development of the Isthmus of Tehuantepec and the Peninsula of Baja California. For more information on the Echeverría administration's regional development policy, see Rébora (1978) and Unikel (1975).

4. In 1976 a series of important reforms were made to the Constitution relating to human settlements policies and the municipality's participation in this matter. These reforms empowered municipalities to propose laws and regulations concerning the problems of urban administration and human settlements; in addition, municipalities were to participate with the state and federal governments in planning and regulating all population centers. These constitutional reforms became the basis for the Law of Human Settlements, in which the municipality played a most important role. For a detailed account of the changes in the constitutional provisions dealing with municipalities, particularly in Article 115, see Valadés Ríos (1985).

5. The main objectives of the PNDU were "to rationalize population distribution and the distribution of economic activities throughout Mexican territory; to promote integrated and balanced urban development; to favor conditions allowing the population to satisfy its needs for urban land, housing, public services, and urban infrastructure and facilities; and to improve and preserve the environment of such human settlements" (*Comercio Exterior* December 1978: 494).

6. As Merilee Grindle (1981: 37–38) concludes, "partisans of the two programs continually sniped at each other. According to followers of COPLAMAR, it had fallen heir to PIDER's original functions which PIDER was not able to carry out. Partisans of PIDER questioned the integrated nature of COPLAMAR's activities and decried its lack of attention to productive activities. In both cases, these tensions inhibited cooperative activity." In addition, even if PIDER was the most comprehensive effort of the Echeverría administration for regional-rural areas, it was ineffective because occasionally it applied incompatible investment criteria; for instance, financial resources were often allocated to those areas where serious manifestations of social protest occurred, even if those areas were unproductive; preference was frequently given to irrigation areas where the highest yields were assured; or PIDER simply gave in to the World Bank's pressures to grant loans to seasonal zones. COPLAMAR hoped to correct some of those problems.

7. Well over a dozen such programs were designed under elaborate names and with equally elaborate objectives. For a description of the content of these programs, see *Comercio Exterior* (December 1978): 496–499.

8. In a speech at the unveiling of the Global Plan, de la Madrid stated that "efforts will be made to control the excessive growth of the largest cities, to strengthen the cities of intermediate size, and to give a boost to those on the coast and in the border zones. This scheme of spatial distribution seeks to achieve more balanced regional development, to reinforce the federal pact" (*Comercio Exterior* 25, no. 11 [November 1979]: 195). De la Madrid's speech reflects the plan's concern with urbanization and gives an early indication of his concern with decentralization.

9. The plan called for an annual increase of 20 percent in regional funds to be channeled through both PIDER and COPLAMAR as well as the Convenios Únicos de Coordinación (Coordination Agreements, or CUCs, the predecessors of de la Madrid's Convenios Únicos de Desarrollo [Development Agreements, CUDs] and Salinas's Convenios de Desarrollo Social [Social Development Agreements, CDSs]), and an overall annual increase of 11 percent in the expenditures of all state enterprises. The revenues from petroleum exports would pro-

vide part of the funds. The plan also called for rationalization of purchases, wiping out corruptive practices, ending the excessive fragmentation of public works, integrating federalism with strong state planning, and increased efficiency through program budgeting mechanisms (SPP 1980: 28–29).

10. With the exception of the *maquiladora* border industrialization program, which increased substantially during the 1980s (Sklair 1989), most industry continued to locate in and around the major metropolitan areas in order to enjoy the agglomeration economies therein and the large markets they represented. Only until substantial industrial restructuring began in order to feed a global market (i.e., post-1986) did new industrial location imperatives emerge, stimulating the growth of intermediate-sized cities and strengthening decentralization and social policy initiatives.

11. For example, between 1970 and 1975 alone, the percentage of industrial establishments in the Federal District and the state of Mexico increased from 32.2 percent to 34.9 percent, the economically active industrial population from 45.6 percent to 46.7 percent, and the manufacturing production from 50.6 percent to 52.1 percent. The population of the metropolitan area of Mexico City increased at an estimated rate of 5.5 percent annually, which means that a population of 8.8 million in 1970 jumped to 11.5 million in 1975 (SPP 1978; Unikel and de la Peña 1976). Many other indicators also illustrate this point; for instance, the twin-plant program, whose purpose was to support regional industrial development, stipulated that these plants could not be located in areas of high industrial concentration, yet over 50 percent of the 107 twin plants registered in the program between 1972 and 1975 were located in or near the three largest metropolitan areas (Cardiel 1976).

12. See SPP (1983). A more detailed discussion of his decentralization efforts can be found in SPP 1984: 89–98.

13. The predecessor to this program was the Programa Nacional de Descentralización Administrativa (National Program for Administrative Decentralization), formulated after the Ley Orgánica de la Administración Pública Federal (the comprehensive legal code of the federal government) was revised on December 29, 1982. The 1984 general decentralization program included the widely publicized Programa de Simplificación Administrativa (Program for Administrative Simplification), designed to eliminate, or at least to reduce, red tape. The program also sought to provide the public with easier access to the services of federal agencies.

14. For example, the Comisión Nacional de Zonas Áridas (National Commission for Arid Zones) was relocated in Saltillo, Coahuila; the Centro Nacional de Investigaciones Agrarias (National Center for Agrarian Research) moved to Cuernavaca, Morelos; the Centro Regional de Investigaciones e Infraestructura Hidráulica (Regional Center for Hydraulic Research and Infrastructure) to the capital of Tlaxcala; the administrative offices of the Empresa Nuevo Vallarta to Puerto Vallarta, Jalisco; and the Centro Internacional de Adiestramiento de Aviación Civil (International Center for Civil Aviation Training) to Santa Lucía in the state of Mexico. These are only some of the programs designated for relocation. One of the more widely publicized and successfully relocated institutions was the Instituto Nacional de Estadística, Geografía e Informática (National Institute for Statistics, Geography, and Information, INEGI) to Aguascalientes, where it is still located.

15. For varying perspectives on the government's responses to the earthquakes, see the special issue of the *Revista Mexicana de Ciencias Políticas y Sociales* (January–March 1986), entitled "Desastre y Reconstrucción."

16. For the decentralization of these sectors, see, for example, Reyes (1986), González Block et al. (1989), Jeannetti Dávila (1986), Street (1984). The Ministry of Health also pub-

lished a series of five volumes entitled *Cuadernos de Descentralización* (1985), which discuss in detail the sector's decentralization policies and programs.

17. The DIF itself embarked on a very successful decentralization program, which also provided large political payoffs. At the beginning of de la Madrid's presidency only the national DIF and several state DIFs existed, with none at the municipal level; by the end of his term, 1,838 municipal DIFs had been created. For a detailed discussion of the DIF's decentralization, see Daigle (1995), Rodríguez (1987).

18. Within each CUD five major programs were subsumed, including PIDER, the Programas Estatales de Inversión (State Investment Programs, or PEI), the Programa de Atención a Zonas Marginadas (Program for Marginalized Areas, or PAZM), the Programas Sectoriales Concertados (Sectoral Programs, or PROSEC), and the Programas de Desarrollo Estatal (State Development Programs, or PRODES). The implementation of these CUD programs met with varying success.

19. The PDR was specifically charged with administering three programs: the Programa de Infraestructura Básica de Apoyo (Program of Basic Infrastructure, or PIBA), to provide services such as electricity, telephones, and roads; the Programa de Infraestructura para el Desarrollo (Program of Development Infrastructure, or PID), to provide rural and urban communities with nutritional, medical, social security, housing, and educational services; and the Programa Productivo (Productive Program) to develop self-sufficiency in rural areas through the provision of supplies and basic needs.

20. The *calpulli* was the Aztecs' system of social and political community administration and is the first sketch of municipal government in Mexico. *Calpullis* were somewhat similar to today's municipalities in that they covered a population in a specified territory and had a group of public officials charged with maintaining order. They were efficient and well-organized institutions that endured until the early colonial period.

21. The argument of promoting decentralization as a measure to increase responsiveness to local needs and conditions is well documented in the literature. Cohen et al., for instance, emphasize that "decentralization aims at making the government more responsive to the varying needs and preferences of the population" (1981: 36), and that "decentralization may improve the application of general, national plans to local areas because they can be implemented in a way that specifically reflects local conditions" (1981: 41). Similarly, Rondinelli (1981) argues that governments are able to perform more efficiently if they have a clear understanding of varying local conditions, and that such understanding can be obtained only at the local level. See also Bennett (1990), Cheema and Rondinelli (1983).

22. The precise origins of the term, or why it was selected, are ambiguous. Obviously, the term lends itself well to the idea of solidarity between government and the governed and has been used in this capacity by representatives of different parties at various points in time; the PAN argues that it was the first to use it, while others recall that in 1982 López Portillo called for solidarity to confront the crisis. Also important was its association with the Polish workers' movement, Solidarnosc, which established a solid link between working classes and drew world attention.

23. In part this was because Salinas did not trust many of the governors' willingness to disburse resources to these groups, particularly in those states where the groups were sympathetic to the opposition or were not well disposed to the governor. Salinas realized that the negative impact of both austerity and the restructuring program on which he had embarked would need to be cushioned by an effective antipoverty program. He could not afford any

margin of error from recalcitrant governors. Subsequently, many of these governors were removed from office.

24. The evidence indicates, however, that PRONASOL never reached even 20 percent of federal spending, as will be shown in Chapter 5.

25. The CUD became CDS in 1992, but still served as the coordinating mechanism for planning intergovernmental programs and investment. The only visible difference is that the CDS emphasized the links between planning and social development and incorporated the funding for carrying out these policies through Ramo 0026. The COPLADEs have had no changes in their composition and functions since 1983.

26. The Programa Nacional de Desarrollo Urbano 1995–2000 developed from a background of growing deregulation and insertion into a global economy. The basic premises of the program are the following: (1) interrelation of economic and urban development; (2) interrelation of planning and investment; (3) economic efficiency with equity; (4) federalism and decentralization; (5) public (social) participation in urban development; (6) coordination and assistance in regional projects; and (7) sustainability of urban development. Numbers 4, 5, and 7 are notable and substantially new in the document when compared to their predecessors. The program offers four strategic programs: (1) 100 Cities; (2) Consolidation of Metropolitan Zones; (3) Territorial Planning and Promotion of Urban Development; and (4) Program to Promote Public Participation in Urban Development (SEDESOL 1996).

Chapter 5

1. As defined by Reagan and Sanzone, "Categorical grants are by and large intended for specifically and narrowly defined purposes, leaving very little discretionary room on the part of a recipient government. Block grants . . . are broader in scope, and although tied to a clearly stated area (such as health, social services, or community development), they do not specify the exact subjects of permitted expenditure and hence create much larger zones of discretion on the part of the receiving government or agency" (1981: 57).

2. The main reason for the reform of 1990 was that total revenue from the IVA, which since 1983 had been collected by the states, had declined consistently. As tax evasion increased, IVA collection fell by 50 percent. Indeed, the revenue-sharing system had been reformed in 1983 precisely in order to transfer to the states the collection of the IVA. While collection at the local level generated great liquidity for the states, it had an adverse effect on the central government, mostly because the states would send to Mexico City only what remained after they deducted what they thought was owed them in *participaciones*. Inadvertently, a genuine system of decentralization had been created. The 1990 reform reinstated the collection of the IVA to the federal government. Many states, particularly those with more efficient taxation systems, continuously demand that the collection of the IVA be returned to them.

3. INDETEC is located in Guadalajara and assists states and municipalities in all matters pertaining to public finance, particularly fiscal issues. Among its activities, it conducts training workshops and seminars for municipal presidents and their financial administration personnel. For the most part, these workshops are conducted throughout the country, rather than in Guadalajara alone, have an average duration of nine weeks, and bring together various municipal officials of the region where the workshop takes place. It has a rather impres-

sive list of publications and also produces a bimonthly magazine (*Revista INDETEC*) with timely and informative articles.

4. Federal taxes included in the FGP, as determined by the LCF, are the IVA, the income tax, and the *impuesto especial sobre producción y servicios* (tax on liquor, beer, gasoline, and tobacco), among others. Of these taxes, the IVA and the income tax are the strongest in monetary terms, but the tax on liquor, beer, gasoline, and tobacco is more significant in that it is the one that determines how much a state will receive in federal allocations. In other words, this latter tax, not the IVA or income tax, is the one that is considered in the formula for distribution. The IVA was collected by the states from 1983 to 1990. As mentioned earlier, this practice was changed by the 1990 reform of the LCF, in which the federal government, rather than the states, was given the authority to collect the IVA.

5. *Impuestos asignables* include both state and federally collected taxes, and thus there are *impuestos asignables federales* and *impuestos asignables estatales*. Most federal and state taxes, however, are not *asignables*. For example, the IVA and the income tax do not figure in the calculation for the distribution of *participaciones*, as they are not *asignables*, but states do get a share of them because they are *participables*. The most important *impuesto asignable federal* is the tax on liquor, beer, gasoline, and tobacco. At the state level, the *impuestos asignables* include a variety of taxes, e.g., vehicle registration (*tenencia*) and a tax on new vehicles, but do not include the payroll tax, the most promising state tax in terms of revenue-raising ability.

6. Once again, this third element demonstrates the nature of the paradox identified at the outset, giving the states and municipalities the opportunity to increase their revenues but at a cost of no longer receiving those revenues as *participaciones*. In effect, however, most states and municipalities would be willing to forgo that loss of revenue sharing, since it is so small in the overall scheme.

7. There is a major contradiction in the information obtained about what, exactly, is included in the Programa Normal, specifically, whether it encompasses *only* investment, or the costs of operation and maintenance as well. For example, according to some officials, the Programa Normal for agriculture will include agricultural investments as well as the cost of maintaining an agency unit in that state, whereas others will categorically affirm that it is exclusively investment.

8. Formerly, these were expressed in Roman numerals. The custom now is to use Arabic numbers.

9. The poverty index is calculated by CONAPO using nine socioeconomic indicators (e.g., literacy, dwelling, environment, wage levels), the relative weights of which are calculated by principal components analysis (see CONAPO 1990: 291–304).

10. The states were arranged from those receiving the most to those receiving the least revenue per capita, and both population and revenue received were transformed into accumulated percentage points. The thirty-one states were plotted for four years (1989–1992), thereby producing four curves. Perfect equity would be a straight line from zero population to 100 percent *participaciones*; the Gini coefficient is calculated to measure the area between the actual distribution and the perfect equity curve.

11. Some programs, especially in the education sector, were channeled through Solidarity but did not appear in Ramo 0026; however, they did not amount to a high percentage of the Solidarity budget.

12. As part of the Convenio de Desarrollo Social, every November the state presents its budget (the Programa Operativo Anual) requesting social development funds for the following year.

13. See Fox and Aranda (1994) and Fox and Moguel (1995) for a thorough assessment of the implementation of the Municipal Funds program in Oaxaca and its impact on local community participation.

14. In addition to the 20 percent required by law, Coahuila distributes another 15 percent of the FGP to its municipalities, thereby raising its total distribution to 35 percent. However, the additional 15 percent is earmarked exclusively for education (*Revista INDETEC*, no. 83 [July–August 1993]: 96).

15. The poverty level is often similar to the poverty index calculated by CONAPO based on a variety of social and economic indicators, including, for example, income per capita, literacy, number of houses with water and drainage. Following the federal pattern of rewarding those states that raise more revenues from the collection of taxes by increasing their share of *participaciones*, some states also reward municipalities in the same fashion.

16. For Veracruz, see Decree no. 39, *Gaceta Oficial* (January 28, 1993): 2. For Chiapas, see Decree no. 33, *Periódico Oficial* (February 1, 1989):17.

17. A bias against small municipalities does not mean that no small municipalities will be favored in the distribution (for example, all the municipalities on the right end of the Guerrero distribution between Acapulco and Chilpancingo are small and on the most-favored end of the scale), but, rather, that on average inhabitants in a small municipality are less likely to receive less per capita than those people living in larger municipalities. Another interesting, but hardly surprising, fact is that marginality, percentage rural, and smallness appear to go hand in hand. Biases favoring small municipalities appear also to favor poorer and more rural ones.

18. The payroll tax is limited by federal law to 2 percent of the business payroll. For example, the State of Hidalgo taxes all businesses that have between thirty and one hundred employees at a rate of .65 percent of its payroll, and those with more than one hundred employees at a rate of 1.43 percent. Most states have started only recently to enforce the payroll tax, although it has great revenue-raising potential.

19. Estimates for the actual costs of water provision will be discussed in Chapter 6, where the costs of operation and maintenance of water supply systems will be taken into account when evaluating the revenues raised from water fees.

20. Tabasco showed an increase of 1300 percent, but this was on an anomalously low base level in 1989.

21. Under the federal Constitution, state governments are not allowed to incur debt with international lending institutions, and thus they secure loans from national (largely government) institutions like BANOBRAS (Banco Nacional de Obras y Servicios Públicos, National Bank for Utilities and Public Works). Many of these loans are designed to find ways of increasing the states' own sources of revenue and to reduce their dependence on federal support. One example is the 100 Cities program, designed to update and modernize the cadastral system of the states and to promote decentralization by revising the cadastre of large and medium cities throughout the country. This modernized cadastre would potentially result in the generation of more revenue from property taxes. This forms a key element of latest government thinking (SEDESOL 1996).

Chapter 6

1. An additional function of municipal and state governments, of course, is to elaborate urban development plans, which, in theory at least, are the blueprints that govern zoning and

land use. In Mexico there were major advances in this field between 1977 and 1984, after which regional development planning gained paramountcy (see Aguilar 1987; Campbell and Wilk 1986; Ward 1986). While urban development plans have become more commonplace in Mexican cities, my analysis focuses on regional development planning.

2. The COPLADE is made up of an *asamblea plenaria* (executive body), the COPLADE's highest authority, which approves all programs and is presided over by the governor; a *comisión permanente* (permanent commission), the COPLADE's administrative arm, which formulates the yearly program and prepares the yearly reports; and several subcommittees and working groups.

3. Many municipalities, with the approval of the state legislature, have increased the fees charged for water in an effort not only to increase the revenue it potentially represents, but also to encourage conservation.

4. Two classic readings on the theory of participatory democracy and representation are Pateman (1970) and Pitkin (1969).

5. For an excellent description and analysis of the evolution of the PRI's popular sector, see Craske (1994).

6. See, for example, Cornelius, Craig, and Fox (1994), Dresser (1991), Fox and Aranda (1994), Fox and Moguel (1995).

7. The same applies for PRI municipal presidents under PAN governors. In Mexicali, for example, there was no significant change in the proportion of *participaciones* received after Ruffo assumed office in 1989. One difference, however, is the greater availability of investment income for PRI municipal presidents who approach the federal government directly (Rodríguez and Ward 1994a).

8. For a discussion of the "new PRI," see Rodríguez and Ward (1996). For an overview of the trend toward technocratic forms of government in Mexican municipalities, see Ward (1996).

9. In 1989 and 1990, the shortfall was made up by major federal transfers in support of the decentralization of government institutions, especially INEGI, as mentioned in Chapter 4.

10. Property taxes are usually considered a local tax used by governments to charge for infrastructure and public services. In 1992, all states in Mexico collected US$798 million in property taxes, although the collection effort varied widely among states. For example, the eight poorest states (listed on Table 5.10), with 32 percent of Mexico's population, collected less than 10 percent of its property tax. This amounts to US$2.97 and US$9.82 per capita for the poorest states and for the federation as whole, respectively. These figures are somewhat low by international standards: in Chile, municipalities collect on average US$16.30 per capita; in Brazil, a country where municipalities are allowed to tax economic activity and thus give little thought to property tax, property tax revenue averages about US$17.30 in the state capitals (although the figure for the country as a whole would be lower, and probably not far above the Mexican average).

11. When I asked the late Dr. Salvador Nava during an interview why he had not raised property taxes dramatically as municipal president of San Luis Potosí, he replied somewhat acerbically, "Of course I could have raised them; but I wouldn't have been municipal president very long."

Bibliography

Acosta Romero, Miguel. 1982. "Mexican Federalism: Conception and Reality." *Public Administration Review* 42 (5): 399–404.

Aguilar Camín, Héctor, and Lorenzo Meyer. 1993. *In the Shadow of the Mexican Revolution: Contemporary Mexican History, 1910–1989.* Austin: University of Texas Press.

Aguilar Martínez, Guillermo. 1987. "Urban Planning in the 1980s in Mexico City: Operative Process or Political Façade?" *Habitat International* 11 (3): 23–38.

_____. 1988. "Community Participation in Mexico City: A Case Study." *Bulletin of Latin American Research* 7 (1): 22–46.

Aguilar Villanueva, Luis. 1994. "El federalismo mexicano: Funcionamiento y tareas pendientes." Mexico City: El Colegio de México. Mimeo.

Aitken, Rob, Nikki Craske, Gareth A. Jones, and David E. Stansfield, eds. 1996. *Dismantling the Mexican State?* London: Macmillan.

Alvarado, Arturo, ed. 1987. *Electoral Patterns and Perspectives in Mexico.* Monograph Series, no. 22. La Jolla: Center for U.S.-Mexican Studies, University of California, San Diego.

Ames, Barry. 1977. "The Politics of Public Spending in Latin America." *American Political Science Review* 21 (1): 149–176.

Anderson, Bo, and James Cockcroft. 1966. "Control and Cooptation in Mexican Politics." *International Journal of Comparative Sociology* 7 (1): 11–28.

Armida Graham, Pablo. 1983. *Federalismo fiscal: El caso de México.* B.A. thesis. Mexico, ITAM.

Ashford, Doug. 1976. *Democracy, Decentralization and Decisions.* Beverly Hills, Calif.: Sage.

Aziz Nassif, Alberto. 1987. *Prácticas electorales y democracia en Chihuahua.* Cuadernos de la Casa Chata, no. 151. Mexico City: Centro de Investigación y Estudios Superiores de Antropología Social.

_____. 1987a. "Electoral Practices and Democracy in Chihuahua, 1985." In Arturo Alvarado, ed., *Electoral Patterns and Perspectives in Mexico.* Monograph Series, no. 22. La Jolla: Center for U.S.-Mexican Studies, University of California, San Diego. 181–206.

Bailey, John. 1984. "Public Budgeting in Mexico, 1970–1984." *Public Budgeting and Finance* 4 (1): 76–90.

_____. 1988. *Governing Mexico.* New York: St. Martin's Press.

_____. 1992. "Fiscal Recentralization in Mexico, 1979–1991." Paper presented at the meeting of the Latin American Studies Association. Los Angeles.

_____. 1994. "Centralism and Political Change in Mexico: The Case of National Solidarity." In Wayne Cornelius, Ann Craig, and Jonathan Fox, eds., *Transforming State-Society Relations in Mexico: The National Solidarity Strategy.* La Jolla: Center for U.S.-Mexican Studies, University of California, San Diego. 97–119.

Baja California. 1990. *Bases generales del programa de descentralización para el fortalecimiento municipal.* Mexicali, B.C.N.: Gobierno del Estado.

Banco de México. 1984. *Indicadores económicos.* Mexico City: Subdirección de Investigación Económica.

_____. 1988. "La política económica y la evolución de la economía en 1987." *Comercio Exterior* 38 (5): 431–444.

Barberán, José, et al. 1988. *Radiografía del fraude: Análisis de los datos oficiales del 6 de julio.* Mexico City: Nuestro Tiempo.

Barros Horcasitas, José Luis, Javier Hurtado, and Germán Pérez Fernández, eds. 1991. *Transición a la democracia y reforma del estado en México.* Mexico City: Miguel Angel Porrúa/FLACSO.

Bartra, Roger, et al. 1975. *Caciquismo y poder político en el México rural.* Mexico City: Siglo XXI.

Basáñez, Miguel. 1990. *El pulso de los sexenios: 20 años de crisis en México.* Mexico City: Siglo XXI.

Beltrán, Ulises, and Santiago Portilla. 1986. "El proyecto de descentralización del gobierno mexicano (1983–1984)." In Blanca Torres, ed. *Descentralización y democracia en Mexico.* Mexico City: El Colegio de México. 91–117.

Beltrán del Río, Pascal. 1990. "Solidaridad, oxígeno para el PRI en el rescate de votos." *Proceso* (718) (August 6): 8–11.

_____. 1993. *Michoacán, ni un paso atrás.* Mexico City: Libros de *Proceso.*

Bennett, Robert J., ed. 1990. *Decentralization, Local Governments and Markets: Towards a Post-Welfare Agenda.* Oxford: Oxford University Press.

Bennett, Vivienne. 1995. *The Politics of Water: Urban Protest, Gender, and Power in Monterrey, Mexico.* Pittsburgh: University of Pittsburgh Press.

Benson, Nettie Lee. 1958. "Spain's Contribution to Federalism in Mexico." In Thomas Cotner and Carlos Castañeda, eds., *Essays in Mexican History: The Charles Wilson Hacket Memorial Volume.* Austin: Institute of Latin American Studies, University of Texas. 90–103.

Beyer de Roalandini, Carmen E. 1985. "La legislación hacendaria municipal y la coordinación fiscal." *Estudios Municipales* 1: 23–36.

Bezdek, Robert. 1995. "Democratic Changes in an Authoritarian System: *Navismo* and Opposition Development in San Luis Potosí." In Victoria E. Rodríguez and Peter M. Ward, eds., *Opposition Government in Mexico.* Albuquerque: University of New Mexico Press. 33–61.

Borja, Jordi. 1989. *Estado, descentralización y democracia.* Bogotá: Ediciones Foro Nacional por Colombia.

Borja, Jordi, Fernando Calderón, María Grossi, and Susana Peñalva, eds. 1989. *Descentralización y democracia: Gobiernos locales en América Latina.* Santiago de Chile: CLACSO.

Brandenburg, Frank. 1964. *The Making of Modern Mexico.* Englewood Cliffs, N.J.: Prentice-Hall.

Brown, Anthony. 1980. "Technical Assistance to Rural Communities: Stopgap or Capacity Building?" *Public Administration Review* 40 (1): 18–23.

Bruhn, Kathleen, and Keith Yanner. 1995. "Governing under the Enemy: The PRD in Michoacán." In Victoria E. Rodríguez and Peter M. Ward, eds., *Opposition Government in Mexico.* Albuquerque: University of New Mexico Press. 113–131.

Cabrero, Enrique. 1995. *La nueva gestión municipal en México: Análisis de experiencias innovadoras en gobiernos locales.* Mexico City: Miguel Angel Porrúa/CIDE.

_____, ed. 1996. *Los dilemas de la modernización municipal: Estudios sobre la gestión hacendaria en municipios urbanos de México.* Mexico City: Miguel Angel Porrúa/CIDE.

Cámara de Diputados del Congreso de la Unión, LII Legislatura. 1983. *Proceso legislativo de la iniciativa presidencial de reformas y adiciones al Artículo 115 de la Constitución Política de los Estados Unidos Mexicanos.* Colección Documentos. Mexico City.

Camp, Roderic A. 1974. "Mexican Governors since Cárdenas: Education and Career Contacts." *Journal of Inter-American Studies and World Affairs* 16 (4): 454–481.

_____. 1976. "A Reexamination of Political Leadership and Allocation of Federal Revenues in Mexico, 1934–1973." *Journal of Developing Areas* 10 (2): 193–211.

_____. 1991. "Mexico's 1988 Elections: A Turning Point for Its Political Development and Foreign Relations?" In E.W. Butler, and J.A. Bustamante, eds., *Sucesión Presidencial: The 1988 Mexican Presidential Elections.* Boulder, Colo.: Westview Press. 95–114.

_____. 1993. *Politics in Mexico.* New York: Oxford University Press.

_____. 1995. *Mexican Political Biographies, 1935–1993.* 3rd ed. Austin: University of Texas Press.

Campbell, Tim, and David Wilk. 1986. "Plans and Plan Making in the Valley of Mexico." *Third World Planning Review* 8 (4): 287–313.

Cantú Segovia, Eloy, et al. 1982. "The Challenge of Managing Mexico: The Priorities of the 1982–1988 Administration." *Public Administration Review* 42 (5): 405–409.

Cárdenas, Leonard, Jr. 1963. "The Municipality in Northern Mexico." *Southwestern Studies,* no. 1. El Paso: Texas Western Press.

_____. 1964. *Municipal Administration in Mexican Border States.* Austin: University of Texas Press.

Cardiel, E. 1976. *Viabilidad económica que ofrece la zona interior del país para el establecimiento de la industria maquiladora.* Mexico City: Universidad Nacional Autónoma de México.

Carpizo, Jorge. 1978. *El presidencialismo mexicano.* Mexico City: Siglo XXI.

_____. 1983. "El sistema federal mexicano." *Gaceta de Administración Pública Estatal y Municipal.* Mexico City: INAP.

Carrillo Huerta, Mario M. 1986. *Los programas regionales de empleo en México. Su impacto en el empleo, los ingresos y el bienestar familiar.* Puebla: El Colegio de Puebla.

Castro Sariñana, María Cristina. 1985. "La reforma municipal en Quintana Roo y los problemas internos de la estructura de los ayuntamientos." *Estudios Municipales* 2: 121–135.

Centeno, Miguel Angel. 1994. *Democracy within Reason: Technocratic Revolution in Mexico.* University Park: Pennsylvania State University Press.

Centeno, Miguel Angel, and Sylvia Maxfield. 1992. "The Marriage of Finance and Order: Changes in the Mexican Political Elite." *Journal of Latin American Studies* 24 (1): 57–85.

Centro Nacional de Estudios Municipales (CNEM). 1985a. *El desafío municipal.* Mexico City: Secretaría de Gobernación.

_____. 1985b. *El municipio mexicano.* Mexico City: Secretaría de Gobernación.

Chávez, E. 1992. "Michoacán: cada voto del PRI costó 239,188 pesos; cada voto del PRD costó 6,916 pesos." *Proceso* (821) (July 27): 22–27.

Cheema, Shabbir G., and Dennis Rondinelli. 1983. *Decentralization and Development: Policy Implementation in Developing Countries.* Beverly Hills, Calif.: Sage.

Cockroft, John D. 1983. *Mexico: Class Formation, Capital Accumulation and the State.* New York: Monthly Review Press.

Cohen, Stephen S., et al. 1981. *Decentralization: A Framework for Policy Analysis.* Berkeley: Project on Managing Decentralization, Institute of International Studies, University of California.

CONAPO (Consejo Nacional de Población). 1990. *Indicadores socioeconómicos e índice de marginación municipal 1990.* Anexo A. Mexico City.

———. 1993. *La marginación en México.* Mexico City.

———. 1994. *La población en los municipios de México, 1950–1990.* Mexico City.

Conde Bonfil, Carola. 1996. *Innovación financiera y participación ciudadana: El caso de Naucalpan de Juárez.* Toluca, Mexico: El Colegio Mexiquense.

Conklin, John G. 1973. "Elite Studies: The Case of the Mexican Presidency." *Journal of Latin American Studies* 5 (2): 247–269.

Consejo Consultivo del Programa Nacional de Solidaridad. 1990. *El combate a la pobreza: Lineamientos programáticos.* Mexico City: El Nacional.

Convergencia de Organismos Civiles por la Democracia. 1992. "Informe de observación electoral." *Perfil de la Jornada* (August 16).

Conyers, Diane. 1983. "Decentralization: The Latest Fashion in Development Administration?" *Public Administration and Development* 3: 97–109.

Cook, Maria Lorena. 1990. "Organizing Opposition in the Teachers' Movement in Oaxaca." In Joe Foweraker and Ann Craig, eds., *Popular Movements and Political Change in Mexico.* Boulder, Colo.: Lynne Rienner Publishers.

———. 1996. *Organizing Dissent: Unions, the State, and the Democratic Teachers' Movement in Mexico.* University Park: Pennsylvania State University Press.

COPLAMAR (Coordinación General del Plan Nacional de Zonas Deprimidas y Grupos Marginados) and Presidencia de la República. 1982. *Necesidades esenciales en México. Situación actual y perspectivas al año 2,000.* Vol. 5 of *Geografía de la marginación.* Mexico City: Siglo XXI.

Corbett, Jack. 1976. "Aspects of Recruitment to Civil Office in a Mexican Community." *Anthropological Quarterly* 49 (3): 160–173.

———. "The Transformation of Community Political Systems in Mexico, 1940–1980." 1984. Paper presented to the Annual Meeting of the Southwestern Council on Latin American Studies, Edinburg, Texas.

Cornelius, Wayne A. 1973. "The Impact of Governmental Performance on Political Attitudes and Behavior: The Case of the Urban Poor in Mexico City." In Francine F. Rabinovitz and Felicity M. Trueblood, eds., *Latin American Urban Research*, vol. 3. Beverly Hills, Calif.: Sage. 217–255.

———. 1975. *Politics and the Migrant Poor in Mexico City.* Stanford: Stanford University Press.

———. 1987. "The Political Economy of Mexico under de la Madrid: The Crisis Deepens, 1985–1986." In Abraham Lowenthal, ed., *Latin America and the Caribbean Contemporary Record*, vol. 5 (1985–1986). New York: Holmes and Meier.

Cornelius, Wayne A., and Ann L. Craig. 1984. *Politics in Mexico: An Introduction and Overview.* Research Reports and Monographs in U.S.-Mexican Studies, Reprint Series, 1. La Jolla: Center for U.S. Mexican Studies, University of California, San Diego.

———. 1991. *The Mexican Political System in Transition.* Monograph Series, 35. La Jolla: Center for U.S.-Mexican Studies, University of California, San Diego.

Cornelius, Wayne A., Ann L. Craig, and Jonathan Fox, eds., 1994. *Transforming State-Society Relations: The National Solidadrity Strategy.* U.S.-Mexico Contemporary Perspectives Series, 6. La Jolla: Center for U.S.-Mexican Studies, University of California, San Diego.

Cornelius, Wayne A., Judith Gentleman, and Peter Smith, eds. 1989. *Mexico's Alternative Political Futures.* Monograph Series, 30. La Jolla: Center for U.S.-Mexican Studies, University of California, San Diego.

Corona Rentería, Alfonso. 1974. *La economía urbana: Ciudades y regiones mexicanas.* Mexico City: Instituto Mexicano de Investigaciones Económicas.

Craske, Nikki. 1994. *Corporatism Revisited: Salinas and the Reform of the Popular Sector.* Institute of Latin American Studies Research Papers. London: University of London.

Crespo, José Antonio. 1995. "Governments of the Opposition: The Official Response." In Victoria E. Rodríguez and Peter M. Ward, eds., *Opposition Government in Mexico.* Albuquerque: University of New Mexico Press.

"Cuadro comparativo del Artículo 115 constitucional." 1985. *Estudios Municipales* 5: 137–148.

Cumberland, Charles C. 1974. *Mexican Revolution: The Constitutionalist Years.* Austin: University of Texas Press.

Daigle, Lesley. 1995. "Bread and Ballots: Social Assistance and the Influence of Politics on the DIF in Mexico." Master's thesis. University of Texas at Austin.

"Decreto de Creación del Centro National de Estudios Municipales." 1985. *Estudios Municipales* 5: 131–135.

"Desastre y reconstrucción." 1986. Special issue of the *Revista Mexicana de Ciencias Políticas y Sociales,* Nueva Época 32 (123).

Diesing, Paul. 1962. *Reason in Society.* Chicago: University of Illinois Press.

Desarrollo Integral de la Familia (DIF). 1986. *Ley sobre el sistema nacional de asistencia social.* Mexico City.

Drake, Paul W., and Eduardo Silva, eds. 1986. *Elections and Democratization in Latin America.* 1980–1985. La Jolla, Calif.: Center for Iberian and Latin American Studies, Center for U.S. Mexican Studies, and Institute of the Americas, University of California, San Diego.

Dresser, Denise. 1991. *Neopopulist Solutions to Neoliberal Problems. Mexico's National Solidarity Program.* Current Issues Brief no. 3. La Jolla: Center for U.S.-Mexican Studies, University of California, San Diego.

———. 1992. "Pronasol: Los dilemas de la gobernabilidad." *El cotidiano* (49) (July–August).

Eckstein, Susan. 1988. *The Poverty of Revolution: The State and the Urban Poor in Mexico.* Princeton: Princeton University Press.

Esman, Milton. 1980. "Development Assistance in Public Administration: Requiem or Renewal?" *Public Administration Review* 40 (5): 426–431.

Fagen, Richard R., and William S. Tuohy. 1972. *Politics and Privilege in a Mexican City.* Stanford: Stanford University Press.

Favela, Alejandro. 1992. "El gobierno salinista y la reforma del estado." *Estudios Políticos* 3 (9): 55–73.

Foro nacional hacia un auténtico federalismo. Memoria. 1995. Comité Organizador del Foro Nacional hacia un Auténtico Federalismo. León, Guanajuato.

Foweraker, Joe. 1988. "Transformism Transformed: The Nature of Mexico's Political Crisis." Essex Papers in Politics and Government, 46. Department of Government, University of Essex.

———. 1993. *Popular Mobilization in Mexico: The Teachers' Movement 1977–1987.* Cambridge: Cambridge University Press.

———. 1995. *Theorizing Social Movements.* London: Pluto Press.

Foweraker, Joe, and Ann Craig, eds. 1990. *Popular Movements and Political Change in Mexico.* Boulder, Colo.: Lynne Rienner Publishers.

Fox, Jonathan. 1992. *The Politics of Food in Mexico: State Power and Social Mobilization.* Ithaca, N.Y.: Cornell University Press.

_____. 1993. "The Difficult Transition from Clientelism to Citizenship: The Politics of Access to Solidarity's Indigenous Programs." In Wayne Cornelius, Ann Craig, and Jonathan Fox, eds., *Transforming State-Society Relations in Mexico: The National Solidarity Strategy.* La Jolla: Center for U.S.-Mexican Studies, University of California, San Diego.

Fox, Jonathan, and Josefina Aranda. 1994. "Analysis of the Distribution of Municipal Funds among the Municipalities of Oaxaca." Paper prepared for the World Bank, Project on Decentralization and Regional Development.

Fox, Jonathan, and Luis Hernández. 1992. "Mexico's Difficult Democracy: Grassroots Movements, NGOs and Local Government." *Alternatives* 17 (2) (Spring): 165–208.

Fox, Jonathan, and Julio Moguel. 1995. "Pluralism and Anti-Poverty Policy: Mexico's National Solidarity Program and Left Opposition Municipal Governments." In Victoria E. Rodríguez and Peter M. Ward, eds., *Opposition Government in Mexico.* Albuquerque: University of New Mexico Press. 189–204.

García del Castillo, Rodolfo, and Manuel Díaz Flores. 1995. "Análisis de capacidades de innovación en la gestión financiera de estados y municipios. El caso de Aguascalientes." Mexico City: CIDE. Mimeo.

Garrido, Luis Javier. 1989. "The Crisis of *Presidencialismo.*" In Wayne Cornelius, Judith Gentleman, and Peter Smith, eds., *Mexico's Alternative Political Futures.* La Jolla: Center for U.S.-Mexican Studies, University of California, San Diego. 417–434.

_____. 1993. *La ruptura. La corriente democrática del PRI.* Mexico City: Grijalbo.

Garza, Gustavo. 1986. "Ciudad de México: Dinámica industrial y perspectivas de descentralización después del terremoto." In Blanca Torres, ed., *Descentralización y democracia en México.* Mexico City: El Colegio de México. 219–236.

Garza, Gustavo, and Martha Schteingart. 1978. "Mexico City: The Emerging Megalopolis." In Wayne A. Cornelius and Robert W. Kemper, eds., *Latin American Urban Research*, vol. 6. Beverly Hills, Calif.: Sage.

Gibson, Charles. 1978. *Los aztecas bajo el dominio español.* Mexico City: Siglo XXI.

Gilbert, Alan. 1984. "Community Action by the Urban Poor: Democratic Involvement, Community Self-Help, or a Means of Social Control?" *World Development* 12 (8): 769–782.

_____. 1989. "Moving the Capital of Argentina. A Further Example of Utopian Planning?" *Cities* 6 (3): 27–34.

Gilbert, Alan, and Peter Ward. 1985. *Housing, the State and the Poor: Policy and Practice in Three Latin American Cities.* Cambridge: Cambridge University Press.

Godwin, Kenneth R. 1977. "Mexican Population Policy: Problems Posed by Participatory Democracy in a Paternalistic Political System." In Lawrence E. Koslow, ed., *The Future of Mexico.* Tempe: Center for Latin American Studies, Arizona State University.

González Block, Miguel, et al. 1989. "Health Services Decentralization in Mexico: Formulation, Implementation and Results of Policy." *Health Policy and Planning* 4 (4): 301–315.

González Casanova, Pablo. 1970. *Democracy in Mexico.* New York: Oxford University Press.

González Oropeza, Manuel. 1983. *La intervención federal en la desaparición de poderes.* Mexico City: Universidad Nacional Autónoma de México.

_____. 1986. "La autonomía municipal vista por las legislaturas locales." *Cuadernos del Instituto de Investigaciones Jurídicas* 1 (2): 501–512.

Gortari Rabiela, Hira de. 1994. "El federalismo en la construcción de los estados." In Jaime Rodríguez, ed., *Mexico in the Age of Democratic Revolutions, 1750–1850.* Boulder, Colo.: Lynne Rienner Publishers. 209–222.

Graham, Lawrence S. 1971. *Mexican State Government: A Prefectural System in Action.* Austin: LBJ School of Public Affairs, University of Texas at Austin.

_____. 1984. "Intergovernmental Relations in Mexico: The View from Below." Paper presented to the Annual Meeting of the Southwest Social Science Association, Fort Worth, Texas.

_____. 1990. *The State and Policy Outcomes in Latin America.* New York: Praeger.

_____. 1993. "Rethinking the Relationship between the Strength of Local Institutions and the Consolidation of Democracy: The Case of Brazil." *In Depth: A Journal for Values and Public Policy* 3 (1): 177–193.

Granados Chapa, Miguel. 1992. *¡Nava Sí, Zapata No!* Mexico City: Grijalbo.

Grindle, Merilee S. 1977. *Bureaucrats, Politicians, and Peasants in Mexico: A Case Study in Public Policy.* Berkeley and Los Angeles: University of California Press.

_____. 1981. *Official Interpretations of Rural Underdevelopment: Mexico in the 1970s.* Working Papers in U.S.-Mexican Studies, 20. La Jolla: Center for U.S.-Mexican Studies, University of California, San Diego.

_____, ed. 1980. *Politics and Policy Implementation in the Third World.* Princeton: Princeton University Press.

Guadarrama, Graciela. 1987. "Entrepreneurs and Politics: Businessmen in Electoral Contest in Sonora and Nuevo León, July 1985." In A. Alvarado Mendoza, ed., *Electoral Patterns and Perspectives in Mexico.* La Jolla: Center for U.S.-Mexican Studies, University of California, San Diego. 81–110.

Guillén López, Tonatiuh. 1992. "Baja California, una Década de Cambio Político." In Tonatiuh Guillén López, ed., *Frontera norte: Una década de política electoral.* Tijuana: El Colegio de la Frontera Norte. 139–185.

_____. 1993. *Baja California 1989–92: Balance de la transición democrática.* Tijuana: El Colegio de la Frontera Norte.

_____. 1995. "Finanzas municipales, federalismo y desarrollo. El caso de Tijuana, B.C." Mexico City: El Colegio de la Frontera Norte. Mimeo.

Hansen, Roger D. 1974. *The Politics of Mexican Development.* 2nd. ed. Baltimore, Md.: Johns Hopkins University Press.

Harvey, Neil. 1989. "Personal Networks and Strategic Choices in the Formation of an Independent Peasant Organization: The OCEZ of Chiapas, Mexico." *Bulletin of Latin American Research* 7 (2): 299–312.

Hayner, Norman S. 1945. "Mexico City: Its Growth and Configuration." *The American Journal of Sociology* 50 (1).

Hellman, Judith. 1978. *Mexico in Crisis.* New York: Holmes and Meier.

Hernández Claro, Edmundo. 1995. "Análisis de capacidades de innovación en la gestión financiera de estados y municipios. El caso de Ciudad Guzmán, Jalisco." Guadalajara: Universidad de Guadalajara. Mimeo.

Hoyo D'Addona, Roberto. 1985. "La hacienda pública municipal." *Estudios Municipales* 1: 13–21.

Huntington, Samuel. 1968. *Political Order in Changing Societies.* New Haven: Yale University Press.

IEPES-PRI (Instituto de Estudios Políticos, Económicos y Sociales del Partido Revolucionario Institucional). 1982. *Diagnóstico para el fortalecimiento municipal.* Mexico City.

———. 1988. *Compromisos. Carlos Salinas de Gortari.* Mexico City.

———. 1988a. *Perfiles del programa de gobierno. 1988–1994. Carlos Salinas de Gortari.* Mexico City.

———. 1988b. "Federalismo y descentralización." *Diálogo Nacional. Revista de la Consulta Popular* 17.

———. 1988c. "Desarrollo regional y fortalecimiento municipal." *Diálogo Nacional. Revista de la Consulta Popular* 32.

INEGI (Instituto Nacional de Estadística, Geografía e Informática). 1991. *Estados Unidos Mexicanos. Perfil demográfico, XI censo general de población y vivienda, 1990.* Mexico City.

———. 1992. *El ingreso y gasto público en México.* Mexico City.

Instituto Nacional de Solidaridad. 1992. "Espacio de convergencia de fuerzas populares." *Gaceta de solidaridad* 3 (53) (June 15).

Jeannetti Dávila, Elena. 1986. "Descentralización de los servicios de salud." In Blanca Torres, ed., *Descentralización y democracia en Mexico.* Mexico City: El Colegio de México. 175–189.

Johnson, Kenneth F. 1978. *Mexican Democracy: A Critical View.* Rev. ed. New York: Praeger.

Jones, Gareth. 1991. "The Impact of Government Intervention on Land Prices in Latin American Cities: The Case of Puebla, Mexico." PhD dissertation. Cambridge University.

Jones, Gareth, Edith Jiménez, and Peter Ward. 1993. "The Land Market in Mexico under Salinas: A Real Estate Boom Revisited?" *Environment and Planning A* 25: 627–651.

Keefe, Eugene K. 1976. *Area Handbook for Austria.* Washington, D.C.: American University.

Klesner, Joseph. 1991. "Challenges for Mexico's Opposition in the Coming *Sexenio*." In E. Butler and J. Bustamente, eds., *Sucesión presidencial.* Boulder, Colo.: Westview Press. 149–175.

Lajous, Alejandra, et al. 1984, 1985. *Las razones y las obras. Crónica del sexenio de Miguel de la Madrid.* 2 vols. Mexico City: Unidad de la Crónica Presidencial, Fondo de Cultura Económica.

Landau, Martin. 1969. "Redundancy, Rationality, and the Problem of Duplication and Overlap." *Public Administration Review* 29 (4): 346–348.

Landau, Martin, and Eva Eagle. 1981. "On the Concept of Decentralization." Unpublished paper. Berkeley: Project on Managing Decentralization, Institute of International Studies, University of California.

Leonard, David K. 1982a. "Analyzing the Organizational Requirements for Serving the Rural Poor." In David K. Leonard and Dale Rogers Marshall, eds., *Institutions of Rural Development for the Poor: Decentralization and Organizational Linkages.* Berkeley: Institute of International Studies, University of California. 1–39.

———. 1982b. "Choosing among Forms of Decentralization and Linkage." In David K. Leonard and Dale Rogers Marshall, eds., *Institutions of Rural Development for the Poor: Decentralization and Organizational Linkages.* Berkeley: Institute of International Studies, University of California. 193–226.

Leonard, David K., and Dale Rogers Marshall, eds. 1981. *Linkages to Decentralized Units.* Berkeley: Project on Managing Decentralization, Institute of International Studies, University of California.

_____. 1982. *Institutions of Rural Development for the Poor: Decentralization and Organizational Linkages.* Berkeley: Institute of International Studies, University of California.

Levy, Daniel, and Gabriel Székely. 1983. *Mexico: Paradoxes of Stability and Change.* Boulder, Colo.: Westview Press.

Lowder, Stella. 1991. "The Context of Urban Planning in Secondary Cities." *Cities* 8 (1): 54–65.

Lustig, Nora. 1992. *Mexico: The Remaking of an Economy.* Washington, D.C.: Brookings.

_____. 1994. "Solidarity as a Strategy of Poverty Alleviation." In Cornelius, Craig, and Fox, eds., *Transforming State-Society Relations: The National Solidadrity Strategy.* U.S.-Mexico Contemporary Perspectives Series, 6. La Jolla: Center for U.S.-Mexican Studies, University of California, San Diego. 79–96.

Mabry, Donald J. 1973. *Mexico's Acción Nacional: A Catholic Alternative to Revolution.* Syracuse, N.Y.: Syracuse University Press.

_____. 1974. "Mexico's Party Deputy System: The First Decade." *Journal of Inter-American Studies and World Affairs* 16 (2): 221–233.

Maddick, Henry. 1963. *Democracy, Decentralization and Development.* Bombay: Asia Publishing House.

Madrid, Miguel de la. 1982. *Manual síntesis de pensamiento político.* Mexico City: Partido Revolucionario Institucional, Coordinación General de Documentación y Análisis.

_____. 1984. "Protesta de ley como presidente constitucional de los Estados Unidos Mexicanos, 1º. de diciembre de 1982." In *Testimonio político.* Mexico City: Presidencia de la República, Dirección General de Comunicación Social.

Malloy, James, ed. 1977. *Authoritarianism and Corporatism in Latin America.* Pittsburgh: University of Pittsburgh Press.

Marshall, Dale Rogers. 1982. "Lessons from the Implementation of Poverty Programs in the United States." In David K. Leonard and Dale Rogers Marshall, eds., *Institutions of Rural Development for the Poor: Decentralization and Organizational Linkages.* Berkeley: Institute of International Studies, University of California. 40–72.

Martínez Assad, Carlos, ed. 1985. *Municipios en conflicto.* Mexico City: Instituto de Investigaciones Sociales, Universidad Nacional Autónoma de México.

Martínez Assad, Carlos, and Alicia Ziccardi. 1987. "El municipio entre la sociedad y el estado." *Mexican Studies/Estudios Mexicanos* 3 (2): 287–318.

_____. 1989. "Política y gestión municipal en México." 1989. In Jordi Borja et al., eds., *Descentralización y democracia: Gobiernos locales en América Latina.* Santiago de Chile: CLACSO. 285–336.

Martínez Cabañas, Gustavo. 1992. *La administración estatal y municipal de México.* 2nd ed. Mexico City: INAP.

Mecham, J. Lloyd. 1938. "The Origins of Federalism in Mexico." *Hispanic American Historical Review* 18.

Merino, Mauricio, ed. 1994. *En busca de la democracia municipal. La participación ciudadana en el gobierno local mexicano.* Mexico City: El Colegio de México.

Meyer, Lorenzo. 1986. "Un tema añejo siempre actual: El centro y las regiones en la historia mexicana." In Blanca Torres, ed., *Descentralización y democracia en Mexico.* Mexico City: El Colegio de México. 23–32.

Middlebrook, Kevin. 1986. "Political Liberalization in an Authoritarian Regime: The Case of Mexico." In Paul W. Drake and E. Silva, eds., *Elections and Democratization in Latin America, 1980–1985.* La Jolla: Center for Iberian and Latin American Studies, Center for U.S.-

Mexican Studies, and Institute of the Americas, University of California, San Diego. 73–104.

_____, ed. 1991. *Unions, Workers, and the State in Mexico*. La Jolla: Center for U.S.-Mexican Studies, University of California, San Diego.

Molinar Horcasitas, Juan. 1986. "The Mexican Electoral System: Continuity by Change." In Paul W. Drake and E. Silva, eds., *Elections and Democratization in Latin America, 1980–1985*. La Jolla: Center for Iberian and Latin American Studies, Center for U.S.-Mexican Studies, and Institute of the Americas, University of California, San Diego. 105–114.

_____. 1991. *El tiempo de la legitimidad. Elecciones, autoritarismo y democracia en México*. Mexico City: Cal y Arena.

Molinar Horcasitas, Juan, and Jeffrey Weldon. 1994. "Electoral Determinants and Effects of Pronasol." In Wayne Cornelius, Ann Craig, and Jonathan Fox, eds., *Transforming State-Society Relations in Mexico: The National Solidarity Strategy*. La Jolla: Center for U.S.-Mexican Studies, University of California, San Diego. 123–141.

Montaño, Jorge. 1976. *Los pobres de la ciudad de México en los asentamientos espontáneos*. Mexico City: Siglo XXI.

Mondragón Carrillo, Guillermo. 1985. "Tipología municipal en la perspectiva del nuevo municipio." *Estudios Municipales* 2: 87–98.

Morales, Cesáreo, and Samuel Palma. 1995. *Colosio, la construcción de un destino*. Mexico City: Rayuela.

Morris, Arthur, and Stella Lowder, eds. 1992. *Decentralization in Latin America*. New York: Praeger.

Moser, Caroline. 1989. "Community Participation in Urban Projects in the Third World." *Progress in Planning* 32: 71–133.

Moya Palencia, Mario. 1981. "Federalismo y descentralización administrativa." *Investigación Jurídica*. Mexico City: UNAM-ENEP Acatlán.

"Municipio libre y descentralización de la vida nacional." 1984. *Gaceta Mexicana de Administración Pública Estatal y Municipal*. Mexico City: INAP.

Nathan, Richard P. 1989. "The Role of the States in American Federalism." In Richard P. Nathan, ed., *The State of the States*. Washington, D.C.: Congressional Quarterly Press. 15–32.

Nathan, Richard P., and Margarita M. Balmaceda. 1990. "Comparing Federal Systems of Government." In Robert J. Bennett, ed., *Decentralization, Local Governments and Markets: Towards a Post-Welfare Agenda*. Oxford: Oxford University Press. 59–77.

Nava, Guadalupe. 1973. *Cabildos de la Nueva España*. Mexico City: SEP.

Navarrete, Ifigenia Martínez de. 1970. "La distribución del ingreso en México: Tendencias y perspectivas." In David Ibarra, et al., eds., *El perfil de México en 1980*. Vol. 1. Mexico City: Siglo XXI. 15–71.

Needler, Martin C. 1971. *Politics and Society in Mexico*. Albuquerque: University of New Mexico Press.

Niemeyer, E.V., Jr. *Revolution at Querétaro: The Mexican Constitutional Convention of 1916–1917*. Austin: University of Texas Press.

Oates, Wallace. 1990. "Decentralization of the Public Sector: An Overview." In Robert J. Bennett, ed., *Decentralization, Local Governments and Markets: Towards a Post-Welfare Agenda*. Oxford: Oxford University Press. 43–58.

Ochoa Campos, Moisés. 1979. *La reforma municipal*. Mexico City: Porrúa.

_____. 1986. "La estrucutra del municipio mexicano." *Estudios Municipales* 10: 133–166.

O'Donnell, Guillermo, and Philippe Schmitter. 1986. *Transitions from Authoritarian Rule: Tentative Conclusions about Uncertain Democracies.* Baltimore, Md.: Johns Hopkins University Press.

Olloqui, José Juan de. 1983. "La descentralización del gobierno federal: Un punto de vista." *Trimestre Económico* 50: 401–418.

Olmedo, Raúl. 1984. *Iniciación a la economía de México. Descentralización, principios teóricos y ejemplos históricos.* Mexico City: Grijalbo.

Ordoño Pérez, Alejandro, and Fernando Azpeitia. 1996. "Principales modificaciones a la Ley de Coordinación Fiscal 1996." *Federalismo y Desarrollo* 9 (53): 60–62.

Ortega Lomelín, Roberto. 1988. *El nuevo federalismo: La descentralización.* Mexico City: Editorial Porrúa.

_____. 1995. "Federalismo fiscal en México." *Federalismo y Desarrollo* 9 (52): 59–66.

Ortiz, M. 1991. "Comentarios al nuevo sistema de participaciones federales a estados y municipios." *Revista Indetec* (April–May): 11–16.

Paas, D., et al., eds. 1991. *Municipio y democracia: Participación de las organizaciones de la sociedad civil en la política municipal.* Mexico City: Fundación Friedrich Naumann.

Padgett, Leon Vincent. 1966. *The Mexican Political System.* Boston: Houghton-Mifflin.

Pardo, María del Carmen. 1986. "La descentralización administrativa: Decisión para fortalecer el federalismo." In Blanca Torres, ed., *Descentralización y democracia en Mexico.* Mexico City: El Colegio de México. 119–133.

Partido Revolucionario Institucional (PRI), Comité Ejecutivo Nacional. 1990. *Programa nacional de promoción y gestoría 1990.* Mexico City.

Pastor, Robert A. 1990. "Post-Revolutionary Mexico: The Salinas Opening." *Journal of Inter-American Studies and World Affairs* 32 (3): 1–22.

Pateman, Carole. 1970. *Participation and Democratic Theory.* Cambridge: Cambridge University Press.

Peralta Burelo, Francisco. 1985. "Orígenes del municipio in México." *Estudios Municipales* 3: 73–80.

Pérez García, Arturo. 1985. "El impuesto predial." *Estudios Municipales* 1: 83–90.

Pichardo Pagaza, Ignacio. 1984. *Introducción a la administración pública en México.* Mexico City: INAP/CONACYT.

Pitkin, Hanna, ed. 1969. *Representation.* New York: Atherton Press.

Poder Ejecutivo Federal. 1995. *Plan Nacional de Desarrollo 1995–2000.* Mexico City: Secretaría de Hacienda y Crédito Público.

Presidencia de la República, Dirección General de Comunicación Social. 1983. *El Marco Legislativo para el Cambio.* Mexico City.

_____. 1984. *Participación democrática.* No. 1. Mexico City.

_____. 1985. *Reunión nacional de evaluación de la Reforma Municipal.* Mexico City.

_____. 1986a. *Comisión Nacional de Reconstrucción, Comité de Descentralización.* Mexico City.

_____. 1986b. *Cuarto informe de gobierno, 1986, que rinde ante el H. Congreso de la Unión Miguel de la Madrid, Presidente Constitucional.* Mexico City.

_____. 1988. *Sexto informe de gobierno, 1988, que rinde ante el H. Congreso de la Unión Miguel de la Madrid. Presidente Constitucional.* Mexico City.

_____. 1989a. *First State of the Nation Report. Carlos Salinas de Gortari.* Mexico City.

_____. 1989b. *Plan nacional de desarrollo, 1989–1994.* Mexico City.

_____. 1996. *Second State of the Nation Report. Ernesto Zedillo.* Mexico City.

Presidencia Municipal, Celaya. 1986. *Reglamento interior del H. Ayuntamiento Municipal de Celaya. Gto.* Celaya.

Presidencia Municipal, Chihuahua. 1986. *Ayuntamiento l983–1986.* Chihuahua.

Pressman, Jeffrey, and Aaron Wildavsky. 1979. *Implementation.* 2nd ed. Berkeley and Los Angeles: University of California Press.

Priestley, Herbert Ingram. 1942. "Las municipalidades españolas en América." *Divulgación Histórica* 4.

"Plan nacional de desarrollo 1989–1994." 1989. *Federalismo y Desarrollo* 15: 15–28.

Puertas Gómez, G. 1993. "Some Distinctive Traits of the Mexican Constitution: Description and Commentaries." Paper delivered at the Houston Bar Association–Monterrey Business Lawyers Group, Houston, Texas.

Purcell, Susan Kaufman. 1973. "Decision-Making in an Authoritarian Regime: Theoretical Implications from a Mexican Case Study." *World Politics* 26: 28–54.

_____. 1975. *The Mexican Profit Sharing Decision: Politics in an Authoritarian Regime.* Berkeley and Los Angeles: University of California Press.

Purcell, Susan Kaufman, and John F.H. Purcell. 1980. "State and Society in Mexico: Must a Stable Polity Be Institutionalized?" *World Politics* 32 (2): 194–227.

Rabinovitz, Francine F., ed. 1973. *National-Local Linkages: The Interrelationships of Urban and National Politics in Latin America.* Beverly Hills, Calif.: Sage.

Ralston, Lenore, et. al. 1980. *Local Voluntary Efforts and Decentralized Management.* Berkeley: Project on Managing Decentralization, Institute of International Studies, University of California.

Ramamurti, Ravi, ed. 1996. *Privatizing Monopolies: Lessons from the Telecommunications and Transport Sectors in Latin America.* Baltimore, Md.: Johns Hopkins University Press.

Ramírez Saiz, Juan Manuel. 1986. *El movimiento popular en México.* Mexico City: Siglo XXI.

Reagan, Michael, and John G. Sanzone. 1981. *The New Federalism.* New York: Oxford University Press.

Rébora, Alberto. 1978. "El ordenamiento territorial y urbano en México: Problemas y perspectivas." *Comercio Exterior* 28 (10): 1181–1191.

Resler, Tamara J., and Roger E. Kanet. 1993. "Democratization: The National-Subnational Linkage." *In Depth: A Journal for Values and Public Policy* 3 (1): 5–22.

Reyes, Yolanda de los. 1986. "Descentralización de la educación." In Blanca Torres, ed., *Descentralización y democracia en México.* Mexico City: El Colegio de México. 161–174.

Reyna, José Luis, and Richard S. Weinert, eds. 1977. *Authoritarianism in Mexico.* Philadelphia: ISHI Press.

Riding, Alan. 1985. *Distant Neighbors.* New York: Knopf.

Riordan, William L. 1948. *Plunkitt of Tammany Hall.* New York: Knopf.

Rodríguez, Jaime. 1992. "The Struggle for the Nation: The First Centralist-Federalist Conflict in Mexico." *The Americas* XLVIV (1): 1–22.

_____, ed. 1994. *Mexico in the Age of Democratic Revolutions, 1750–1850.* Boulder, Colo.: Lynne Rienner Publishers.

Rodríguez, Victoria E. 1987. "The Politics of Decentralization in Mexico: Divergent Outcomes of Policy Implementation." PhD dissertation. University of California, Berkeley.

_____. 1992. "Mexico's Decentralization in the 1980s: Promises, Promises, Promises . . ." in Arthur Morris and Stella Lowder, eds., *Decentralization in Latin America.* New York: Praeger. 127–143.

_____. 1993. "The Politics of Decentralization in Mexico: From *Municipio Libre* to *Solidaridad.*" *Bulletin of Latin American Research* 12 (2): 133–145.

_____. 1994. *Municipal Government in Mexico*. World Bank, Working Paper no.3, Project on Decentralization and Regional Development II. Washington, D.C.

_____. 1995. "Municipal Autonomy and the Politics of Intergovernmental Finance: Is It Different for the Opposition?" In Victoria E. Rodríguez and Peter M. Ward, eds., *Opposition Government in Mexico*. Albuquerque: University of New Mexico Press. 153–172.

_____. 1997. "Opening the Political Space in Mexico: Local Elections and Electoral Reform." In Henry Dietz and Gil Shidlo, eds., *Elections and Democratization in Latin America*. Wilmington, Del.: Scholarly Resources.

Rodríguez, Victoria E., and Peter M. Ward. 1991. "Opposition Politics, Power and Public Administration in Urban Mexico: The Experience and Future of Opposition Parties in Government." *Bulletin of Latin American Research* 10 (1): 23–36.

_____. 1992. *Policymaking, Politics, and Urban Governance in Chihuahua: The Experience of Recent Panista Governments*. Austin: LBJ School of Public Affairs, University of Texas at Austin.

_____. 1994a. *Political Change in Baja California: Democracy in the Making?* Monograph Series, 40. La Jolla: Center for U.S.-Mexican Studies, University of California, San Diego.

_____. 1994b. "Disentangling the PRI from the Government in Mexico." *Mexican Studies/Estudios Mexicanos* 10 (1): 163–186.

_____. 1994c. "The PRD in Power: Missed Opportunities in the Spotlight." Working Paper. University of Texas at Austin.

_____. 1996. "The New PRI: Recasting Its Identity." In Aitken et al., eds., *Dismantling the Mexican State*. London: Macmillan. 92–112.

_____, eds. 1995. *Opposition Government in Mexico*. Albuquerque: University of New Mexico Press.

_____, et al. 1996. *New Federalism, State and Local Government in Mexico: Memoria of the Bi-National Conference*. Austin: Mexican Center of the Institute of Latin American Studies, University of Texas at Austin.

Roett, Riordan, ed. 1993. *Political and Economic Liberalization in Mexico: At a Critical Junction?* Boulder: Lynne Rienner Publishers.

Rojas, Carlos, et al. 1991. *Solidaridad a debate*. Mexico City: El Nacional.

Romano Ibarra, Julio. 1975. "El proceso de desconcentración de la hacienda pública." *Pensamiento Político* 20: 187–194.

Rondinelli, Dennis A. 1978. "National Investment Planning and Equity Policy in Developing Countries: The Challenge of Decentralized Administration." *Policy Sciences* 10 (1): 45–74.

_____. 1981. "Government Decentralization in Comparative Perspective: Theory and Practice in Developing Countries." *International Review of Administrative Science* 47 (2): 133–145.

_____. 1989. "Decentralizing Public Services in Developing Countries: Issues and Opportunities." *Journal of Social, Political, and Economic Studies* 14 (1): 77–99.

_____. 1990. *"Decentralizing Urban Development Programs: A Framework for Analyzing Policy*. Washington, D.C.: U.S. Agency for International Development.

Rondinelli, Dennis A., and John R. Nellis. 1986. "Assessing Decentralization Policies in Developing Countries, Public and Private Roles in Urban Development: A Case for Cautious Optimism." *Development Policy Review* 4 (1): 3–23.

Roth, G. 1987. *The Private Provision of Public Services.* Washington, D.C.: Oxford University Press/World Bank.

Rousseau, Mark, and Raphael Zariski, eds. 1987. *Regionalism and Regional Devolution in Comparative Perspective.* New York: Praeger.

Salinas de Gortari, Carlos, et al. 1982. "La política en la formación del estado nacional." *Revista Mexicana de Sociología* 44 (1): 263–284.

Sánchez Gutiérrez, Arturo, ed. 1992. *Las elecciones de Salinas. Un balance crítico a 1991.* Mexico City: Plaza y Valdés/FLACSO.

Sánchez Susarrey, Jorge. 1991. "México: ¿Perestroika sin Glasnost?" *Vuelta* (176) (July): 47–51.

Sanderson, Steven E. 1983. "Presidential Succession and Political Rationality in Mexico." *World Politics* 35 (3): 315–334.

San Pedro: Tres años de resultados. 1991. San Pedro Garza García, Nuevo León.

Santos Zavala, José. 1995. "Actividad financiera municipal de León: Innovación con sentido empresarial." Mexico City: CIDE. Mimeo.

Savas, E.S. 1987. *Privatization: The Key to Better Government.* Chatham, N.J.: Chatham House Publishers.

Schers, D. 1972. "The Popular Sector of the PRI in Mexico." PhD dissertation. University of New Mexico.

Schmitter, Phillipe. 1974. "Still the Century of Corporatism?" In Fredrick Pike and Thomas Stritch, eds., *The New Corporatism.* Notre Dame, Ind.: University of Notre Dame Press. 85–131.

Schryer, Frans. 1976. "Faccionalismo y patronazgo del PRI en un municipio de la Huasteca hidalguense." *Cuadernos del CES* 16. Mexico City: El Colegio de México.

Scott, D.C. 1992. "Mexico's Public-Works Program Bolsters President as It Aids the Poor." *Christian Science Monitor* (September 16).

Scott, Robert E. 1959. *Mexican Government in Transition.* Urbana: University of Illinois Press.

Secretaría de Agricultura y Recursos Hidráulicos (SARH). 1985. *Programa Nacional de Desarrollo Rural Integral.* Mexico City.

Secretaría de Asentamientos Humanos y Obras Públicas (SAHOP). 1978. *Plan Nacional de Desarrollo Urbano.* 5 vols. Mexico City.

Secretaría de Desarrollo Social (SEDESOL). 1992. *Programa de 100 ciudades.* Mexico City.

———. 1993. *Fondos municipales de Solidaridad. Proyecto de descentralización y desarrollo regional. Guía técnica.* Mexico City.

———. 1994. *Solidaridad. Seis años de trabajo.* Mexico City.

———. 1996. *Programa Nacional de Desarrollo Urbano 1995–2000.* Mexico City.

Secretaría de Desarrollo Social (SEDESOL)/World Bank. 1993. *Intergovernmental Relations in Mexico.* Report to assist the preparation of the Project on Decentralization and Regional Development.

Secretaría de Desarrollo Urbano y Ecología (SEDUE). 1984. *Programa Nacional de Desarrollo Urbano y Ecología. 1984–1988.* Mexico City.

Secretaría de Gobernación. 1983. *Democratización integral: Consulta popular para la reforma municipal. Memorias.* 13 vols. Mexico City.

Secretaría de Programación y Presupuesto (SPP). 1980. *The Global Development Plan. 1980–82. Synopsis.* Mexico City.

_____. 1982. *Sistema Nacional de Planeación Democrática. Principios y organización.* Mexico City.

_____. 1983a. *Convenio Unico de Desarrollo: Instrumento de desarrollo regional.* Mexico City.

_____. 1983b. *Plan Nacional de Desarrollo. 1983–1988.* Mexico City.

_____. 1983c. *Programa de Desarrollo de la Zona Metropolitana de 1a Ciudad de México y Región Centro.* Mexico City.

_____. 1984a. *Plan Nacional de Desarrollo: Informe de ejecución. 1983.* Mexico City.

_____. 1984b. *Memoria institucional. 1983.* Mexico City.

_____. 1985. *Programa de Descentralización de la Administración Pública Federal.* Mexico City.

_____. 1986. *Presupuesto de egresos de la federación 1986.* Mexico City.

_____. 1988. *México: Desarrollo regional y descentralización de la vida nacional. Experiencias de cambio estructural 1983–1988.* Mexico City.

Secretaría de Salud, Subsecretaría de Planeación. 1984. *Programa Nacional de Salud. 1984–1988.* Mexico City.

_____. 1985. *Cuadernos de Descentralización.* 5 vols. Mexico City.

"Segundo Informe de Gobierno, Carlos Salinas de Gortari." 1990. *Comercio Exterior* 40 (11).

Sepúlveda Amor, Alejandro. 1985. "Reforma fiscal municipal." *Estudios Municipales* 1: 57–65.

Sherwood, F. 1969. "Devolution as a Problem of Organizational Strategy." In R.T. Darland, ed., *Comparative Urban Research.* Beverly Hills, Calif.: Sage.

Short, John. 1984. *An Introduction to Urban Geography.* London: Routledge.

Silverman, Jerry. 1992. *Public Sector Decentralization: Economic Policy and Sector Investment Programs.* Washington, D.C.: The World Bank.

Skidmore, Thomas E., and Peter H. Smith. 1989. *Modern Latin America.* 2nd ed. New York: Oxford University Press.

Skinner, Reinhard, and Michael Rodell, eds. 1983. *People, Poverty and Shelter: Problems of Self-Help Housing in the Third World.* London: Methuen.

Sklair, Leslie. 1989. *Assembling for Development: The Maquila Industry for Mexico and the United States.* Boston: Unwin Hyman.

Smith, B.C. 1985. *Decentralization: The Territorial Dimension of the State.* Boston: Allen and Unwin.

Smith, Peter H. 1979. *Labyrinths of Power: Political Recruitment in Twentieth Century Mexico.* Princeton: Princeton University Press.

Steinberg, Samuel. 1984. *Understanding American Government and Politics.* Rev. ed. New York: Sadlier-Oxford.

Stevens, Evelyn P. 1974. *Protest and Response in Mexico.* Cambridge, Mass: MIT Press.

_____. 1975. "Protest Movements in an Authoritarian Regime: The Mexican Case." *Comparative Politics* 7(3).

_____. 1977. "Mexico's PRI: The Institutionalization of Corporatism?" In James Malloy, ed., *Authoritarianism and Corporatism in Latin America.* Pittsburgh: University of Pittsburgh Press. 227–258.

Story, Dale. 1986. *The Mexican Ruling Party: Stability and Authority.* New York: Praeger.

Street, Susan. 1984. "Los distintos proyectos para la transformación del aparato burocrático de la SEP." *Perfiles Educativos* UNAM 7.

Teichman, Judith A. 1988. *Policymaking in Mexico: From Boom to Crisis*. Boston: Allen and Unwin.

Teune, Henry. 1982. "Decentralization and Economic Growth." *Annals of the American Academy of Political and Social Science* 459: 93–102.

Torres, Blanca, ed. 1986. *Descentralización y democracia en México*. Mexico City: El Colegio de México.

Townroe, Peter, and David Keen. 1984. "Polarization Reversal in the State of Sao Paulo, Brazil." *Regional Studies* 18 (1): 45–54.

Tuohy, William, and David Ronfeldt. 1969. "Political Control and the Recruitment of Middle Level Elites in Mexico: An Example from Agrarian Politics." *Western Political Quarterly* 22 (2): 365–374.

Ugalde, Antonio. 1970. *Power and Conflict in a Mexican Community*. Albuquerque: University of New Mexico Press.

Unikel, Luis. 1975. "Políticas de desarrollo regional en México." *Demografía y Economía* 9 (26): 143–181.

⸻. 1978. *El desarrollo urbano de México: Diagnóstico e implicaciones*. Mexico City: El Colegio de México.

Unikel, Luis, and R. de la Peña. 1976. "Consideraciones sobre la concentración económica en México." *Asentamientos Humanos* I. Mexico City: Secretaría de la Presidencia.

Unikel, Luis, and Allan Lavell. 1979. "El problema urbano-regional en México." *Gaceta UNAM* III (August).

United Nations, Dept. of Economic and Social Affairs. 1962. *Decentralization for National and Local Development*. New York.

Valadés Ríos, Diego. 1985. "El desarrollo municipal como supuesto de la democracia y el federalismo mexicano." *Estudios Municipales* 3: 63–71.

Varley, Ann. 1989. "Settlement, Illegality, and Legalization: The Need for Reassessment." In Peter Ward, ed., *Corruption, Development and Inequality*. London: Routledge. 143–174.

⸻. 1993. "Clientalism or Technocracy? The Politics of Urban Land Regularization." In Neil Harvey, ed., *Mexico: Dilemmas of Transition*. London: British Academic Press. 249–276.

Velázquez Carranza, Yolanda. 1985. "La hacienda municipal." *Estudios Municipales* 1: 67–82.

Véliz, Claudio. 1980. *The Centralist Tradition of Latin America*. Princeton: Princeton University Press.

Ward, Peter. 1986. *Welfare Politics in Mexico: Papering Over the Cracks*. London: Allen and Unwin.

⸻. 1989. "Government without Democracy in Mexico City: Defending the High Ground." In Wayne Cornelius, Judith Gentleman, and Peter Smith, eds., *Mexico's Alternative Political Futures*. Monograph Series, 30. La Jolla: Center for U.S.-Mexican Studies, University of California, San Diego.

⸻. 1990a. *Mexico City: The Production and Reproduction of an Urban Environment*. London: Belhaven Press.

⸻. 1990b. "Mexico." In Willem Van Vliet, ed., *International Handbook of Housing Policies and Practices*. New York: Greenwood Press. 407–436.

⸻. 1993. "Social Policy and Political Opening in Mexico." *Journal of Latin American Research* (25): 613–628.

⸻. 1995. "Policy Making and Policy Implementation among Non-PRI Governments: The PAN in Ciudad Juárez and in Chihuahua." In Victoria E. Rodríguez and Peter M.

Ward, eds., *Opposition Government in Mexico*. Albuquerque: University of New Mexico Press. 135–152.

_____. 1996. "From Machine Politics to the Politics of Technocracy: Charting the Decline of Partisanship in the Mexican Municipality." Paper presented at the Simposio Internacional sobre Desarrollo Municipal: Retos y Posibilidades. Toluca, Mexico: Colegio Mexiquense.

_____, ed. 1989. *Corruption, Development and Inequality*. London: Routledge.

_____, et al. 1994. *Mexico's Electoral Aftermath and Political Future: Memoria of the Bi-National Conference*. Austin: Mexican Center of the Institute of Latin American Studies, University of Texas at Austin.

Weintraub, Sidney. 1990. *A Marriage of Convenience: Relations between Mexico and the United States*. New York: Oxford University Press.

Wilkie, James Wallace. 1970. *The Mexican Revolution: Federal Expenditure and Social Change since 1910*. 2nd ed. rev. Berkeley and Los Angeles: University of California Press.

_____. 1977. *Money and Politics in Latin America*. Los Angeles: UCLA Latin American Center Publications.

Williams, Walter. 1980. *The Implementation Perspective: A Guide for Managing Social Service Delivery Programs*. Berkeley and Los Angeles: University of California Press.

Wilson, Patricia. 1992. *Exports and Local Development: Mexico's New Maquiladoras*. Austin: University of Texas Press.

Wilson, Robert H., and Reid Cramer, eds. 1994. *International Workshop on Good Local Government*. First Annual Proceedings. Austin: LBJ School of Public Affairs, University of Texas at Austin and the Ford Foundation.

Wolman, Harold. 1990. "Decentralization: What It Is and Why We Should Care." In Robert J. Bennett, ed., *Decentralization, Local Governments and Markets: Towards a Post-Welfare Agenda*. Oxford: Oxford University Press. 29–42.

World Bank. 1993. *Intergovernmental Relations in Mexico: An Examination Focusing on Disadvantaged States and Municipalities*. Internal report prepared for the second Decentralization and Regional Development Project. Washington, D.C.

Wyman, Donald L., ed. 1983. *Mexico's Economic Crisis: Challenges and Opportunities*. Monograph Series, 12. La Jolla: Center for U.S.-Mexican Studies, University of California, San Diego.

Ziccardi, Alicia, ed. 1995. *La tarea de gobernar: Gobiernos locales y demandas ciudadanas*. Mexico City: Miguel Angel Porrúa/UNAM.

About the Book and Author

This book assesses the impact of decentralization on Mexico's intergovernmental relations and examines the constraints upon the devolution of political power from the center to the lower levels of government. It also discusses the distribution of power and authority to governments of opposition parties within the context of a more open political space. Victoria Rodríguez uncovers a new paradox in the Mexican political system: retaining power by giving it away. She argues that since the de la Madrid presidency (1982–1988), the Mexican government has embarked upon a major effort of political and administrative decentralization as a means to increase its hold on power. That effort continued under Salinas, but paradoxically led to further centralization. However, since Zedillo assumed the presidency, it has become increasingly clear that the survival of the ruling party and, indeed, the viability of his own government require a genuine, de facto reduction of centralism.

Victoria E. Rodríguez is associate professor at the Lyndon B. Johnson School of Public Affairs at the University of Texas at Austin. In addition to her joint work with Peter M. Ward on opposition governments in Mexico, she is currently engaged in a research project on women in contemporary Mexican politics.

Index